OLD LONDON
Haymarket to Mayfair

THE
'VILLAGE LONDON'
SERIES
from
THE ALDERMAN PRESS

THE VILLAGE LONDON SERIES

Other titles already published in hard back are:

VILLAGE LONDON Volume I
VILLAGE LONDON Volume II
LONDON RECOLLECTED Volume I
LONDON RECOLLECTED Volume II
LONDON RECOLLECTED Volume III
LONDON RECOLLECTED Volume IV
LONDON RECOLLECTED Volume V
LONDON RECOLLECTED Volume VI
VILLAGE LONDON ATLAS

Other titles already published in paperback:

VILLAGE LONDON Pt. 1 West and North
VILLAGE LONDON Pt. 2 North and East
VILLAGE LONDON Pt. 3 South-East
VILLAGE LONDON Pt. 4 South-West

OLD FLEET STREET
CHEAPSIDE AND ST. PAUL'S
THE TOWER AND EAST END
SHOREDITCH to SMITHFIELD
CHARTERHOUSE to HOLBORN
STRAND to SOHO
COVENT GARDEN and the THAMES to WHITEHALL
WESTMINSTER to ST. JAMES'S
HAYMARKET to MAYFAIR
HYDE PARK to BLOOMSBURY

The above ten titles are extracts from the hardback edition of London Recollected.

OLD LONDON

Haymarket to Mayfair
by

EDWARD WALFORD

THE ALDERMAN PRESS

British Library Cataloguing in Publication Data

Walford, Edward, *1823–1897*
   Old London: Haymarket to Mayfair
   l. London, history
   I. Title
942.1

ISBN 0-946619-37-9

This edition published 1989

The Village Press Ltd.,
7d Keats Parade
Church Street,
Edmonton,
London N9 9DP

Printed and bound in Great Britain
by Redwood Burn Ltd, Yeoman Way,
Trowbridge, Wiltshire

CONTENTS.

---◆---

CHAPTER XVII.

WATERLOO PLACE AND HER MAJESTY'S THEATRE.

CHAPTER XVIII.

THE HAYMARKET.

CHAPTER XIX.

PALL MALL EAST, SUFFOLK STREET, &c.

CHAPTER XX.

GOLDEN SQUARE AND ITS NEIGHBOURHOOD.

CONTENTS.

CONTENTS.

CHAPTER XXVII.

GROSVENOR SQUARE AND ITS NEIGHBOURHOOD.

PAGE

CHAPTER XXVIII.

MAY FAIR.

CHAPTER XXIX.

APSLEY HOUSE AND PARK LANE.

LIST OF ILLUSTRATIONS.

CHAPTER XVII.

WATERLOO PLACE AND HER MAJESTY'S THEATRE.

"Hic alta theatris
Fundamenta locant."—*Virgil, "Æn.," i.*

PREVIOUS to the year 1560, the tract of ground which we are about to traverse, and indeed as far north and north-west as the parish of St. Mary-lebone, was a vast extent of fields. There were no houses, excepting three or four in the immediate neighbourhood of what is now called Pall

Mall East. In the time of Charles I., the whole of the district was unbuilt upon, and was known by the name of "St. James's Fields." In the middle of these fields stood a solitary dwelling, called "Pickadilly," mentioned by Clarendon, in his "History of the Rebellion," as "a fair house for entertainment and gaming," with handsome gravel walks and shade, and where there was an upper and a lower bowling-green, whither many of the nobility and gentry of the best quality resorted for exercise and recreation. In Charles Knight's "Old London" reference is made to a petition from Colonel Thomas Panton, read in 1671, before the Privy Council, setting forth that the petitioner having been at great charge in purchasing "a parcel of ground lying at Pickadilly," part of it being two bowling-greens fronting the Haymarket, the other lying on the north of the Tennis Court, on which several old houses were standing, and praying for leave to build on this ground, notwithstanding the royal proclamation against building on new foundations within a certain distance of London. No doubt the colonel must have had influential friends about him, for we find that, "in consequence of Sir Christopher Wren's favourable report, he obtained leave to erect houses in Windmill Street, on the east corner towards the Haymarket, and also in the two bowling-greens between the Haymarket and Leicester Fields."

In the reign of Charles II., mention is made of the Hay Market and Hedge Lane; but they were at that time literally lanes, bounded by hedges. In Faithorne's plan of London, published in 1658, no traces of houses are to be found in the north, except a single one, called the Gaming House, at the end next to Piccadilly. In the upper part of this district, on the north side of Jermyn Street, and on the site now partly covered by the Criterion Restaurant and Theatre and Lower Regent Street, a market was established in 1664. Malcolm tells that the market for all sorts of provisions was proclaimed "to be kept in St. James's Fields on Mondays, Wednesdays, and Saturdays; and for all kinds of cattle in the Hay Market, in the parish of St. Martin-in-the-Fields." According to Gay's "Trivia," St. James's Market was famous for its supply of veal. From Pepys we learn that the market owed its foundation to Jermyn, Earl of St. Albans, whose name is still preserved in Jermyn Street.

At the "Mitre Tavern," in the market, the mother of the charming and accomplished actress, Mrs. Oldfield, was living when the latter was quite young. One day the girl was overheard reading a play with so much power and expression, that Sir John Vanbrugh obtained for her an introduction to Rich, the patentee of Covent Garden Theatre, by whom she was engaged. Here she soon made herself a name, and became so popular, that she obtained access to the first circles. She became the mistress of General Churchill, a nephew of the great Duke of Marlborough, by whom she had a son, who married a natural daughter of Sir Robert Walpole, and obtained the rank and precedence of an earl's daughter. In the end Mrs. Oldfield had the honour of a funeral in Westminster Abbey.

In the house which stood at the corner of Market Street, in St. James's Market, at the shop of a linen-draper named Wheeler, lived Hannah Lightfoot, the early flame of King George III., and indeed, if report may be credited, privately married to him. The fair Quakeress—for such was Hannah—is said to have contracted her marriage with royalty in 1759, in Kew Church. She afterwards married a Mr. Axford, and died in obscurity. The story of Hannah Lightfoot has been thoroughly sifted and discussed by Mr. W. J. Thoms in the pages of *Notes and Queries*, the conclusion arrived at leaving little or no doubt as to the legality of her union with the young Prince.

"The 'Hoop and Bunch of Grapes,'" says Mr. Larwood, "was the sign of a public-house in St. Albans Street (now part of Waterloo Place), kept, at the beginning of the present century, by the famous Matthew Skeggs, who obtained his renown from playing, in the character of Signor Bombasto, a concerto on a broomstick at the Haymarket Theatre, adjoining. His portrait was painted by King, a friend of Hogarth, engraved by Houston and published by Skeggs himself."

About the year 1815, some low and mean houses that stood between the market and Pall Mall were demolished, and these were soon afterwards followed by the market itself, in order to form the broad and spacious thoroughfares of Lower Regent Street and Waterloo Place. At the upper or northern end of Lower Regent Street a junction is formed right and left with Piccadilly. In that part of Piccadilly lying to the east is the "Criterion" Restaurant and Theatre. This handsome building, which combines under one roof the advantages of a restaurant on an unusually large scale, reading, billiard, hair-dressing rooms, cigar divan, concert-hall, ball-room, and theatre, was built for Messrs. Spiers and Pond, in 1873, from a design by Mr. Thomas Verity. The sum originally named as the probable cost, exclusive of decorations and fittings, was £25,000, but the actual expense to the proprietors, before the vast establishment was opened, is said to have exceeded £80,000.

The "Criterion" has two façades; the principal one, in Piccadilly, is of Portland stone, decorated in the style of the French Renaissance. The doorway is arched and deeply recessed, the arch being supported by four handsome bronze columns. Figures, beautifully sculptured, representing the seasons, are placed in niches above. The frontage in Jermyn Street is of brick, picked out with Portland stone. The great dining-room, capable of accommodating 200 persons, is on the right of the central vestibule; on the left is the refreshment-buffet, at the south end of which is the smoking-divan. The grand staircase leads to the ball-room, which occupies the entire width of the Piccadilly frontage. The whole interior is richly decorated; mosaics, parquetry, painted frescoes, mirrors, gildings, and carvings, meet the eye in every direction. The upper floor is occupied by kitchens and sculleries. The right-hand entrance in Piccadilly leads to the grill-room, also to the balcony and orchestra stalls of the theatre, while the entrance to the amphitheatre stalls and parterre is from Jermyn Street, the whole theatre being below ground. It will accommodate 800 persons, and is fitted up in the most luxurious manner. It was opened on the 21st of March, 1874, with two new pieces—*An American Lady*, by Mr. H. J. Byron; and *Topsyturveydom*, by Mr. W. S. Gilbert. The company being an excellent one, and principally consisting of popular favourites, and the two authors being equally well and favourably known, the opening night was a triumphant success, giving a favourable augury of its future career. The entertainments since given have been principally of the class known as *opera bouffe*.

The "Criterion" stands on the site of an inn, the "White Bear," which for a century and more was one of the busiest coaching-houses in connection with the west and south-west of England. Mr. Larwood, in his "History of Sign-boards," tells us that at this inn Benjamin West, the future President of the Royal Academy, put up and spent the night on his first arrival in London from America. Here, too, he tells us, died Luke Sullivan, the engraver of some of Hogarth's most famous works, and another engraver, Chatelain—the latter in such poverty, that he was buried, at the expense of friends who had known him in better days, in the poor-ground attached to St. James's workhouse.

A few doors to the eastward of the "Criterion" stood for many years a house notorious from the commencement of the present century as "The Piccadilly Saloon," a house of refreshment and gambling, which was open nearly all night, and formed a scene of dissipation which, even at that time, was unparalleled in London. Its aristocratic patrons, however, did not protect it from the fate which awaits all such dens sooner or later, and it is now a thing of the past.

On the eastern side of Lower Regent Street is a large building, which till recently bore the name of the "Gallery of Illustration." It was erected from the designs of Mr. Nash, who intended it as a residence for himself. It was used occasionally for dramatic readings, and also for a class of amusements popularly known as "drawing-room entertainments." The northern wing of the building, formerly the Parthenon Club-house, is now the home of the Raleigh Club; the other portion of the edifice (formerly the Gallery of Illustration) has been converted into a restaurant, and bears the name of the "Pall Mall." The long gallery was decorated from a *loggia* of the Vatican at Rome.

St. Philip's Chapel, or, as it is often called, Waterloo Chapel, on the opposite side of the street, was built in 1820 from the designs of Mr. Repton. The tower is a reproduction of the Choragic Monument of Lysicrates, at Athens. The front is adorned with a portico, supported by four Doric columns. The interior has the appearance of a public secular assembly-room rather than of a church, being nearly square, with a double gallery, supported below by heavy piers, and above by Corinthian columns of scagliola. The ceiling is formed of a double cove, and is lighted from above.

Crossing Regent Street, and extending from St. James's Square to the Haymarket, is Charles Street. Here Burke was living in the year 1781, when he received from a poor and friendless young man, named George Crabbe, a letter asking for aid. Burke read the note, and at once responded; asked Crabbe to call on him; read, and admired his verses. "From that hour," writes Mr. Serjeant Burke, "Crabbe was a made man. Burke not only relieved his more pressing necessities, but domesticated him in his own house, introduced him to a large circle of noble and literary friends, afforded him the inestimable advantage of his critical advice, and, having established his poetical reputation to the world, finally crowned the most ardent aspirations of his *protégé* by getting him admitted into the Church." Such deeds of kindness deserve to be recorded to the honour of the great orator.

Here, too, in 1806, the sculptor Chantrey, then quite a young man, was living; and whilst residing here he exhibited some of his early busts.

The Junior United Service Club, of which we have already spoken in our chapter on "Clubland," stands at the corner of Charles Street and Regent Street.

Waterloo Place, which we now enter, was, like Regent Street, built from the designs of Mr. Nash. Some time after the death of the architect, the *New Monthly Magazine* gave the following eulogium on his memory :—" Whether the stranger traverses the splendid line of Regent Street, the Quadrant, and Portland Place, until he reaches the Regent's Park—beautifully disposed, and laid out in walks and groves, ornamented with sheets of water, dotted with elegant villas, and encircled by rows of houses of noble elevation, from classic architectural designs —or takes his way from Waterloo Place towards Somerset House, and sees before him streets, and places, and arcades, occupying the sites of the filthiest courts imaginable, and finds himself in front of the splendid parish church of St. Martin-in-the-Fields—able to admire its beauties, because cleared away from the wretched dwellings by which it was surrounded—we think his first inquiry will be—to whose taste, genius, and enterprise, are these improvements owing ? He will be answered by being told that they are all attributable to the genius, energy, and talent of Mr. Nash, to abuse and ridicule whom was the fashion of the time in which he lived. This is the best answer to the senseless cry raised against him by those whose enmity arose from their jealousy of the estimation in which he was held by the munificent monarch in whose regency and reign these wonderful changes in this part of the metropolis were effected. Mr. Nash is in his grave ; and, standing in the midst of the vast alterations for which we are indebted to him, we feel inclined to say, in the words of Wren's epitaph, *Si monumentum requiris, circumspice.*"

On the eastern side was, in 1851, and for some time afterwards, Mr. Catlin's American Indian Collection, one of the most interesting and successful of the many exhibitions that have been opened in London.

In the centre of Waterloo Place, facing the Duke of York's Column, stands the Guards' Memorial, which was erected from the designs of Mr. John Bell. It consists of a massive granite pedestal, the front of which, some eleven feet from the ground, is occupied by three bronze figures, representing a Grenadier, a Fusilier, and one of the Coldstream Guards, " in their full marching costume, as they fought at Inkerman." These figures are about eight feet high, and behind them are placed their respective flags, thus forming a pyramidal group. The front of the pedestal is inscribed with the word "Crimea." Upon this pedestal rises a smaller one, having upon either side the words "Alma," " Inkerman," " Sebastopol;" whilst

the back of this upper block of granite is ornamented with a pyramidal pile of cannon—the *actual* broken Russian guns, burst and mutilated, as they were found in Sebastopol—having beneath it this inscription :—" To the memory of 2,162 officers and men of the Brigade of Guards who fell during the war with Russia, 1854, 1855, 1856." The whole is surmounted with a bronze figure of Honour, with her arms extended wide, and having in her hands and on her arms wreaths of laurel ; and immediately beneath this figure is inscribed—" Honour to the brave."

Eastward of Waterloo Place stands Her Majesty's Theatre, or, as it is generally called, the Opera House. The building occupies a vast space of ground, with its eastern side in the Haymarket, and extends north and south from Charles Street to Pall Mall.

The species of dramatic performance which we now style an opera, in which the various emotions incidental to the action of the piece are interpreted by the aid of music, vocal and instrumental, is supposed to have originated with the Chinese. Their dramas, almost interminable (a single representation of one being an affair of many nights, and sometimes even of weeks), instead of being declaimed in the natural voice, have been, from time immemorial, delivered in a carefully intoned recitative, mingled with songs. The first work of this description produced in Europe was *The Conversion of St. Paul*, composed by an Italian artist, Francisco Barbarini, and performed in Rome in 1470. England was at that period by no means a musical nation ; and it was not until about the commencement of the eighteenth century that, as Colley Cibber writes, " the Italian opera began first to steal into England, but in as rude a disguise as possible, in a lame hobbling translation, with metre out of measure to its original notes, sung by our own unskilful voices, with graces misapplied to almost every sentiment and action."

In 1704 a subscription was started by Sir John Vanbrugh to build a theatre for this special purpose, and £3,000 was raised in shares of £100 from each of thirty persons, who, in addition to their interest in the building, were to have an admission ticket for life to all public entertainments given therein. The foundation-stone was inscribed with the words, " Little Whig," in honour of Lady Sunderland, the most celebrated Whig toast and beauty of her day. The theatre was opened April 9th, 1705, with an Italian opera, *The Triumph of Love*, which was so far from being a " triumph," that it was withdrawn after having been performed three times before a mere handful of spectators. Sir John Vanbrugh and his associate Congreve, the dramatist, were not long in retiring from a management so little profitable to themselves, and the theatre was transferred to a Mr. McSwiney. The first Italian singer who made his mark on these boards was Valentini, who, on his first appearance, sang through his part in his own language, the rest of the company singing in English! The effect must have been grotesque in the extreme, and may partially account

It appears that this species of entertainment has never been truly popular in England. The first masquerade given in London upon the foreign plan, uniting, after the Venetian fashion, elegance with rude mirth and revelry, was given by Henrietta, the queen of Charles I.; but, as it was unfortunately fixed for a Sunday, the populace in front of the Banqueting House, Whitehall, loudly complained of the profanation of the Lord's Day. A scuffle

THE YARD OF THE OLD "WHITE BEAR" INN, PICCADILLY, ABOUT 1820.
From an Original Drawing by Shepherd, in the Crace Collection. (*See page* 208.)

for the fact that, during the first twenty-five years of its existence, the Opera House was but very poorly supported, and was frequently made a subject for satire in the *Spectator* and *Tatler*. Under these discouraging circumstances a subscription was raised for its support, and £50,000 was thus obtained, King George I. contributing £1,000 (afterwards continued annually) : from this time the theatre assumed the name of "The King's."

In 1729, says Hughson, the Grand Jury of Middlesex "presented" the fashionable and wicked diversion called masquerade, and "particularly the contriver and carrier on of masquerades at the King's Theatre in the Hay Market, in order to be punished according to law."

ensued between the soldiers and the people, in which half a dozen of the latter and two or three of the former were killed.

The most splendid masquerade ever known in England, as we learn from Colburn's "Kalendar of Amusements," took place at the Opera House in 1717, and was provided by Mr. Heidegger. It was allowed to exceed anything that had been known in Italy or any other country. The masquerades formerly given at the Pantheon were very celebrated. In 1783 Delphini, the famous clown, got up a grand masquerade there, in honour of the birthday and coming of age of the Prince of Wales. The tickets were sold at three guineas each, yet Delphini was a loser by the speculation.

In 1724 the Bishop of London preached a sermon against masquerades, which made such an impression, that orders were issued for their discontinuance. After the lapse of some years they were again introduced. Some excellent reasons for the renewal of the prohibited amusement appeared in the *Morning Chronicle*, March 7, 1770. We have already spoken of masquerades in our account of Mrs. Cornelys' house in Soho Square.

The first oratorio ever performed in England

Fetonte. "It is," writes he, "in what they call the French manner, but about as like it as my Lady Pomfret's hash of plural persons and singular verbs was to Italian. They sing to jigs, and dance to church-music. 'Phaeton' is run away with by horses that go a foot's pace, like the 'Electress's' coach, with such long traces, that the postilion was in one street and the coachman in another. Then comes 'Jupiter' with a farthing candle, to light a squib and a half; and that they call fireworks. 'Regi-

PICCADILLY CIRCUS, FROM COVENTRY STREET.

was Handel's *Esther*, which was produced at this theatre in 1732, and followed, later in the same year, by his *Acis and Galatea*. The opera must, by this time, have made vast strides in the estimation of the public, as in the year 1734 we find the famous Farinelli—at whom the newspapers of the day directed many a pointed sarcasm—receiving for the season a salary of £15,000, as well as a free benefit, which realised an additional profit of £2,000. Such, however, is the uncertain tenure of the public favour, that scarcely two years later Farinelli had the mortification of singing to a house containing but £35.

Horace Walpole, in a letter written in 1747, gives a piquant criticism upon Vaneschi's opera of

nello,' the first man, is so old and so tall, that he seems to have been growing ever since the invention of operas. The first woman has had her mouth let out to show a fine set of teeth, but it lets out too much bad voice at the same time. Lord Middlesex, for his great prudence in having provided such very tractable steeds to 'Prince Phaeton's' car, is going to be Master of the Horse to the Prince of Wales ; and, for his excellent economy in never paying the performers, is likely to continue in the Treasury."

In the year 1789 the usual fate of theatres befell the Opera House, which was burnt to the ground on the night of the 17th of June. The fire was supposed to have been the work of an

incendiary, and suspicion attached to Pietro Carnivalli, the leader of the orchestra, who owed a
grudge to Signor Ravelli, the manager, for whose
benefit the performance was to have taken place
the evening after the catastrophe. The company
were at rehearsal when the fire broke out, and
the wife of Signor Ravelli owed her life to the
intrepidity of the firemen. In this conflagration
the favourite opera of *La Laconda*, by Paesiello, was
destroyed—score, separate parts, and all. It is said
that Mazzinghi, who then presided at the harp-
sichord, undertook to reproduce from memory the
whole of the instrumental accompaniments, and
this he did successfully. There still exists a print
of the original building, taken from a drawing made
on the spot by W. Capon, published in Smith's
" Historical and Literary Antiquities." It shows the
front of the edifice, much as it must have been
when built by Sir John Vanbrugh, in the reign of
George I. It was a dull plain building, not unlike
a Quaker's meeting-house. The front was " of
red brick, rusticated with good gauged work." It
had three circular-headed doorways, with three
windows of a similar shape above; in the second
floor, instead of windows, were three oblong re-
cesses of a very heavy character, and the roof was
covered with black glazed tiles. The front was
thirty-four feet in width. Over the entrance-hall
was " Ridant's Fencing Academy," shown by a conspicuous notice in the print. On the piers below
are seen some handbills of the time, including the
name of Signor Rauzzini, and of Signora Carnivalli,
the wife of the man whose hand is supposed to
have set fire to the theatre.

The first stone of the succeeding structure, the
entrance to which is shown on page 216, was
laid in April, 1790, by the Earl of Buckinghamshire, the architect being Michael Novosielski.
The new theatre commenced its career under
weighty liabilities, for which it was by no means
fairly responsible, and of which there will be occasion to speak more in detail in our history of the
Pantheon. Chancery or the Insolvent Court generally terminated the career of its first half-dozen
managers, as, in addition to its hopeless load of
debt, the current expenses were so enormous as to
swallow up all the receipts.   '

The great English tenor, John Braham—as mentioned in our notice of the St. James's Theatre—
made his *début* here in 1796, and rose at one step
to the height of public favour. The year 1806 was
distinguished by two great events in the history of
this theatre—the introduction of Mozart's music,
never before performed in England, and the *début*
of Madame Catalani. This marvellous singer, the

versatility of whose talents rendered her equally
admirable in a tragic or comic *rôle*, received the
sum of £15,000 for the season of 1809, her benefit
and the various concerts which she gave amounting
to £11,000 more.

Catalani is pronounced by Captain Gronow, who
well recollected her, the greatest vocalist that he
ever heard. He writes : " In her youth she was
the finest singer in Europe, and she was much
sought after by all the great people during her *séjour*
in London. She was extremely handsome, and was
considered a model as wife and mother. Catalani
was very fond of money, and would never sing
unless paid beforehand. She was asked, with her
husband, to pass some time at Stowe, where a
numerous but select party had been invited ; and
Madame Catalani, being asked to sing soon after
dinner, willingly complied. When the day of her
departure came, her husband placed in the hands
of the Marquis of Buckingham the following little
billet—' For seventeen songs, seventeen hundred
pounds.' This large sum was paid at once without
hesitation, proving that Lord Buckingham was a
refined gentleman in every sense of the word."

" I visited Catalani in town," writes Cyrus
Redding, " and always found her the same elegant
and amiable creature, with the same sweet simple
smile and modest manners. She stood unrivalled
in her profession. As an actress she was by no
means remarkable ; yet she looked so attractive on
the boards, that the audience forgave any little fault
of action. And then her voice was transcendent.
She sang in a private room more charmingly than
in the theatre. I had known her previously. Of
all the females attached to the opera, before or
since, that I have seen, she pleased me most. She
was a kind generous creature, without a particle of
pretension, an excellent mother, and exemplary wife,
wedded to a narrow-minded man, who sometimes
got her an ill name from his avarice. He managed
all her money transactions, and used to call her
' ma poule d'or.' I hear her now singing 'God
save the King,' with her heavenly voice and pretty
foreign accent, set off by a person, one of the
sweetest on the stage I ever saw. For mind she
was not remarkable ; I never met with a singer of
either sex that was so. There was an openness
and candour about her quite charming. ' Monsieur
Redaing, I speak no language propre. I speak
one Babylonish tongue. I speak not my own
tongue, nor French, nor your tongue propre.'

" Her husband, before Junot entered Lisbon,
used to blaze away in the pit of the opera in a
dashing French uniform, speculating upon his future
poule d'or, which to him she afterwards most fully

proved. He was rarely invited with his wife to the houses of people of consideration. A person I knew, half a Roman, said one day to Catalani, 'My dear half-countrywoman, how did you come to marry Valabreque?'—'I will tell you. I was at Lisbon; the Portuguese are fond of music. Great men, princes, and counts talk to me of love, and a number of fine things, but none of them talk of marrying. M. Valabreque talked of marriage—I marry M. Valabreque.'"

Captain Gronow writes thus in his "Anecdotes and Reminiscences:"—"When George IV. was Regent, this theatre was conducted on a very different system from that which now prevails. Some years previous to the period to which I refer, no one could obtain a box, or a ticket for the pit, without a voucher from one of the lady patronesses, who, in 1805, were the Duchesses of Marlborough, Devonshire, and Bedford, Lady Carlisle, and some others. In their day, after the singing and ballet were over, the company used to retire into the concert-room, where a ball took place, accompanied by refreshments and a supper. There all the rank and fashion of England were assembled, on a sort of neutral ground. At a later period the management of the Opera House fell into the hands of Mr. Waters, when it became less difficult to obtain admittance; but the strictest etiquette was still kept up as regarded the dress of the gentlemen, who were only admitted with knee-buckles, ruffles, and *chapeau-bras*. If there happened to be a drawing-room, the ladies would appear in their court dresses as well as the gentlemen; and on all occasions the audience of Her Majesty's Theatre was stamped with aristocratic elegance. In the boxes of the first tier might have been seen the daughters of the Duchess of Argyle, four of England's beauties; in the next box were the equally lovely Marchioness of Stafford and her daughter, Lady Elizabeth Gower, now the Duchess of Norfolk; not less remarkable were Lady Harrowby and her daughters, Lady Susan and Lady Mary Ryder. The peculiar type of female beauty which these ladies so attractively exemplified is such as can be met with only in the British isles: the full round, soul-inspired eye of Italy, and the dark hair of the sunny South, often combined with that exquisitely pearly complexion which seems to be concomitant with humidity and fog. You could scarcely gaze upon the peculiar beauty to which I refer without being as much charmed with its kindly expression as with its physical loveliness."

The theatre was reconstructed, in 1818, by Messrs. Nash and Repton, with great improvements. The interior was the first in England to be modelled in the horse-shoe shape, so favourable both for sight and sound. The dimensions were within a few feet of those of the Grand Opera House at Milan. The length from the front of the curtain to the back of the boxes was 102 feet; the extreme width, 75 feet; the stage measured 60 feet in length and 80 in width. The edifice was of brick and Bath stone, with a bas-relief on the Haymarket front representing Apollo and the Muses. It was in this year that the music of Rossini was first presented to the English public.

A French nobleman remarks, in a letter to an English friend, in 1823—"I must acknowledge that the whole universe does not offer a more splendid *coup d'œil* than that which is presented by the Italian Opera in London on a Saturday night. The beauty of the theatre, the richness of the decorations, the loveliness of the women, the variety and brilliancy of their dresses and jewels, the blaze of light, the number of distinguished characters who are often found in the ranks of the audience, the general appearance of wealth and prosperity, and the total absence of all features of an opposite kind, form altogether such a picture of gaiety and magnificence as is indeed unrivalled."

From 1824 to 1840 the history of the King's Theatre is that of a series of triumphs. Pasta, Veluti (the wonderful male soprano), Sontag, Grisi, Rubini, Tamburini, Lablache, and Mario successively appeared upon the stage; the five last named, who were all in their zenith about the same time, forming a brilliant constellation of talent unequalled before or since.

In 1837 the name of the theatre was changed to "Her Majesty's," in honour of the accession of Queen Victoria. The year 1841 witnessed the "Omnibus" row, almost as famous in history as the O. P. riots. The manager, Laporte, who had long been at issue with several of the talented quintette, who were the glory of his establishment, and who had formed a *clique* against him, had declined the further services of Tamburini. His choice of a victim was determined by the fact that he was enabled to replace the great baritone by Coletti, a singer who had achieved a great success at La Scala. But Laporte had miscalculated his power. Madame Grisi, at whose fair shrine all the *jeunesse dorée* of that day bowed down, induced her aristocratic admirers to organise a disturbance, which burst out on the appearance of Coletti in the place of Tamburini. The omnibus boxes were crowded with lords of high degree, foremost among whom was a prince of the blood; and Coletti was saluted with yells, hisses, and cries of "Off, off!" "Tamburini!" "Laporte!" shouted with all the force of aristocratic lungs ; and finally the whole party, headed by the scion of royalty, leaped upon the stage, and the curtain fell on their shouts of "Victory." Negotiations were subsequently entered into with Tamburini, through the good offices of Count D'Orsay, and the discarded baritone was persuaded to overlook the affront and resume his place.

This battle royal is handed down to posterity in the "Ingoldsby Legends," as "A Row in an Omnibus (Box) :"—

> " Dol-drum, the manager, sits in his chair,
> With a gloomy brow and dissatisfied air ;
> And he says, as he slaps his hand on his knee,
> ' I'll have nothing to do with Fiddle-de-dee.
> Though Fiddle-de-dee sings loud and clear,
> And his tones are sweet, yet his terms are dear.
>   The glove won't fit !
>   The deuce a bit—
> I shall give an engagement to Fal-de-ral-tit !'
>
> " The prompter bow'd, and he went to his stall ;
> And the green baize rose at the prompter's call ;
> And Fal-de-ral-tit sang fol-de-rol-lol ;
>   But scarce had he done,
>   When a row begun ;
> Such a noise was never heard under the sun.
>   ' Fiddle-de-dee,
>   Where is he ?
> He's the *artiste* whom we all want to see.
>   Dol-drum ! Dol-drum !
>   Bid the manager come !
> It's a scandalous thing to exact such a sum
> From boxes and gallery, stalls and pit,
> And then fob us off with Fal-de-ral-tit !'"

The manager, being thus peremptorily summoned by the audience—

> " Smooth'd his brow,
>   As he well knew how ;
> And he walk'd on, and made a most elegant bow ;
> And he paused, and he smiled, and advanced to the
> In his opera hat, and his opera tights.   [lights,
> ' Ladies and gentlemen,' then said he,
> ' Pray what may you please to want with me ? '
>   ' Fiddle-de-dee !
>   Fiddle-de-dee !'
>
> " Folks of all sorts, and of every degree,
> Snob, and snip, and haughty grandee,
> Duchesses, countesses, fresh from their tea,
> And shopmen who had only come there for a spree,
> Halloo'd, and hooted, and roared with glee—
>   ' Fiddle-de-dee,
>   None but he !
> Subscribe to his terms, whatever they be !
> Agree, agree, or you'll very soon see,
> In a brace of shakes, we'll get up an O. P. !'"

M. Laporte, who must have had rather a hard time of it among his imperious *troupe*, resigned his uneasy throne in 1842, and was succeeded by Mr. Lumley, who had long been his colleague.

The year 1847 was an eventful one for Her Majesty's Theatre, which had been for more than half a century the only temple of Italian opera in London. Then took place the secession of Grisi, Mario, Persiani, and Tamburini, with the mighty Costa, to the new Opera in Covent Garden ; then began the struggle to solve the problem whether two Italian Opera Houses could be made to pay in London—a vexed question, which seems hardly settled even yet.

The same year (1847) witnessed also the first appearance of Jenny Lind, who had been persuaded to break her engagement with Mr. Bunn, the lessee of Drury Lane, in favour of Mr. Lumley. No words can describe the *furore* excited by this far-famed lady from the night of her *début* until the time when she finally quitted the stage. As much as £30 was frequently paid for a stall on a "Jenny Lind night." As Lumley tells us in his "Reminiscences:"—" The newspapers teemed with descriptions of wild scenes of ' crushing, crowding, and squeezing ; of ladies fainting in the pressure, and even of gentlemen carried out senseless ; of torn dresses, and evening coats reduced to rags.' " These triumphs were, however, partially counterbalanced by the result of an action brought by Mr. Bunn against the *prima donna*, for her breach of contract with him. He laid the damages at £10,000, and gained a verdict for £2,500—a loss which fell entirely on Mr. Lumley, who had undertaken to bear the vacillating fair one scathless. The operatic career, however, of the celebrated songstress was as brief as it was brilliant ; for on the 18th of May, 1849, Jenny Lind made her last appearance upon any stage, as "Alice," in *Roberto il Diavolo*.

In 1850 the chief stars of the Italian opera at Her Majesty's were native artists, Mr. Sims Reeves and Miss Catherine Hayes. An attempt was made in the same year to produce a sensation through the introduction of the *Black Malibran*. The lady bearing this pretentious title was Donna Maria Martinez, a negress, who appeared in a *divertissement* called *Les Delices du Serail*, in which she sang quaint Spanish melodies, accompanying herself on the guitar. " Her songs," writes Lumley, " were full of original charm, her execution excellent, her voice sweet, pure, and true ; but the whole performance was small almost to meagreness, and, although it might well be regarded as a piquant musical curiosity, it failed in any real power of attraction." In 1852 Mdlle. Titiens, the only worthy successor of Grisi in such parts as " Norma," " Lucrezia Borgia," or " Semiramide," appeared as " Valentina " in *Les Huguenots*.

The year 1856 produced another " great sensation" in the young, charming, and high-born Marietta Piccolomini, of whom Lumley writes:— " Once more frantic crowds struggled in the lobbies of the theatre; once more dresses were torn and hats crushed in the conflict. In what lay the charm of this new fascinator of all hearts? It would be difficult to tell, although this much is undeniable, that she exercised an almost magical power over the masses. The statistics of a 'treasury' are indisputable facts. Her voice was a high and pure soprano, with all the attraction of youth and freshness, not wide in range, sweet rather than powerful, and not gifted with any perfection of flexibility. Her vocalisation was far from being distinguished by its correctness or excellence of school; to musicians she appeared a clever amateur, but never a really great artist." This fascinating little lady created an equal *furore* in Paris, yet the French criticisms on her performance seem to agree with those of Lumley—as, for example, the following:—" Mdlle. Piccolomini sings with infinite charm, but is not a *cantatrice*. She acts with talent, but is not an actress. She is a problem—an enigma!"

Pecuniary difficulties having terminated Mr. Lumley's long managerial career, Mr. E. T. Smith became the lessee of Her Majesty's Theatre in 1860, to be succeeded, two years afterwards, by Mr. Mapleson.

Mdlle. Christine Nilsson appeared in 1867 with great success; perhaps the only *artiste* who has ever succeeded in realising to the full the poet's exquisite conception of " Marguerite," in *Faust*. This triumph was the last reserved for the old " King's Theatre," which was once more destroyed by fire on the 6th of December, 1867. At the time of the catastrophe the Earl of Dudley, as assignee of Mr. Lumley, was the lessee under the Crown, on a lease terminating in 1891. In 1862 Lord Dudley had sub-let the theatre to Mr. Mapleson for twenty-one years, at a yearly rental of £8,000, payable in advance. The earl was fully insured; but Mr. Mapleson, who unfortunately was not so, was a loser to the extent of £10,000. The great organ, valued at £800. the chandeliers, scenery, costumes, interior fittings, the whole of the musical library, besides several invaluable manuscripts of Rossini, were all destroyed. The origin of the fire was never ascertained.

Lord Dudley having decided upon rebuilding the theatre without loss of time, the site was cleared early in 1868, and the works were commenced at midsummer. The architect was Mr. Charles Lee, and the contractors Messrs. George Trollope and Sons, who undertook to complete their task in forty weeks, under a penalty of £1,000 for every following week in case of failure. This promise was so strictly fulfilled, that before the end of March, 1869, the new theatre, complete at all points, at a cost of about £50,000, was in a condition to open its doors to the public. The old edifice having been considered deficient in stage accommodation, care had been taken in the present case to increase the size of the stage, which had been effected, as it was stated, without materially lessening the area of the auditorium. There are four tiers of boxes in front of the stage, and five tiers on either side; the space above the fourth tier in front being occupied by amphitheatre stalls, with a spacious amphitheatre behind them. As in the case of Covent Garden Theatre, the partitions between the boxes are constructed in such a manner as to be easily removed, so as to form the ordinary dress circle of a theatre, if required. Every possible precaution has been adopted to reduce the risk by fire, throughout the whole of the building, to a minimum. It is calculated that the new theatre will accommodate about 1,800 for operatic, and 2,500 for dramatic performances. So much stress had been laid upon the completion of the new edifice by the contractors before the commencement of the opera season of 1869, that both the public and the press were daily speculating upon the probable date of the opening night; when the *Times* of the 24th of March, 1869, published a notice from the " Directors " of Her Majesty's Theatre, to the effect that no performances would be given there during that season. Great was the surprise and consternation at this announcement, and higher still rose popular amazement when the solution of the enigma leaked out by degrees. The construction of the interior is such that, the greater part of the boxes and stalls being held on lease, the expenses must necessarily be in excess of the receipts, even in the case of a full attendance every night. In 1874 the theatre was advertised for sale by public auction; but it does not appear that any sale was effected. In 1875 the theatre was hired for the " revival " services of Messrs. Moody and Sankey, and since 1876 it has been under the management of Mr. Mapleson, and has been occasionally used for the performance of English, Italian, and German Opera.

Even the Italian Opera House has had its "ups and downs "—its days of popularity and the reverse. It went out of fashion, through the caprice of the day, in the reign of George II., the nobility supporting their own favourite house in Lincoln's Inn Fields. What the Court then patronised was but in ill odour with the rest of the aristocracy.

"The opera, on its first introduction into England," writes a well-known author, "divided the
wits, literati, and musicians of the age. By those
esteemed the best judges, the English language
was thought too rough and inharmonious for the
music of the opera; and by men of common sense
a drama in a foreign and unknown tongue was
considered very absurd. However, Addison, who
opposed the Italian opera on the London stage,
wrote the English of *Rosamond*, which seemed an
attempt to reconcile the discordant opinions. But
this, though a beautiful poem, is said by Dr. Burney
to have shown Addison's total ignorance of the
first principles of music."

ENTRANCE TO THE OLD OPERA HOUSE, 1800.

CHAPTER XVIII.

THE HAYMARKET.

"From the Haymarket canting rogues in grain."—"*Rejected Addresses.*"

The Old Market for Hay and Straw—A Seller of ' Sea Coal"—Foreign Ambassadors in Peril—Rogues "in Grain"—Addison in a Garret—
Thackeray on Addison—Sir John Suckling's Heroine—Tiddy Dol and his Gingerbread—Lord Eldon's Pint of Wine—Dr. Wolcott and
Madame Mara—Michael Kelly's Wine Vaults—Assault on Sir John Coventry—Baretti: his Trial for Murder—Shows in the Haymarket—
The Animal Comedians—The Cat's Opera—O'Brien, the Irish Giant—Weeks's Museum—The "Little Theatre in the Haymarket:" its
History—Foote: his "Cat Music"—Anecdotes of Foote—"Romeo" Coates—The Theatre in Colman's Hands—A Sad Accident—Reconstruc-
tion of the Theatre by Nash—Liston's Appearance in *Paul Pry*—Subsequent Managers and Actors at the Haymarket: Mr. Benjamin
Webster, Mr. Buckstone, Mr. Charles Mathews—"Lord Dundreary."

THE broad street denominated the Haymarket,
connecting Pall Mall East with the eastern end of
Piccadilly, was a place for the sale of farm-produce
as far back as the reign of Elizabeth; and in
Aggas's plan it appears under its present name
It was then evidently a rural spot, as there were
hedgerows on either side, and few indications of
habitations nearer than the "village of Charing."

At that time, as may be gathered from an inspection of the plan referred to, the air was so pure and clear, that the washerwomen dried their linen by spreading it upon the grass in the fields, as nearly as possible on the spot where now stands Her Majesty's Theatre. Down to the reign of found to violate a part of the Charter granted by Edward III. to the City of London, and was accordingly annulled. At the beginning of the eighteenth century we find the Crown, however, leasing the tolls of the Haymarket for ninety-nine years to one Derick Stork. The market for hay and straw, three

JOSEPH ADDISON. *From an Authentic Portrait.* (*See page* 218)

William III. it was the public highway, in which carts loaded with hay and straw were allowed to stand for sale toll-free; but in 1692 the street was paved, and a tax levied on the carts according to their loads. But this was not the first market held here; for, as far back as the reign of Charles II., John Harvey and another person received a grant empowering them, and their heirs after them, to hold markets here for the sale of oxen and sheep on Mondays and Wednesdays; but the grant was times a week, continued to be held here as lately as the reign of George IV., when it was removed to Cumberland Market, near Regent's Park.

In 1708 Hatton speaks of the Haymarket as "a very spacious and public street, in length 340 yards, where is a great market for hay and straw;" and it is described by Malcolm in 1807 as "an excellent street, 1,020 feet in length, of considerable breadth, and remarkably dry, occasioned by the descent from Piccadilly."

Apart from the obstruction arising from the heavy-laden carts, which on certain days occupied the middle of the street, the Haymarket, and especially its eastern side, is described by Malcolm as a "pleasant promenade;" and he speaks of that side as being occupied by several eminent tradesmen's houses and the "Theatre Royal," of which we shall have to say more presently.

On the opposite, or western side, he adds, is the "King's Theatre for Italian operas," which he describes as "fronted by a stone basement in rustic work, with the *commencement* of a very superb building of the Doric order, consisting of three pillars, two windows, an entablature, pediment, and balustrade." "This," he adds, "if it had been continued, would have contributed considerably to the splendour of London; but the unlucky fragment is fated to stand as a foil to the vile and absurd edifice of brick pieced to it, which I have not patience to describe." How little could he anticipate the future glories of the Italian opera on this very spot!

One of the earliest tradesmen in the Haymarket appears to have been a coal-merchant, or, as he was then styled, a vendor of sea-coal. A "token" used by him is in the British Museum; it bears this inscription—"Nathanil Robins, at the Sea-coale seller, 1666." Reverse—"Hay Markett, in Piccadilla, his half-penny." About half-way down, on the east side, at the south-west corner of James Street, and on the site of the building now known as Clarence Chambers, stood till very recently a large house which dated from the time of Charles II.; tradition says that it was frequented by that monarch and the Duke of York, who used to walk through it to the Tennis Court at the back.

During the riots which ensued on the accession of William and Mary to the throne vacated by James II., the house of the minister of the Duke of Florence, which was in this street, had a narrow escape of being burnt and sacked by the mob, as was also that of the Spanish ambassador. Sir Henry Ellis, in his second series of "Original Letters," quotes one from an eye-witness, dated December 13, 1688, who describes the scene, the "train-bands coming up only just in time to save the house from destruction, and that only after the officer at their head being shot through the back." The attack, however, was renewed a day or two afterwards, when Macaulay tells us that the house above mentioned was destroyed by the infuriated mob, who paraded the streets, almost unchecked, with oranges on the top of their drawn swords and naked pikes. "One precious box," he adds, "the Tuscan minister was able to save from the marauders. It contained some volumes of memoirs written in the hand of King James himself."

The authors of the "Rejected Addresses," in their imitation of Crabbe, as shown in the line quoted as a motto for this chapter, would seem to give a bad name to the Haymarket and its inhabitants, on the score of moral character, if we are to take literally the expression "rogues in grain." But if the meaning of the adjective "canting" as applied to them is to be understood in its ordinary sense, some explanation of it is certainly required; for we never heard of the Haymarket assuming even the appearance of rigid virtue.

In a garret in this street, literally up "three pair of stairs," was living Joseph Addison, when he was waited on by the Hon. H. Boyle, Chancellor of the Exchequer under Lord Godolphin, and requested to write a poem on the battle of Blenheim. The Whig hack jumped at the offer, and penned "The Campaign," which led to his immediate appointment as a Commissioner of Appeals, and to his subsequent advancement by the Whig party. Unfortunately, it is impossible, by the help of letters or of the parish rate-books, to identify the house in which Addison actually lived here; for though Pope visited the house for that purpose, and "made a note of it," saying to his companion, "In this garret Addison wrote his 'Campaign,'" yet he has forgotten to record its exact whereabouts. D'Israeli, in his "Curiosities of Literature," in noticing this incident, adds—"Nothing less than a strong feeling impelled the poet to ascend this garret—it was a consecrated spot to his eye; and certainly a curious instance of the power of genius contrasted with its miserable locality! Addison, whose mind had fought through 'a campaign' in a garret, could he have called about him 'the pleasures of imagination,' had probably planned a house of literary repose, where all parts would have been in harmony with his mind. Such residences of men of genius have been enjoyed by some; and the vivid descriptions which they have left us convey something of the delightfulness which charmed their studious repose."

Thackeray, in his own peculiar manner, thus deals with this incident in Addison's career:—"At thirty-three years of age that most distinguished wit, scholar, and gentleman was without a profession and an income. His book of 'Travels' had failed; his 'Dialogue on Medals' had no particular success; his Latin verses, even though reported the best since Virgil, or Statius, at any rate, had not brought him a Government place; and Addison was living up two shabby pair of stairs in the Haymarket, in a poverty over which old Samuel Johnson rather chuckles, when in these shabby rooms an emissary from Government and fortune came and found him. A poem was wanted about the Duke of Marlborough's victory of Blenheim. Would Mr. Addison write one? Mr. Boyle, afterwards Lord Carleton, took back to Lord Treasurer Godolphin the reply that Mr. Addison would. When the poem had reached a certain stage, it was carried to Godolphin; and the last lines which he read were these :—

> "'But oh, my muse! what numbers wilt thou find
> To sing the furious troops in battle join'd?
> Methinks I hear the drum's tumultuous sound
> The victor's shouts and dying groans confound;
> The dreadful burst of cannon rend the skies,
> And all the thunders of the battle rise.
> 'Twas then great Marlborough's mighty soul was proved,
> That in the shock of charging hosts unmov'd,
> Amidst confusion, horror, and despair,
> Examined all the dreadful scenes of war,
> In peaceful thought the field of death surveyed,
> To fainting squadrons lent the timely aid,
> Inspired repulsed battalions to engage,
> And taught the doubtful battle where to rage.
> So when an angel by Divine command,
> With rising tempests shakes a guilty land,
> Such as of late o'er pale Britannia passed,
> Calm and serene he drives the furious blast;
> And, pleased th' Almighty's orders to perform,
> Rides on the whirlwind and directs the storm.'

"Addison," continues Thackeray, "left off at a good moment. That simile was pronounced to be one of the greatest ever produced in poetry. That angel, that good angel, flew off with Mr. Addison, and landed him in the place of Commissioner of Appeals! . . . . In the following year Mr. Addison went to Hanover with Lord Halifax, and the year after was made Under-Secretary of State. Oh! angel-visits! you come 'few and far between' to literary gentlemen's lodgings! Your wings seldom quiver even at second-floor windows now!"

The "Hay Market" originally stretched down to Charing Cross; for Northumberland House was really the scene of the wedding of the young lady so prettily celebrated in the cavalier song of Sir John Suckling, in which occur the oft-quoted lines :—

> "Her feet beneath her petticoat
> Like little mice stole in and out
> As if they fear'd the light;
> But oh! she dances such a way!
> No sun upon an Easter day
> Is half so fine a sight."

The place is identified by the second verse, which runs thus :—

> "At Charing Cross, hard by the way,
> Where we (thou know'st) do sell our hay,
> There is a house," &c.

Among the eccentric characters who had their haunts in and about the Haymarket, was "Tiddy Dol," the celebrated vendor of ginger-bread and the king of itinerant dealers in such wares, who figures in Hogarth's picture of the "Idle Apprentice" at Tyburn. His proper name was Ford; and Mr. Frost, in his "Old Showmen," records the fact that he was so well-known a character, that once, being missed from his usual stand in the Haymarket on the occasion of a visit which he paid to a country fair, a "catch-penny"* account of his alleged murder was printed, and sold in the streets by thousands.

But in spite of its alleged production of "rogues in grain," we find that, in the reigns of Anne and of George I., the Haymarket was inhabited by a few of "the quality." Thus, Lord Sackville was born in 1716 in the Haymarket, where his father, he is careful to tell us, then resided.

Cyrus Redding tells us that he well remembered Lord Eldon often stealing into the "George Coffee House" at the top of the Haymarket, to get a pint of wine, as Lady Eldon did not permit him to enjoy it in peace at home. Redding did not like Eldon, either as a Tory or as a man. "His words," he writes, "were no index of his real feelings. He had a sterile soul for all things earthly except money, doubts, and the art of drawing briefs."

The Haymarket is said to have been the scene of the meeting between Dr. Wolcott ("Peter Pindar") and Madame Mara, with reference to the sale of the manuscript of the song, "Hope told a Flattering Tale," which the doctor had written expressly for Madame Mara, and which she had sung for the first time at one of her own benefits. The next day she sold the manuscript. The doctor, it appears, had already done the same, and the two purchasers, after a long dispute, which neither had the power to settle, agreed to wait on Mara, and solicit her interference. She consented; and, as she was going in search of Dr. Wolcott, he happened here to cross her path. He had already heard of the circumstance, and, like the *prima donna*, was not disposed to refund the money he had received. "What is to be done?" said Mara. "Cannot you say you were intoxicated when you sold it?" "Cannot you say the same of yourself?" replied the satirist; "one story would be believed as soon as the other."

Dr. Wolcott, whose fondness for liquor of all kinds was notorious, might possibly at the time have been making his way to the house of Michael Kelly, the once popular singer and composer, who was in business in this street as a wine merchant. The singer had written over his door in conspicuous letters—"Michael Kelly, Composer of Music and

Importer of Wine." Sheridan, it is said, suggested the following alteration—"'Michael Kelly, Importer of Music and Composer of Wine;' for," observed the wit, "none of his music is original, and all his wine is, since he makes it himself." Sheridan's favourite haunt at this time, it may be remarked, was the "One Tun Tavern" in Jermyn Street, close by.

Hard by was the scene of the famous assault on Sir John Coventry, which occasioned the passing of the "Coventry Act," Sir John being waylaid here on his way to or from his lodgings, and having his nose slit by some young men of high rank for an ill-timed, and perhaps ill-judged, reflection on the theatrical amours of his sovereign.

This episode of Sir John Coventry is mentioned by Sir Walter Scott, in his "Life of Dryden," as a parallel to the assault on that poet by hired ruffians in Rose Street, which we have already mentioned. He observes, that "in the age of the second Charles, a high and chivalrous sense of honour was esteemed Quixotic, and that the Civil War had left traces of ferocity in the manners and sentiments of the people. Encounters where the assailants took all advantages of number and weapons were as frequent, and were held as honourable, as regular duels." The assault on Sir John Coventry, he adds, "caused the famous statute against maiming and wounding, called the 'Coventry Act;' an act highly necessary, since so far did our ancestors' ideas of manly forbearance differ from ours, that Killigrew introduces the hero of one of his comedies, a cavalier and the fine gentleman of the piece, as lying in wait for and slashing the face of a poor courtesan who had cheated him."

On the 3rd of October, 1769, as we learn from Boswell's "Life of Johnson," another assault of a very similar nature to the above took place here. It appears that Mr. Baretti, the author of the well-known "Italian Dictionary," was going hastily up the street, when he was accosted by a woman, who behaving with great rudeness, he was provoked to give her a blow on the hand; upon which three men immediately interfering and endeavouring to push him from the pavement, with a view to throw him into a puddle, he was alarmed for his safety, and rashly struck one of them with a knife (which he constantly wore for the purpose of cutting fruit and sweetmeats), and gave him a wound, of which he died the next day. Baretti was arraigned at the Old Bailey for murder, and among the numerous witnesses called to give evidence as to character, appeared Dr. Johnson himself. This, his biographer supposes, was the only time in his life that the doctor ever appeared as a witness in a court of justice. "Never," he adds, "did such a constellation of genius enlighten the awful Sessions-house, emphatically called Justice-hall; there were Mr. Burke, Mr. Garrick, Mr. Beauclerk, and Dr. Johnson: and undoubtedly their favourable testimony had due weight with the court and jury. Johnson gave his evidence in a slow, deliberate, and distinct manner, which was uncommonly impressive. It is well known that Mr. Baretti was acquitted."

Situated in the centre of the pleasure-going West-end population, the Haymarket is a great place for hotels, supper-houses, and foreign *cafés;* and it need hardly be added here, that so many of its taverns became the resort of the loosest characters, after the closing of the theatres, who turned night into day, and who were so constantly appearing before the sitting magistrates in consequence of drunken riots and street rows, that the Legislature interfered, and an Act of Parliament was passed, compelling the closing of such houses of refreshment at twelve o'clock.

The street and its neighbourhood have long been noted for places of amusement, and for those kinds of entertainment which are generally known as "popular." About the year 1750 a collection of performing dogs and monkeys from Italy, and exhibited under the name of the "Animal Comedians" at a place in the Haymarket known as "Mrs. Midnight's Oratory," became so famous that they were made the subject of a paper in the *Adventurer*. The writer discourses in a most learned style on the various animal prodigies and strange biped performers that had lately appeared "within the bills of mortality"—such as the "modern Colossus;" the "female Samson;" the "famous negro, who swings about his arms in every direction;" the "noted ox with six legs and two bellies;" the "beautiful panther-mare;" the "noted fire-eater, smoking out of red-hot tobacco pipes, champing lighted brimstone, and swallowing his infernal mess of broth;" the "most amazing new English *chien savant;*" the "little woman that weighs no more than twenty-three pounds;" the "wonderful little Norfolk man;" the "wonderful Stentor;" the "wonderful man who talks in his belly;" the "wire-dancer;" the "five dancing bears;" and the "much-applauded stupendous ostrich."

In 1758, or the following year, Bisset, the famous animal-trainer, hired here a room, in which he announced a public performance of the "Cat's Opera," supplemented by tricks of a horse, a dog, and some monkeys. Mr. Frost, in his "Old Showman," tells us that, "besides the organ-grinding and rope-dancing performances, the monkeys took wine together, and rode on the horse, pirouetting and somersaulting with the skill of a practised acrobat. One of them also," he adds, "danced a minuet with the dog. The 'Cat's Opera' was attended by crowded houses, and Bisset cleared a thousand pounds by the exhibition in a few days. He afterwards taught a hare to walk on its hind legs and beat a drum; a feathered company of canaries, linnets, and sparrows to spell names, tell the time by the clock, &c.; half-a-dozen turkeys to execute a country dance; and a turtle (or more probably a tortoise) to write names on the floor, having its feet blackened for the purpose. After a successful season in London, he sold some of the animals, and made a provincial tour with the rest, rapidly accumulating a considerable fortune." "At the Opera Room in the Haymarket," in the reign of George II., were exhibited by Fawkes, the showman, some waxwork figures, which went through the comical tragedy of "Tom Thumb."

According to a placard immortalised by Mr. John Timbs in his "Romance of London," at No. 61 in this street, O'Brien, the Irish Giant, whose skeleton is to be seen in the Museum of the College of Surgeons, as already stated by us,* was exhibited in 1804. He is thus described:—"He is indisputably the tallest man ever shown; is a lineal descendant of Brian Boru, and resembles that great potentate. All the members of the family are distinguished by their immense size. The gentleman alluded to measures near nine feet high." Owing to his great height he was most unwieldy, and could scarcely walk up an incline, so that he had to rest his hands for support on the shoulders of two men in walking up Holborn Hill. When he wished to light his pipe, Mr. Timbs tells us, he used to take the top off a street-lamp. Once on a journey in his own carriage he was stopped by a robber; but when he looked out of the window, the thief rode off, frightened at his height. He exhibited himself for more than twenty years, and realised a large sum; and we are told that he was seldom absent from Bartlemy Fair. He died in 1806.

Another of the principal places of amusement in the Haymarket, in the early part of the present century, was Weeks's Museum. The grand room, which was upwards of one hundred feet in length, was hung entirely with blue satin, and contained a variety of figures, which exhibited the powers of mechanism.

At the top of the street, at the north-east corner, facing Weeks's Museum, stood a place of public amusement — in fact, a gaming-house, familiar

to the readers of the comedies of the time as "Shaver's Hall;" its name being derived from the barber of Lord Pembroke, who built it out of his earnings. It occupied the whole of the southern side of Coventry Street from the Haymarket to Hedge Lane. It is described by Garrow in a letter to Lord Strafford, in 1635, as "a new Spring Garden, erected in the fields beyond the Mews." For the following minute description of it we are indebted to the industry and research of John Timbs :— From a survey of the premises made in 1650, we gather that Shaver's Hall was strongly built of brick, and covered with lead; its large cellar was divided into six rooms; above these were four rooms, and the same in the first storey, to which there was a balcony commanding a view of the bowling-alleys that sloped to the south. In the second storey were six rooms, and over the same a walk with leads, and enclosed with rails, "very curiously carved and wrought," as was also the staircase throughout the house. On the west were large kitchens and coal-house, with lofts over it. At the entrance-gate to the upper bowling-green was a "parlour-lodge," close to which a double flight of steps led down to the lower bowling-alley. There was still beyond this another bowling-alley, and an orchard well planted with choice fruit-trees, as also "one pleasant banqueting house, and one other fair and pleasant apartment called the Green Room, and one other Conduit House, and two turrets adjoining the walls." Beyond, to the south, was also "one fair Tennis Court, of brick, tiled, well accommodated with all things fitting for the same." This is the Tennis Court which till recently stood at the corner of James Street, the last building shown on Faithorne's plan in 1658.

On the east side of the upper part of the Haymarket, in the year 1720, if not still later, was living the widow of Colonel Thomas Panton, the successful gamester, who, having realised a sudden fortune as the keeper of a gaming-house in Piccadilly, had the good sense to invest his gains in a house and land, and abandon cards and the dice-box. His name is still kept up in that of Panton Street, and of Panton Square; but the bulk of his wealth was carried by his daughter on her marriage into the family of Lord Arundell of Wardour, who gave his name to Arundell Street adjoining, and also, as we have said, to Wardour Street, in Soho.

On the same side of the street, opposite Charles Street, stands the Haymarket Theatre. Its early history runs as follows :—

In the year 1720 an enterprising carpenter named John Potter built a small playhouse in the Haymarket, on the site of the "King's Head Inn."

The cost of the building was £1,000, and Potter further expended £500 in decorations, scenery, and dresses. He leased the theatre, immediately after its completion, to a company of French actors, who were at that time much favoured by the English aristocracy, and who performed under a temporary licence from the Lord Chamberlain. This company styled themselves "The French Comedians of his Grace the Duke of Montague," that nobleman dropped from the clouds." His opening piece was entitled *Pasquin*, and, being a social satire of the most caustic nature, it achieved great popularity, and had a run of more than fifty nights. Elated by his success, Fielding produced a second piece, called *The Historical Register*, a political satire, which contained so audacious a caricature of Sir Robert Walpole, under the name of "Quidam," that the Prime Minister's resentment led to the

THE OLD HAYMARKET THEATRE.

being their principal patron, and opened the new house on the 29th of December, 1720, with the comedy of *La Fille à la Morte, ou le Badeaud de Paris*. At this time, and for several years afterwards, Potter's speculation was known to the play-going world as "The New French Theatre." About ten years later, being then occupied by an English company, it began to be spoken of as "The Little Theatre in the Haymarket"—a title which it retained until the original edifice was pulled down in 1820, having just completed a century of existence. Its site is now occupied by the "Café de l'Europe." In 1734 it was in the occupation of Henry Fielding, the great novelist and dramatist, with a congenial band, styled in the play-bills "The Great Mogul's Company, recently

passing of that Act which requires all dramatic pieces to be submitted to the approval of the Lord Chamberlain before they can be performed.

We are told by Mr. Frost, in his "Old Showmen," already quoted, that "Punch's celebrated company of comical tragedians from the Haymarket performed the most comical and whimsical tragedy that ever was tragedised by any tragical company of comedians, called *The Humours of Covent Garden*, by Henry Fielding, Esq."

In 1745 the "Little Theatre," having passed through the hands of several managers, each of whom had only a temporary licence, was opened without the ceremony of a licence of any sort by Theophilus Cibber, who succeeded in evading the usual penalty by the manner in which his advertisements were worded. They ran thus :—"At Cibber's Academy, in the Haymarket, will be a concert; after which will be exhibited *gratis* a rehearsal in the form of a play, called *Romeo and Juliet.*" It is probable, however, that in spite of this ingenious artifice, Mr. Cibber received an

Apropos of Foote's entertainment, a good story of the silly Duke of Cumberland is told by Mr. W. C. Hazlitt, in his "New London Jest Book." One night he was in the green-room here. "Well, here I am, Mr. Foote," said he, "ready to swallow all your good things." "Your royal highness,"

SAMUEL FOOTE.

official hint which induced him to announce, in the autumn of the same year, that "Mr. Cibber's company, being busily employed in reviving several pieces, are obliged to defer playing until further notice."

In 1747 the house was daily crowded by fashionable audiences to witness Samuel Foote's humorous entertainments, entitled "Foote giving Tea," &c., which included life-like imitations of the most notable characters of the day.

answered the witty actor, "must have the digestion of an ostrich, for I never knew you to throw up any again !"

When Foote first opened this theatre, amongst other projects, he proposed to entertain the public with an imitation of cat music. For this purpose he engaged a man famous for his skill in mimicking the mewing of cats. This person was called "Cat Harris." As he did not attend the rehearsal of this odd concert, Foote desired Shuter would endeavour to find him out and bring him with him. Shuter was directed to some court in the Minories where this extraordinary musician lived; but not being able to find the house, Shuter began a cat solo; upon this the other looked out of the window, and answered him with a cantata of the same sort. "Come along," said Shuter, "I want no better information that you are the man. Mr. Foote stays for us—we cannot begin the cat opera without you."

All sorts of stories are told of Foote, and some of them on very good authority. A few of them will bear repeating here.

Foote could not bear to see anybody or anything succeed in the Haymarket but himself and his own writings, and forgot that a failure of the new scheme might possibly endanger the regular payment of his annuity. His pique broke out sometimes in downright rudeness. One morning he came hopping upon the stage during the rehearsal of the *Spanish Barber*, then about to be produced; the performers were busy in that scene of the piece where one servant is under the influence of a sleeping draught, and another of a sneezing powder. "Well," said Foote, dryly, to the manager, "how do you go on?" "Pretty well," was the answer; "but I cannot teach one of these fellows to gape as he ought to do." "Can't you?" replied Foote; "then read him your last comedy of *The Man of Business*, and he'll yawn for a month."

On another occasion he was not less coarse, though more laughable, to an actor than he had been to the manager. This happened when Digges, of much celebrity out of London, and who had come to town from Edinburgh, covered with Scottish laurels, made his first appearance in the Haymarket. He had studied the antiquated style of acting; in short, he was a fine bit of old stage-buckram, and "Cato" was therefore selected for the first essay. He "discharged the character" in the same costume as it is to be supposed was adopted by Booth when the play was originally acted; that is, in a shape, as it was technically termed, of the stiffest order, decorated with gilt leather upon a black ground, with black stockings, black gloves, and a powdered periwig. Foote had planted himself in the pit, when Digges stalked on before the public thus formidably accoutred. The malicious wag waited till the customary round of applause had subsided, and then ejaculated, in a pretended under-tone, loud enough to be heard by all around him, "A Roman chimney-sweeper on May-day!" The laughter which this produced in the pit was enough to knock up a *débutant*, and it startled the old stager personating the Stoic of Utica; the sarcasm was irresistibly funny, but Foote deserved

to be kicked out of the house for his cruelty and insolence too.

The theatre barely escaped being destroyed, in 1749, by an enraged mob, the victims of a hoax planned by the eccentric Duke of Montague, who had caused an advertisement to appear, stating that, "on the 16th of January, a conjurer would jump into a quart bottle at the Little Theatre." On the appointed day thousands of persons were assembled in and around the theatre to witness the exploit, and a furious riot was the result of their disappointment.

In 1766 the Duke of York, who was Foote's staunch patron, obtained for him a royal patent for his life, in virtue of which the "little" playhouse became a "Theatre Royal," and Foote, who had leased it as a summer theatre since 1762, now purchased the premises on which it was built, and greatly altered and enlarged the building. It is said that on one occasion, when out on a party of pleasure with the Duke of York and other illustrious personages, Foote met with an accident which in the end was overruled to his advantage. He was thrown from his horse, and his leg being broken, he was forced to submit to amputation. It was in consequence of this accident the duke obtained for him the patent above mentioned. "Strange as it may appear, with the aid of a cork leg he performed his former characters with no less agility and spirit than before, and continued by his laughable performances to draw together crowded houses."

Remarkable for his wit as well as for his marvellous power of mimicry, neither friend nor patron was sacred from Foote's merciless satire, provided the person were sufficiently well known to be worth the trouble. It must, however, be urged in his defence, that his friends were no more troubled with scruples of delicacy than himself, and seem to have considered gross personalities to be the soul of wit. Foote's uncle, Captain Goodere, having been executed for the murder of his brother, Sir John Goodere, Mr. Cooke, the translator of "Hesiod," once presented Foote to a select society, with the agreeable introductory remark, "This is the nephew of Captain Goodere, the gentleman who was lately hung in chains for murdering his brother."

Another little episode in the annals of the Haymarket Theatre is perhaps worth mentioning here. In the early days of the Regency—about the year 1810—there suddenly appeared at the West-end a wealthy gentleman, of middle age, and of West Indian extraction, named Robert Coates. He was of good-figured appearance, dressed well, and even showily, and always wore a quantity of fur. At evening parties, to which he gained an entrance, his buttons and knee-buckles were studded with diamonds. There was a great mystery about his antecedents, and the public curiosity was heightened by the announcement that he proposed to appear at the Haymarket Theatre in the character of "Romeo." By hook or by crook he contrived to arrange for this appearance, and on the night the house was crowded to suffocation, the play-bill having given out that an "amateur of fashion" had consented to perform "for one night only;" and it was generally whispered that the rehearsal gave unmistakable signs that the tragedy would be turned into a comedy. But his appearance outdid all expectations. Mr. Coates's dress was grotesque in the extreme. In a cloak of sky-blue silk, profusely spangled, red pantaloons, a vest of white muslin, and a wig of the style of Charles II., capped by an opera hat, he brought down the whole house with laughter before he opened his lips, and the laughter was increased by the fact that his nether garments, being far too tight, burst in seams which could not be concealed. But when his guttural voice was heard, and he showed his total misapprehension of every part of the play, especially in the vulgarity of his address to "Juliet," and in his equally absurd rendering of the balcony scene, the whole thing was so comic, that gallery and pit were equally convulsed with laughter, and the piece ended in an uproar. It is needless to add that, for the character of the theatre, "Romeo" Coates, as he was afterwards called, was not allowed to appear again upon the stage at the Haymarket, though he possibly amused his friends by amateur performances in private.

To this theatre belongs the somewhat eccentric and amusing story of Lady Caroline Petersham, told by Horace Walpole :—

"Your friend Lady C—— P—— has entertained the town with a new scene. She was t'other night at the play with her court—viz., Miss Ashe, Lord Barnard, M. St. Simon, and her favourite footman, Richard, whom, under pretence of keeping places, she always keeps in her box the whole time to see the play at his ease. Mr. Stanley, Colonel Vernon, and Mr. Vaughan arrived at the very end of the farce, and could find no room but a row and a half in Lady C——'s box. Richard denied their entrance very impertinently. Mr. Stanley took him by the hair of his head, dragged him into the passage, and thrashed him. The heroine was outrageous; the heroes not at all so. She sent Richard to (Sir John) Fielding for a warrant : he could not grant it ; and so it ended." On this incident Lady Lepel Hervey remarks, "Come and hear a little of what is going on in town. . . . . You will

hear of ladies of quality who uphold footmen in insulting gentlemen."

In 1770 the theatre was engaged by one Maddox, a performer on the slack wire ; and it is said that his were the most prosperous entertainments ever carried on in this house. His profits in one season are stated to have amounted to £11,000, being £2,500 more than Garrick's a few years earlier.

In 1776 Foote sold his interest in the theatre to George Colman the elder for an annuity of £1,600, and Colman, on Foote's death, early in the following year, obtained the whole property for £800. And now, for a period of nearly fifty years, the Haymarket Theatre was the property of George Colman, passing, in 1794, on the death of George the elder, into the hands of George the younger, under whose management it was one of the most prosperous theatres in London.

On the 3rd of February, 1794, a dreadful accident happened here, through the pressure of the crowd, who had assembled in great numbers, in consequence of the play on that night having been commanded by their Majesties. On opening the pit door, the rush was so strong, that a number of persons were thrown down, and fifteen persons deprived of life, and upwards of twenty others materially injured by bruises and broken limbs. Most of the sufferers were respectable persons, and among the dead were two of the heralds.

An old lady named Wall, for whom Colman, from early associations, appears to have had a kind consideration, had been an actress in a subordinate situation for many seasons in this theatre. We must all pay the debt of nature ; and, in due time, the old lady died. Somebody from the theatre went to break the intelligence to Colman, who, on hearing it, inquired "whether there had been any bills stuck up !" The messenger replied in the negative, and ventured to ask Mr. Colman why he had put that question. Colman answered, "They generally paste bills on a *dead wall*, don't they?"

In 1820, Colman having sold his entire interest in the theatre, the old edifice was pulled down, and the present building erected, on almost the same site, from a design by John Nash. The front is of stone, and is about sixty feet in length, and nearly fifty in height. The entrance is through a handsome portico, the entablature and pediment being supported by six columns of the Corinthian order ; above are circular windows connected by sculpture of an ornamental character. Under the portico are five doors, leading respectively to the boxes, pit, galleries, and box-office. The shape of the interior differs from that of every other theatre in London, being nearly a square, with the side facing the stage very slightly curved. The expense of the new building was about £20,000. It is a remarkably neat and pretty house, having two tiers of boxes, besides other half-tiers parallel with the lower gallery, and will seat about 1,500 persons with comfort.

The first great success of the new theatre was Poole's comedy of *Paul Pry*, which was produced in 1825, with Liston in the principal character, supported by William Farren, Mrs. Waylett, Mrs. Glover, and Madame Vestris. With such a caste it cannot be a matter of surprise that the piece had a run of 114 nights, and that the price of a box was sometimes paid for a seat in the gallery.

In 1837 Mr. Benjamin Webster became the lessee, and collected around him a brilliant company. Messrs. Macready, Charles Kean, Tyrone Power, Sheridan Knowles, Charles Mathews the younger, Mrs. Glover, Mrs. Nisbet, Miss Ellen Tree, Madame Vestris, Miss Cushman, Miss Helen Faucit, and Mrs. Stirling, were the most notable stars which shone in the Haymarket Theatre during Mr. Webster's management. In 1843 the lessee made a spirited effort in behalf of the modern drama, by offering a competition prize of £500 for the best comedy. The piece selected was *Quid pro Quo*, by Mrs. Gore, which was performed in the year 1844, and turned out a dead failure, a result partly compensated by the enormous success of Charles Mathews in *Used Up*, which was produced here shortly afterwards. Mr. Webster relinquished his connection with the Haymarket in 1853, after having effected great improvements at his own expense. He widened

the proscenium eleven feet, introduced gas at an expense of £500 per annum, and presented the central chandelier to the proprietors. The theatre then passed into the hands of Mr. Buckstone, under whose management it has run a career of uninterrupted prosperity. For several years it was the only house in London where the standard English comedies, such as *The School for Scandal*, *The Rivals*, &c., were regularly performed, the *pièce de résistance* being as regularly followed by a farce in which Mr. Buckstone sustained the principal part. For a quarter of a century since Mr. Buckstone became the lessee of the Haymarket he was the life and soul of his company; and just as in those days his "Tony Lumpkin" and "Bob Acres" seemed the chief features of the old comedies, so now the humours of "My Lord Dundreary" and the exquisite grace of Mr. Gilbert's fairy dramas would be accounted insipid, without the pinch of Attic salt with which the veteran actor flavours the dainty dish.

In a work published in 1808 it is made a subject of complaint that there were only two theatres, whereas London, in the reign of Elizabeth and James I., the golden age of the English drama, was not a tenth part of its then size, and yet nevertheless it contained seventeen theatres. "More theatres are therefore wanted," adds the writer; and he complains bitterly of the restrictions imposed on the dramatic muse by the exclusive privileges conferred on Drury Lane and Covent Garden. It is perhaps worthy of note that the first new theatre to break the ice of these restrictions was the Haymarket, as already related in this chapter.

CHAPTER XIX.

PALL MALL EAST, SUFFOLK STREET, &c.

The University Club-house and the Royal College of Physicians—The Society of Painters in Water-Colours—Benjamin West's *Chefs d'Œuvres*—Messrs. Colnaghi's and Messrs. Graves' Print-shops—The Assassination of Thomas Thynne—Grant of Land to Edward Russell in 1692—The Old Horse-pond—Suffolk House—Suffolk Street—Miss Vanhomrigh and Dean Swift—Stanislaus, King of Poland—Mr. Chenevix's Toy-shop—The "Cock Tavern" and Mr. Pepys—The "Calves' Head Club"—The Gallery of British Artists—Suffolk Place and "Moll Davis"—Dorset Place and Whitcomb Street—Hedge Lane—Supposed Remains of the Old Royal Mews—Oxendon Street Chapel—The Attack on Sir John Coventry—James Street—The Royal Tennis Court—Fawkes, the Conjuror—Orange Street Chapel—Sir Isaac Newton's Residence—Panton Street—Royal Comedy Theatre—Goldsmith's and Burke's Visit to the Puppets—Hamlet, the Jeweller—Messrs. Ambroise and Brunn's Entertainments—The Société Française de Bienfaisance—A Singular Atmospheric Phenomenon—Arundell Street—Coventry Street—Coventry House—Sights and Amusements—Messrs. Wishart's Tobacco and Snuff Manufactory—The Kilted Highlander as a Sign for Snuff-shops.

EXTENDING eastward from the southern end of Her Majesty's Theatre to Trafalgar Square, and skirting the northern end of Cockspur Street, is Pall Mall East. Here, at the corner of Suffolk Street, stands the United University Club-house, of which we have already spoken* in our chapter on "Club-

land," and also the principal front of the Royal College of Physicians, described in the previous volume.†

At No. 5 are the rooms of the old Society of Painters in Water-Colours. Externally the building possesses nothing to call for special mention,

* See above, p. 146.

* See Vol. III., p. 142.

excepting, perhaps, a new and elegant doorway, which was erected in 1875; this, alike in design and workmanship, is worthy of the gallery to which it gives access. The society itself originated in 1808, when its first exhibition of water-colour drawings took place. It was at first blended with that of the Royal Academy; but in 1821 the painters in this branch of art determined to exhibit their productions separately from other artists, and erected the house in Pall Mall East expressly for the purpose. The exhibition is open during the greater part of the year, and comprises usually about 500 pictures of various kinds, among which, as might be expected, landscapes generally predominate. This society has always limited the exhibition entirely to its own members; but the body of artists showed a gradual and steady increase.

Here, in the year 1819, were exhibited the *chefs d'œuvres* of Benjamin West, President of the Royal Academy, including his "Christ rejected by the Jews," and "Death on the White Horse." The former contains nearly two hundred figures, in their appropriate costumes, all these displaying some passion of grief, pity, astonishment, revenge, exultation, or total apathy. The principal figures of Christ, the High Priest, Pilate, and many others, taken as single objects, are scarcely to be equalled in the entire compass of art. It is enriched with a splendid frame, carved after the model of the gate of the Temple of Theseus at Athens.

From its central position, Pall Mall East has always been a favourite locality in the world of art; and the two old-established shops for the sale of prints and engravings—that of Messrs. Colnaghi, adjoining the College of Physicians, and of Messrs. Graves, close by the Royal Opera Arcade—have tended to keep up its reputation in this respect. At No. 9, on the north side of the street, are the offices of the Palestine Exploration Fund, to which Biblical scholars are so largely indebted for bringing to light many objects in Jerusalem and elsewhere, which throw light on the narrative of the Holy Scriptures, as well as on the manners and customs of the Jewish people two thousand years ago.

Nearly opposite the south-west corner of what is now the Opera House, on Sunday, February 12th, 1681, Mr. Thomas Thynne was "most barbarously shot with a musketoon in his coach, and died next day." The instigator of this crime, as we have already related in describing Thynne's monument in Westminster Abbey,* was Count Köningsmark, who was in hopes of gaining the hand of the rich heiress, Lady Elizabeth Ogle, to whom Thynne was either already married or else contracted. The sentiment of Köningsmark on this occasion furnishes a curious insight into the ideas as to violence current in the days of the early Stuarts. We learn from the "State Trials" that he "allowed that the assassination of Mr. Thynne by his bravoes was a stain on his blood, but only such a one as a good action in the wars . . . would easily wash out!" Three of the ruffians whom he hired to do the deed were tried at the Old Bailey, found guilty, and hanged on the spot whereon the murder was committed. The cowardly villain, the Count himself, however, escaped the just punishment of his crime, getting off by securing the favour of a corrupt jury. Strangely enough, the jury who acquitted the real and principal agent, condemned the actual perpetrator of the deed, Colonel Vrats, who was hung, and, being of good family in Holland, was allowed to have his body embalmed and carried thither; so Evelyn, at least, tells us in his "Diary."

Two parcels of waste ground—no doubt, a part of the old site of the Royal Mews, containing about three acres, bounded on the east by the once rural Hedge Lane, by the Haymarket on the west, and by Cockspur Street on the south, including Suffolk and Little Suffolk Streets—were granted by the Crown, in 1692, to Edward Russell, no fine being taken "on account of the eminent services" of the grantee. It may be added, in excuse for the grant, that in the good old days before George III. was king, when Leicester *Square* was Leicester Field—a "dirty place where ragged boys used to assemble to play at chucks"—between the bottom of the Haymarket and "the King's Mews" there was a horse-pond, where stray horses were taken to water, and in which pickpockets were ducked when caught in the act.

Mr. Peter Cunningham considers that in early times there was a town mansion of the Earls of Suffolk on the site of what is now Suffolk Street; and quotes, in support of his views, the commencement of the ballad of Suckling, already given above on page 219. The Suffolks, however, subsequently became possessed of what was afterwards Northumberland, but was for a time called Suffolk, House, at Charing Cross, when they removed to their new quarters.

In this street, which now consists almost entirely of modern houses, and has been transformed partly into Pall Mall East, and partly into Dorset Place, formerly resided the unhappy Miss Vanhomrigh, the poor "Vanessa" of Dean Swift, a lady who died of a broken heart through her unfortunate

* See Vol. III., p. 419.

attachment to the Dean. The witty Dean, when in London on the affairs of the Irish Church, made the acquaintance of this young lady and her mother, the widow of a Dutch merchant, and became so constant a visitor at their house, as to leave there "his best gown and cassock for convenience." As he was a man of middle age, while she was not twenty, it was thought quite a matter

for she was always known by the latter, and never by the former name—that surely "Vanessa" must have been an extraordinary woman to have inspired the Dean to write such fine verses upon her. "That's not at all clear," said the lady, offended with and yet proud of her husband, and hurt besides in her own vanity, "for it is very well known that the Dean could write finely upon a broomstick."

THE COLLEGE OF PHYSICIANS. (*See page* 226.)

of course that he should direct her studies; but this direction of her reading soon ripened into quite another affair, and it was only when Miss Vanhomrigh's affections were deeply and irrevocably engaged that she discovered, on following the Dean back to Ireland, that he had a wife living— his "Stella." This discovery was shortly afterwards followed by the young lady's death.

While the melancholy fate of Miss Vanhomrigh was the common topic of conversation in London circles, and while every one was reading the Dean's "Cadenus and Vanessa," somebody is said to have remarked to Mrs. Swift, or rather to Mrs. Johnson—

Malcolm tells us that the last and most unfortunate King of Poland, Stanislaus Augustus lodged in 1754, in Suffolk Street, at the house of a Mr. Cropenhole. We also learn incidentally that "over against Suffolk Street, Charing Cross," in the reign of George II., was the celebrated toy-shop of Mr. Chenevix, where tickets for most of the West-end "shows" and exhibitions were sold.

In Suffolk Street was an old hostelry, the "Cock," much praised by Samuel Pepys, who thus writes, under date March 15, 1669: "Mr. Hewes and I did walk to the Cocke, at the end of Suffolk Street, where I never was (before): a great ordinary mightily cried up, and there bespoke a pullet; which, while dressing, he and I walked into St. James's Park, and thence back, and dined very handsome, with a good soup and a pullet for 4s. 6d. the whole." It would appear that on the whole the diarist was well pleased with the accommoda-

occasion, was held one of the meetings of this club, which, in the year 1735, produced a serious riot. At this meeting it is said by tradition that a bleeding calf's head, wrapped in an old napkin, was thrown out of the window into the street below, while the members of the club inside were drinking

THE OLD TENNIS COURT, NEAR THE HAYMARKET. (*See page* 231.)

tion; for in less than a month afterwards he took his wife and some other friends thither, where they were "mighty merry," the house being "famous for good meat, and particularly for pease-porridge."

A tavern in this street—possibly the "Cock," already mentioned—appears to have been at one time the head-quarters of the famous, or rather infamous, "Calves' Head Club," established by the Puritans and Roundheads in ridicule of the memory of Charles I. At all events, here, on one

the pious toast of confusion to the Stuart race! Lord Middlesex, however, who was one of those present on the occasion, denies the truth of this indictment in a letter to Mr. Spence, which is published in "Spence's Anecdotes." In this letter he says that there happened to be a bonfire of straw made by some boys in the street under the windows, and that some of the company, "wiser or soberer than the rest," proposed drinking some loyal and popular toasts to the mob outside, and that the only toasts drank by the members were the King, the Queen, the Royal Family, the Protestant Succession, Liberty and Property, and the present Administration. Stones were then flung, the windows of the tavern were broken, and a regular row ensued, which was only suppressed by the arrival, an hour later, of "the justice, attended by a strong body of guards, who dispersed the populace."

The author of the "Secret History of the Calves' Head Club, or the Republicans Unmasked" (supposed to be "Ned Ward," of alehouse memory), ascribes the origin of this association to Milton and other partisans of the Commonwealth, who, in opposition to Bishop Juxon, Bishop Sanderson, and other loyalists, used to meet together on the 30th of every January, having compiled for their own use a form of prayer for the day, not very unlike that which was till lately to be found in the Book of Common Prayer. "After the Restoration," observes the writer of this pamphlet, "the eyes of the Government being on the whole party, they were obliged to meet with a great deal of precaution; but in the reign of King William they met almost in a public manner, apprehending no danger. . . . They kept in no fixed house, but moved about from place to place, as they thought convenient." The place where they met when his informant was present was in a blind alley near Moorfields, where "an axe was hung up in the club-room, and was reverenced as a principal symbol in this diabolical sacrament. Their bill of fare was a large dish of calves' heads, dressed in several ways, by which they represented the king, and his friends who had suffered in his cause; a large pike with a smaller one in his mouth, as an emblem of tyranny; a large cod's head, by which they intended to represent the person of the king singly; a boar's head with an apple in his mouth, to represent the king as bestial, as by their other hieroglyphics they had made him out to be foolish and tyrannical. After the repast was over, one of their elders presented an 'Icon Basilicé,' which was with great solemnity burnt on the table, whilst anthems were being sung. After this, another produced Milton's 'Defensio Populi Anglicani,' upon which all present laid their hands, and made a protestation in form of an oath ever to stand by and maintain the same. After the table-cloth was removed, the anniversary anthem, as they impiously called it, was sung, and a calf's skull, filled with wine or other liquor, and then a brimmer, went about to the pious (?) memory of those worthy patriots who had 'killed the tyrant,' and relieved their country from his arbitrary sway; and lastly, a collection was made for the mercenary

scribbler [probably meaning John Milton], to which every man contributed according to his zeal for the cause and the ability of his purse. The company consisted only of Anabaptists and Independents; and the famous Jeremy White—formerly chaplain to Oliver Cromwell, who, no doubt, came to sanctify with his pious exhortations the ribaldry of the day—said grace before and after dinner." "Although no great reliance," says Wilson, in his "Life of Defoe," "is to be placed upon the faithfulness of Ward's narrative, yet in the frighted mind of a high-flying Churchman, continually haunted by such scenes, the caricature would easily pass for a likeness. It is probable, therefore, that the above account must not be accepted without many grains of salt to qualify it. The name and idea of the club is sufficiently disgusting, and a lasting dishonour, not to the murdered king, but to its founders."

On the east side of Suffolk Street stands the Gallery of British Artists. The building, which was completed in 1824, is entered by a Doric portico, designed by Mr. Nash, and consists of a suite of six octagonal galleries, all on one floor, and lighted from above, designed by Mr. James Elmes.

In consequence of the limited size of the rooms at Somerset House, where the Royal Academy held its exhibitions, the Society of British Artists was instituted in 1823 for the annual display of the works of living artists in the various branches of painting, sculpture, architecture, and engraving. The fund raised for the erection of the building, &c., was by donations and subscriptions, which were divided into eight classes, and admissions awarded in accordance with the amount given or subscribed.

In a notice of the building printed in the *Mirror*, in 1824, it is stated that it was "intended as a building for the reception of ancient models, casts, &c., and students; the ground storey is occupied by a portico of the Grecian Doric, having coupled *antæ*, the proportions, apparently, from the Temple of Theseus, at Athens; the upper storey is a continuation of the *antæ* throughout the front; in the centre is a window with a pediment, frieze, architrave, &c., from the Temple of Erectheus, at Athens, ornamented with *pateræ*, as are also the *antæ*; the ornaments are of terra cotta, the whole surmounted by a bold cornice."

Suffolk Place, leading to Suffolk Street, is mentioned by Strype as consisting of handsome houses. They do not, however, appear to have been aristocratically tenanted. At all events, here lived the notorious "Moll Davis," in a mansion which Charles II. had furnished expensively for her—an arrangement of which even Pepys speaks as "a most infinite shame ;" she kept also, as he tells us, " a mighty pretty fine coach."

Running up northwards from Pall Mall East, in the rear of Suffolk Street, are Dorset Place and Whitcomb Street, its continuation, which leads towards Coventry Street. This follows the course of the old " Hedge Lane," which, till about 1830, commemorated the once rural character of the neighbourhood of the Haymarket and Leicester Fields.

It is related of Steele, Budgell, and Phillips, that one evening, when they were coming out of a tavern or coffee-house in Gerrard Street, they were warned that there were some suspicious characters waiting to waylay any stray foot-passengers in Hedge Lane. " Thank ye," said the wits, and each hurried off home by a different way.

Hedge Lane is marked in the map of Ralph Aggas, *temp.* Elizabeth, and was, even in the days of Charles II., what the name implied—a lane running into the fields, and bordered by hedges. The Duke of Monmouth is said to have lived here before taking up his abode in Soho, where we have already seen him located. According to Mr. Peter Cunningham, Maurice Lowe, the painter, was also a resident of this lane. It was still called Hedge Lane in the days of Dr. Johnson, of whom Boswell tells us that, in April, 1778, on his way to dine at the West-end, he got out of the hackney-coach at the bottom of Hedge Lane in order to leave a letter containing charitable aid for a " poor man in distress," probably a hungry author.

The Royal Mews, already mentioned, in the reign of Henry VIII., as standing near the bottom of the lane, was burnt in 1534, and some remains (or what were supposed to be remains) of its charred walls were discovered in 1821.

In Oxendon Street, which runs parallel to the Haymarket, from north to south, about half way between it and Leicester Square, formerly stood, on its western side, a Nonconformist chapel, which had become historical. It was built by no less a man than that " prince of Independents," Richard Baxter, " adjoining the wall of the house of Mr. Secretary Coventry," to whom Baxter's principles were so unpalatable that it is said he caused the soldiers to beat drums under the chapel windows to drown the preacher's voice. The Secretary was so far successful in this outrageous conduct that he forced Baxter to give up the chapel, which afterwards became a chapel-of-ease to the parish in which it stood. The following curious notice respecting it will be found in the *Spectator*, under date November 30, 1711 : " This is to give notice to all promoters of the holy worship, and to all lovers of the Italian tongue, that on Sunday next, being the 2nd of December, at five in the afternoon, in Oxendon Chapel, near the Haymarket, there will be divine service in the Italian tongue, and will continue every Sunday at the aforesaid hour, with an Italian sermon, preached by Mr. Casotti, Italian minister, author of a new method of teaching the Italian tongue to ladies," &c. Malcolm, in his " Londinium Redivivum," after quoting the advertisement, adds a waggish remark, to the effect that the chapel is still (1807) in use, though " not for the above purpose of teaching the Italian language." The chapel, after serving as a chapel-of-ease to St. Martin's, passed to the " Scottish Secession." It was pulled down about 1875, its connection removing to Haverstock Hill.

It was in this street that Sir John Coventry was living at the time of the attack made on him in the Haymarket, as noticed in the preceding chapter. It appears that Sir John had been supping with some friends at the Cock Tavern in Bow Street, and was, at the time, on his way home. A motion had recently been made in the House of Commons to lay a tax on playhouses. The Court opposed the motion. The players, it was said (by Sir John Birkenhead), were the king's servants, and a part of his pleasure. Coventry asked, " Whither did the king's pleasure lie, among the men or the women that acted ?" perhaps recollecting more particularly the king's visit to Moll Davis in Suffolk Street, where Charles had furnished a house for her, provided her with " a mighty pretty fine coach," and given her a ring of £700, " which," says the page (like Pepys), " is a most infinite shame." The king determined to *leave a mark* upon Sir John Coventry for his freedom of remark, and he was marked on his way home. " He stood up to the wall," says Burnet, " and snatched the flambeau out of the servant's hands ; and with that in one hand, and the sword in the other, he defended himself so well, that he got more credit by it than by all the actions of his life. He wounded some of them, but was soon disarmed, and " they cut his nose to the bone, to teach him to remember what respect he owed to the king." Burnet adds, that " his nose was so well sewed up, that the scar was scarcely to be discerned."

Eastward from the Haymarket, a little north of the theatre, stretches James Street, on the south side of which is a building which was till lately occupied by the Royal Tennis Court. Tennis, if we may trust old writers, derives its name from the French Hand-ball or Palm-play, and was played in London as far back as the sixteenth century, in covered courts erected for that special purpose. Henry VII. and

Henry VIII. were both fond of tennis; the latter added a tennis-court to his palace at Whitehall. James I., we know, recommended tennis to his son as a game well becoming the dignity of a prince. Charles II. was an accomplished master of the game, and had a particular dress which he wore when playing it here. Timbs tells us that there was another tennis-court not far off, in Windmill Street, belonging to and attached to Piccadilly Hall. He also mentions "one called Gibbons's in Clare Market, where Killigrew's comedians sometimes performed," and others in Holborn, Blackfriars, and Southwark, where there were (and possibly still are) small thoroughfares still bearing the name of Tennis Courts. The court in James Street, it may be added, was one of the favourite haunts of Charles II. It was closed about the year 1863, and has lately been converted into a storehouse for military clothing.

In this street, in the reign of George II., the conjuror Fawkes used to locate his "show" in the intervals between the various London and suburban fairs, at which he put in his appearance, anticipating the tricks of Colonel Stodare of our own time.

The eastern end of James Street is continued by Orange Street—so called after the Prince of Orange, William III.—which is crossed by St. Martin's Street, running northwards into the centre of the south side of Leicester Square. The corner of Orange and St. Martin's Street is occupied by a Nonconformist chapel. Next to the chapel stands a house which is still visited by pilgrims from all parts of the world, as having been the last London residence of Sir Isaac Newton. He removed hither in 1710 from Jermyn Street, but did not die here, as is erroneously said by Dr. Burney in an anecdote related to Boswell, and mentioned in his "Life of Johnson." The house is now a school; on its roof was till lately a small observatory built by a subsequent tenant, but often supposed to have been Newton's own. The house had subsequently as its tenants Dr. Burney and his daughter Frances, who here composed her once (and still) popular novel, "Evelina." Frances Burney (Madame D'Arblay) dates from this house many of the letters published in her diaries; and Mr. Henry Thrale—Johnson's friend and host—writing to Miss Burney, playfully styles the inmates of the house his "dear Newtonians."

Panton Street, which forms one of the connecting links between the Haymarket and Leicester Square, was so called after its ground landlord, Colonel Panton, of whom we have spoken in the preceding chapter as having won his money at the card-table, and refusing to touch a card again. It has been said, though erroneously, that the street received its name from a kind of horse-shoe called a panton. At the corner of Panton and Oxendon Streets stands the Royal Comedy Theatre, which was erected in 1881. The class of entertainment given here is implied by the name of the theatre.

In a large room in Panton Street, Messrs. Ambroise and Brunn gave a "variety entertainment," consisting of "Ombres Chinoises," "danses de caractère," and sundry "metamorphoses" by a veritable magician; this being patronised by the Court, the price of admission was raised to five shillings. This same room was occupied, in a subsequent season, by the conjuror Breslau.

Forster tells us in his "Life of Goldsmith" that poor Oliver and Edmund Burke once paid a visit to some very ingenious puppets exhibited here. Burke praised in particular the dexterity of one puppet, who tossed a pike with military precision. "Psha!" remarked Goldsmith, with some warmth, "I could do it better myself." Boswell adds that Goldsmith afterwards went home to supper with Burke, and broke his shin by attempting to show the company how much better he could jump over a stick than the puppets themselves.

It is, perhaps, worth noting that Hamlet, the great jeweller of the time of the Regency, who had nearly all the aristocracy on his books, and of whom we have already spoken in our notice of Cranbourn Alley, Leicester Square, at one time had his business in Panton Street. He made a colossal fortune, but afterwards hastening to be rich in excess, he lost it through unfortunate speculations.

At No. 5 in this street was established, in 1842, a charitable institution, entitled the Société Française de Bienfaisance, for the relief of the distressed French in London. Its chief operations consist in giving temporary help in money and bread to numerous French artisans out of work.

Before quitting Panton Street, we may add, on the authority of Hughson's "London," that in the afternoon of the 9th of June, 1803, a most singular phenomenon happened here. He writes: "The inhabitants were alarmed by a violent and tremendous storm of rain and hail, which extended only to Oxendon Street, Whitcomb Street, Coventry Street, and the Haymarket, a space not exceeding 200 acres. For about seven minutes the torrent from the heavens was so great that it could only be compared to a cataract rushing over the brow of a precipice. In the midst of the hurricane an electric cloud descended in Panton Street, which struck the centre of the coachway, and sunk in to a great depth, forming a complete pit, in which not a vestige of the materials which had before occupied the space could be found. The sulphurous odour from the cloud was so powerful that for several seconds the persons near the spot were almost suffocated. No further damage was done, except filling the neighbouring kitchens and cellars with water, which soon escaped through the gulf formed by the electric fluid."

Arundell Street, which leads from Panton Square to Coventry Street, preserves the memory of its original ground landlord, Lord Arundell of Wardour; and still remains in the possession of the family.

Coventry Street derived its name from Mr. Henry Coventry, Secretary of State in the reign of Charles II., whose private mansion stood on its south side, with a garden wall running down behind what now is the west side of Oxendon Street. In the *London Gazette* for July — August, 1674, is an advertisement offering a reward for the recovery of a white, long-haired land-spaniel, lost between London and Barnet, on application to "the porter at Mr. Secretary Coventry's house in Pickadilly." Coventry House, according to Pennant, stood on the site of a building called in the old plans of London "The Gaming House."

The Secretary, it may be added, died here in 1686, and was buried in the church of St. Martin's-in-the-Fields. Coventry Street was continued eastwards beyond Leicester Square into St. Martin's Lane about the year 1842; the compensation paid to the freeholder of the ground, the Marquis of Salisbury, exceeded £70,000.

Like the rest of this neighbourhood, Coventry Street in its time has had its places of amusement. At one of these, in 1835, was exhibited the "Parisian infernal machine." This extraordinary exhibition comprised a likeness of the murderer Gerard (*alias* Fieschi), before and after the perpetration of his crime, attempting to assassinate the French king and his sons; also a model of the room and of the infernal machinery, taken from drawings made on the spot by distinguished artists, sent to Paris expressly for that purpose. The advertisements announcing this place of entertainment state that "Ladies may visit this exhibition, where the most scrupulous attention has been observed not to wound the most fastidious delicacy."

In 1851, one of the most popular entertainments given here was that of a French wizard, named Robin.

The tobacco and snuff manufactory of Messrs. Wishart, now in the Haymarket, was located in this street for many years. The house has lately been demolished to make room for improvements. The "card" of the firm a century and a half ago, and still used, is a curiosity in its way. A fac-simile of it is here given.

WISHART'S SHOP-CARD.

Mr. J. Larwood humorously remarks in his "History of Sign-boards," "Since the Highlander's love of snuff and whisky was such, that he wished to have a Ben Lomond of the former and a Loch Lomond of the latter, nobody could make a better public-house sign than the 'Highland Laddie,' nor a better sign for a snuff-shop than the kilted Highlander, who generally stands guard at the door of these establishments."

The following skit appeared shortly after the Rebellion of 1745, when every effort was made to suppress the nationality of the Scotch, down to their ballads and their kilts:—"We hear that the dapper wooden Highlanders who so heroically guard the doors of snuff-shops intend to petition the Legislature in order that they may be excused from complying with the Act of Parliament with respect to the change of dress, alleging that they have ever been faithful subjects to his Majesty, having constantly supplied his guards with a pinch out of their mulls when they marched by; and so far from engaging in any rebellion, they have never

In Coventry's known street, near Leicester Fields,
At the 'Two Heads,' full satisfaction yields.
Teeth artificial he fixes so secure,
That as our own they usefully endure;
Not merely outside show and ornament,
But every property of teeth intent;
To eat as well as speak, and form support

SIR ISAAC NEWTON'S HOUSE, 1850. (*See page* 232.)

entertained a rebellious thought: whence they humbly hope that they shall not be put to the expense of buying new clothes."

The "Two Heads" in this street was, in 1760, the sign of an advertising dentist, who thus makes known his profession in the *London Evening Post*:

" Ye beauties, beaux, ye pleaders at the bar,
Wives, husbands, lovers, every one beside
Who'd have their heads deficient rectify'd,
The dentist famed, who by just application
Excels each other operator in the nation,

To falling cheeks and stumps from further hurt.
Nor is he daunted when the whole is gone,
But by an art peculiar to him known,
He'll so supply, you'll think you've got your own.
He scales, he cleans, he draws; in pain gives ease,
Nor in each operation doth fail to please.
Doth the foul scurvy fierce your gums assault?
In this he also rectifies the fault
By a fam'd tincture.   And his powder, nam'd
A Dentifrice, is also justly fam'd.
Used as directed, 'tis excellent to serve
Both teeth and gums—cleanse, strengthen, and preserve.

"Foul mouth and stinking breath can ne'er be lov'd ;
But by his aid these evils are remov'd."

In this street, towards the close of the last century, if the tradition runs aright, there was a famous fish-shop which numbered Sir Joshua Reynolds (who lived hard by in Leicester Square) among its daily customers. The great painter would generally stroll so far before breakfast,

examine the fish that lay on the leads, turn them over and reverse their position ; then, having chosen what was to his taste, he would go back to breakfast, report the state of the fish-market, and send his sister to effect the purchase. " Miss Reynolds," the old fishmonger used to say, " never chose ; Sir Joshua never paid ; and both were good hands at driving bargains."

THE LION BREWERY. (*See page* 239.)

(*See page* 239.)

CHAPTER XX.

GOLDEN SQUARE AND ITS NEIGHBOURHOOD.

" Fallentis semita vitæ."—*Horace, "Epistles."*

The Neighbourhood of Golden Square Two Centuries ago—Great Windmill Street—Piccadilla Hall—Noted Residents—Anatomical School—Argyll Rooms—St. Peter's Church—Golden Square—Lord Bolingbroke—Mrs. Cibber—Angelica Kauffmann—The Residence of Cardinal Wiseman—Chapel for French Refugees—Wardour Street—Dr. Dodd's Residence—Princes Street—The "Star and Crown" and the "Thirteen Cantons" —Berwick Street—St. Luke's Church—Bentinck Street—Sherwin, the Engraver—Broad Street—William Blake—"The Good Woman"— The Lion Brewery- Warwick Street—Roman Catholic Chapel of the Assumption—Carnaby Street—The Pest Houses—Great Marlborough Street—Distinguish.d Inhabitants—Argyll Street—Northcote the Painter—Madame de Staël—The "Good" Lord Lyttelton—Argyll House —Argyll Street Rooms—Chabert, the "Fire King"—The Harmonic Institution—Oxford Street—The Pantheon—Miss Linwood's Ex-hibition of Needlework—The "Green Man and Still"—The "Hog in the Pound"—The "North Pole"—The "Balloon" Fruit-shop.

IN the second year after the Restoration orders were issued for the paving of the way from St. James's northwards, which was a quagmire, and also of the Haymarket "about Piquadillo." The

Piccadilly line of road is said to have formed at its eastern end the line of demarcation between the courtly mansions then in the course of erection in "St. James's Fields," and the mean and small dwellings which, in Sir C. Wren's words, "will prove only a receptacle for the poorer sort, and for offensive trades, to the annoyance of the better inhabitants, the damage of the parishes already too much burdened with poor, the choking of the air of his Majesty's palace and park and the houses of the nobility, and the infecting of the waters." These dwellings were some lately erected in Dog's Fields, Windmill Fields, and the fields adjoining Soho. This is the first mention that we find of the neighbourhood of which Golden Square and Wardour Street now form the western and eastern limits. The property in this vicinity of old belonged to Lord Craven, who erected the famous pest-house here for the reception of those struck by the plague. The lazaretto itself consisted, we are told, of thirty-six small tenements; and near it, at the lower end of Marshall Street, was a common cemetery, in which some thousands of poor persons found a last resting-place during the continuance of that pestilence. "Out of Wardour Street," we are told by Strype, in 1720, "goeth Peter Street, which crosseth Berwick Street, and falleth into waste and unbuilt ground; a street not over-well inhabited. Here is a small court, but the right name is not given. Further northward is Edward Street, which also crosseth Berwick Street, and falleth into waste and unbuilt ground; nor is this street over-well inhabited." Berwick Street, mentioned as running on the west of Wardour Street as far to the north as "Tyburn Road," is described as a "pretty, handsome, straight street, with new well-built houses, much inhabited by the French, where they have a church." About the middle of the street was a place designed for a hay market, and a great part of the low ground raised, with some of the houses built piazza-wise. "Westward of this," adds the annalist, "is a large tract of waste ground, reaching to the wall of the pest-house builded by the Earl of Craven, which runneth from the back side of Golden Square to a piece or close of meadow ground which reacheth to Tyburn Road."

Passing northward from Coventry Street, in a direct line from the Haymarket, is Great Windmill Street, so called from a mill which stood there till the reign of Charles II.; it was designed at one time to be made the main thoroughfare from Charing Cross and the Haymarket to Oxford Street; the removal of Carlton House, however, deflected this to Swallow (now Regent) Street. At the corner of Great Windmill Street formerly stood a noted gaming-house, called Piccadilly Hall, mentioned by Lord Clarendon, in his "History of the Rebellion," under date 1640. Referring

to himself, Clarendon says: "Mr. Hyde going to a house called Piccadilly, which was a fair house for entertainment and gaming, with handsome gravel walks and with shade, and where were an upper and a lower bowling-green, whither very many of nobility and gentry of the best quality resorted for exercise and conversation."

In explanation apparently of this incidental mention, Pennant tells us that "at the upper end of the Haymarket stood Piccadilla Hall, where piccadillas, or turn-overs, were sold, which gave name to that vast street called from that circumstance Piccadilly." This street was completed in 1642 as far westwards as Berkeley Street. The explanation, however, does not solve the mystery which surrounds the word, unless we suppose that the "fair house for entertainment" mentioned by Lord Clarendon derived its name from the articles sold in the neighbouring houses. The tennis-court attached to the hall was not pulled down till our own day. Its last owner was the celebrated and successful gamester, Colonel Panton. The gaming-house itself figures in Faithorne's plan of London, published in 1658, as almost the only house standing in this locality.

In Great Windmill Street lived Colonel Godfrey, whose wife, Arabella Churchill, sister of John, Duke of Marlborough, had been the mistress of James II., when Duke of York.

Here, in the early part of the present century, was the great Anatomical School of the metropolis, in which nearly all the most distinguished surgeons of the last two generations taught as lecturers and professors. This school of surgery owed its establishment to Dr. William Hunter, who erected the building, and in whose "Medical Commentaries" will be found a full account of its origin and progress. Its lecturers were chiefly members of the staff of St. George's Hospital. The list included such names as Sir C. Bell, Sir B. Brodie, Dr. Baillie, and Dr. Wilson. Some interesting details respecting the introduction of Sir Charles Bell to it, and his long connection with it, will be found in a work entitled "Extracts from the Correspondence of Sir Charles with his Brother, Mr. George Joseph Bell." After flourishing with great prestige for half a century or more, it began to decline, mainly owing to the establishment of other schools of the same kind in connection with University and King's College Hospitals. It may be added that the fine museum in which Sir Charles Bell used to lecture, with its miscellaneous collection of curiosa, which the Government refused to buy, was sold to the Royal College of Surgeons at Edinburgh. The house occupied by the Medical School became afterwards a printing-office, and is now a foreign restaurant.

On the site of the tennis-court of Piccadilly Hall stand the Argyll Rooms, which were formerly opened for promenade concerts and dancing ; such, however, was the character that the rooms acquired, that a renewal of the licence was refused about 1878. The place is now known as the "Trocadero." It was for some time a restaurant, but has recently obtained a licence to open as a music-hall. The rooms originally bearing the name of "The Argyll" stood, as we shall presently see, at the corner of Little Argyll Street.

Adjoining the above-mentioned rooms is St. Peter's Church, an edifice of Gothic design, erected in 1861, from the designs of Mr. Raphael Brandon. The church owes its origin mainly to the Rev. J. E. Kempe, the Rector of St. James's, Piccadilly ; the money for the work, amounting to some £12,000, having been chiefly obtained through his influence among his wealthy congregation.

Golden Square, which is connected with Windmill Street by two narrow thoroughfares, called respectively Denman and Brewer Streets, though so close to Regent Street, still lies out of the beaten path, and few Londoners know it, unless business happens to call them in its direction. It has been said of it that it is "not exactly in anybody's way, to or from anywhere." Even in the summer time it wears a dull and dingy look, and seems as if it had seen better days. And yet it stands immortalised, not only in Charles Dickens's "Nicholas Nickleby," but in the older and more venerable pages of "Humphrey Clinker" by Tobias Smollett, whilst the authors of the "Rejected Addresses," in their imitation of Crabbe, speak of "bankrupts from Golden Square and Riches Court." It is said to have derived its name from the person by whom it was laid out for building, and Hatton describes it in the reign of Queen Anne, within a few years of its erection, as a "very new and pleasant square." Pennant, however, says that the name was derived from a neighbouring inn, the "Gelding," which the good taste of its inhabitants changed gradually into "Golden"—a change, it must be owned, for the better, if true in fact. Pennant dismisses it with the remark that it is "of dirty access ;" and certainly none of the thoroughfares which lead into it can be accused of being broad or clean. This square, which was at one time surrounded with wooden rails, was built a little before the Revolution of 1688, as is clear from its being mentioned by that name in an advertisement in the *Gazette* of that year.

One of its earliest inhabitants was the great Lord Bolingbroke, Pope's friend, when holding the office of Secretary-at-War, in the beginning of the last century ; and Mrs. Cibber, the singer, whose name is so well known in connection with that of Lord Peterborough, was living here in the reign of George II. The small and very common-place statue of George II., in the centre of the square, was brought from Lord Chandos's seat at Canons, near Edgware.

In the centre house on the south side of this square resided, for many years, Angelica Kauffmann, one of the original members of the Royal Academy, and who lived till 1807. Of this lady a very amusing story is told, illustrative of female folly and vanity. She was a great coquette, and pretended to be in love with several gentlemen at the same time. Once she professed to be enamoured of Nathaniel Dance ; to the next visitor she would divulge the great secret that she was dying for Sir Joshua Reynolds. However, she was at last rightly served for her duplicity, by marrying a very handsome fellow who pretended to be "Count Horn," an adventurer of the type of the Duc de Roussillon of more recent times. With this alliance she was so pleased, that she made her happy conquest known to Queen Charlotte, who was much astonished that the Count should have been so long in England without coming to Court! However, the real Count's arrival was some time afterwards announced at Dover ; and Angelica Kauffmann's titled husband turned out to be no other than the real Count's *valet de chambre!* He was prevailed upon subsequently to accept a separate maintenance. After this man's death she married an Italian, named Zucchi, and settled in Rome, where she spent her declining years. There is a portrait of Angelica, by Sir Joshua Reynolds, engraved by Bartolozzi.

The large house in the centre of the north side was for many years the residence of the Roman Catholic vicars-apostolic of the London district, as the heads of that communion in England were designated previous to the restoration of the hierarchy in 1850. Here, about 1835, were living Bishops Bramston and Griffiths, who successively held that office ; and the house was the residence of Dr. Wiseman, when he obtained, in 1850, the honour of the archiepiscopal mitre, and the red hat of a cardinal, in spite of Lord John Russell's ineffective opposition.

In 1875, Childs, an old servant of Lord Byron, and the last survivor of his personal attendants, was still acting as a beadle in this square.

In Glasshouse Street, close by the south side of the square, was founded, in 1689, a chapel for one of the French refugee congregations; but it was removed before long to Leicester Fields.

From what we have said, it is evident that the whole of this district was covered with small buildings towards the beginning of the eighteenth century, though here and there on the north there were a few open spaces left. A piece of stone, let into one of the houses in New Street, on the north side of the square, bears the date 1704. Thirty years before, as already stated, Sir C. Wren complained of the small streets which were being run up, and of the poverty of their inhabitants, as if he could foresee the day when St. Giles' and St. James' would be placed in close and painful contrast; and Fielding, in the reign of George II., describes the mob, whom he calls the "fourth estate of the realm," as "encroaching upon people of fashion," and driving them fast from their seats in Leicester, Soho, and Golden Squares, to Cavendish Square and other spots in that more distant locality, where there was more light and fresher air, as the breezes blew across the green lanes of St. Marylebone.

The streets to the north and east of the square were the scene of a very violent outbreak of cholera in the year 1853, on account of the overflowing of cess-pools into a well whence the inhabitants drew their supply of water.

To the east of the square lies Wardour Street, renowned as the head-quarters of the dealers in old furniture, and other curiosities, and which serves as a line of demarcation between this district and the parish of Soho. Here, we may add, lived Dr. Dodd in 1751, when, a little over age, he had married a penniless girl, and had not even yet taken orders. We shall have more to say of his career when we come to Pimlico.

"A large fort with four half bulwarks across the road (now Oxford Street), at the corner of Wardour Street," is mentioned among the fortifications ordered to be set up around London by the Parliament in 1642.

Wardour Street, with Princes Street, opens up a direct line of communication between Oxford Street and Leicester Square. In Princes Street was, in 1785, the "Star and Crown," the sign of a fashionable haberdasher, who, amongst other articles of female luxury, dealt in "dress and undress hoops." Branching off on the east from Princes Street is King Street, where there is a tavern called "The Thirteen Cantons." This sign was put up in compliment to the thirteen Protestant cantons of Switzerland, or more strictly speaking, to the numerous natives of those districts who were settled in the neighbourhood of Soho.

Parallel with Wardour Street, and opening into Oxford Street, is Berwick Street, which is described by Hatton (in 1708) as "a kind of a row;" whilst "the fronts of the houses, resting on columns, make a small piazza." The appearance of the houses in the present day, however, is very much changed. This street was a haunt of artists of little note, and of trades subservient to an artist's requirements. Mr. Peter Cunningham records the fact that Sir Joshua Reynolds's portrait of Sheridan was engraved by a resident in this street, John Hall, a man of some little fame in his day. The only building in this street which merits special mention is St. Luke's Church. This edifice serves as the church of a district cut off from St. James's, Westminster. It was built in 1838-9, from the designs of Mr. Blore, and in the Gothic style of architecture; but it has, nevertheless, a somewhat poor and mean appearance. The cost of the building and the site on which it stands amounted to about £14,000.

In Bentinck Street, which runs out of Berwick Street, was the studio of Sherwin, the engraver. Mr. J. T. Smith tells the following anecdote of this place, which brings up the remembrance of one of the most famous actresses of the last century:—"The Bishop of Peterborough (Dr. Hinchliffe), one of my father's patrons, prevailed on Sherwin to let me in at half-price; and under his roof I remained for nearly three years. Here I saw all the beautiful women of the day; and being considered a lively lad, I was noticed by several of them. Here I received a kiss from the beautiful Mrs. Robinson.

"This impression was made upon me, nearly as I can recollect, in the following way:—It fell to my turn that morning, as a pupil, to attend the visitors, and Mrs. Robinson came into the room singing. She asked to see a drawing which Mr. Sherwin had made of her, which he had placed in an upper room. When I assured her that Mr. Sherwin was not at home, 'Do try to find the drawing of me, and I will reward you, my little fellow,' said she. I, who had seen 'Rosetta,' in *Love in a Village*, the preceding evening, hummed to myself as I went upstairs, 'With a kiss, and a kiss, I'll reward you with a kiss.' I had no sooner entered the room with the drawing in my hand, than she imprinted a kiss on my cheek, and said, 'There, you little rogue.' I remember that Mrs. Berby, her mother, accompanied her, and had brought a miniature, painted by Cosway, set in diamonds, presented by 'a high personage,' of whom Mrs. Robinson spoke with the highest respect to her last hour. The colour of her carriage was a light blue, and upon the centre of each panel a basket of flowers was so artfully painted, that as she drove along it was mistaken for a coronet."

In Broad Street, a little to the north-east of this square, where his father kept a hosier's shop, was born, in 1757, William Blake, the gifted poet and painter, the author of " Songs of Innocence," " Songs of Experience," &c. Here, too, after his marriage, in 1784-7, he established himself as a print-seller and engraver. In the latter year he removed into Poland Street, hard by, and after many wanderings he died at Fountain Court, in the Strand, in 1827. In this street there was a most ill-natured sarcasm levelled against the fair sex on a sign-board, representing a headless female figure, and styled " The Good Woman." No doubt this sign was older than the Reformation, and represented St. Osyth, the Saxon martyr, who is said to have been beheaded. The legend runs that where her head fell a spring of clear water bubbled up. The same sign—said to be the only good woman in Essex—curiously enough, still exists at Widford, near Chelmsford, a parish in which the Priory of St. Osyth formerly held lands. In Broad Street is the Lion Brewery, represented on page 235.

But to return to Golden Square. On its west side, running parallel with Regent Street, and forming a communication between Glasshouse Street and Great Marlborough Street, is Warwick Street, on the eastern side of which stands the Roman Catholic Chapel of the Assumption, long known as the Bavarian Chapel, from having been originally erected, in the time of the penal laws, under the shelter and protection of the Bavarian Embassy. It is probable that it was founded under the later Stuarts, though its registers go back only to 1747. To it most of the noble Roman Catholic families, during the last century, when this was a fashionable quarter of the town, resorted for the celebration of divine service, and of marriages and baptisms. It was burnt down in the Gordon riots of 1780, and not rebuilt, or, at all events, re-opened till eight years afterwards, so great and so real was the panic caused by that outbreak of fanaticism. According to the trust deed, the chapel was built as a sanctuary, not for the West-end of London only, but for the whole Roman Catholic body of England. In 1839 the Auxiliary Catholic Institute was established in connection with this chapel. Here, it is said, the first modern " mission service " was held; and within its walls the first English pilgrimage to Paray le Monial was projected, organised, and sent forth in September, 1873, in honour of the Sacred Heart, a devotion first taught in England very near this

spot by F. Colombiere, chaplain to Queen Mary Beatrice, wife of James II.

The chapel, when rebuilt, stood a little back from the line of the street, being made so to retreat in order to avoid attracting notice, as is or was till lately the case with Roman Catholic chapels even in Dublin. It is a poor, shapeless, and unsightly edifice, built after the commonest type of Nonconformist chapels of the time, with heavy galleries and round-headed windows. The decorations of the interior, especially about the altar, redeem it to some extent from the charge of being hideous; and in 1875 a large subscription was entered into by the Roman Catholic body for the enlargement and adornment of the structure, the old walls being retained as memorials of a state of things which happily has long since passed away.

This chapel, it may be added, serves as a centre of ministration for a very large number of Roman Catholics of the middle classes about the southern parts of Soho. The residence of the priests who officiate in this chapel is in Golden Square, with which it has a communication in the rear. The schools attached to the chapel are among the most efficient in the Roman Catholic arch-diocese of Westminster.

Carnaby Street, which extends from the north side of the square to Great Marlborough Street, is thus described by Strype :—" An ordinary street which goes out of Silver Street, and runs northward almost to the bowling ground. On the east side of this street are the Earl of Craven's pest-houses, seated in a large piece of ground, inclosed with a brick wall, and handsomely set with trees, in which are buildings for the entertainment of persons that shall have the plague, when it shall please God that any contagion shall happen."

Maitland, in his " History of London," mentions the Pest Field in the following terms :—" The site whereon Marshall Street, part of Little Broad Street, and Marlborough Market are now erected, was denominated the Pest Field, from a lazaretto therein, which consisted of thirty-six small houses, for the reception of poor and miserable objects of this neighbourhood that were afflicted with the direful pestilence of 1665. And at the lower end of Marshall Street, contiguous to Silver Street, was a common cemetery, wherein some thousands of corpses were buried that died of that dreadful and virulent contagion." When Carnaby Street and other streets were built, a " field on the Paddington estate " was assigned as a pest-field in place of that which we have described.

The parish authorities of St. James's do not appear to have been very popular with the poor in

GOLDEN SQUARE IN 1750.

the reign of the first Georges, if we may take literally the following paragraph which occurs in the *St. James's Evening Post*, of August 4, 1726 :—"Some days since, while the officers of the parish of St. James, Westminster, were making merry at a tavern, the workhouse in the Pest-Fields (nearly finished) was then "esteemed one of the finest in Europe." The writer adds, however, that its only claim to such a character lies in its length and breadth, "the buildings on each side being trifling and inconsiderable, and the vista ending either way in nothing great or extraordinary." To the eyes of

THE PANTHEON THEATRE. (*See page* 244.)

for the reception of the poor was blown down by a sudden gust of wind, to the no small satisfaction of the lazars, who testified their joy by loud acclamations, bonfires, and other illuminations in the evening."

Great Marlborough Street, which we now enter, runs parallel with Oxford Street, extending from Poland Street to Regent Street. If we may believe the author of the "New Critical Review of the Public Buildings of London," in 1736, this street

persons in the nineteenth century, the street will, we fancy, present little ground for admiration, even of this limited kind : it is a broad, heavy, dull street, and that is all.

A century or so ago the appearance of the street must have been very different from what it is in the present day ; for, as we learn, it formed one of the principal promenades for the belles and beaux of the day, when the piazza in Covent Garden had become deserted by them, and the shady walk along the Mall in St. James's Park had lost for a time its attraction. Its chief literary note arises from the fact that a house on the north side was for many years the publishing office of the late Mr. Henry Colburn, to whom we are so much indebted for cheap light literature. After his death his business passed into the hands of Messrs. Hurst and Blackett.

That talented but unfortunate genius, B. R. Haydon, in the earlier part of his career, had lodgings on the southern side of this street, which at that time had not quite lost its fashionable character. Cyrus Redding tells us, in his "Autobiography," how he breakfasted with Haydon and Wilkie at the "Nassau Coffee House" at the corner of Nassau and Gerrard Streets, close to the home of John Dryden, which we have already mentioned, between Leicester Fields and Soho.

This street had also another distinguished inhabitant, in the person of the miser, John Elwes, who, on one occasion, had a narrow escape of his life here. The story is thus told:—It was the custom of Mr. Elwes, whenever he went to London, to occupy either of his houses that might be vacant. On one occasion when he had come to town, and, as usual, had taken up his abode in one of the empty houses, Colonel Timms (his nephew), who wished much to see him, in vain inquired at his banker's and at other places. Some days elapsed, and he at length learned from a person whom he met by chance in the street that Mr. Elwes had been seen going into an uninhabited house in Great Marlborough Street. The colonel proceeded to the house, knocked very loudly at the door, but could obtain no answer. Feeling alarmed, he sent for a person to join him, and they entered the house together. In the lower part all was shut and silent, but on ascending the stairs they heard the moans of a person seemingly in distress. They went to the chamber, and there on an old pallet-bed they found Mr. Elwes, apparently in the agonies of death. For some time he seemed quite insensible, but on some cordials being administered he recovered.

At the western end of the street, near the Argyll Baths and Argyll Street, is the Marlborough Street Police Court.

Argyll Street, which here branches off from Great Marlborough Street, and forms the connecting link between its western end and Oxford Street, runs northwards parallel with Regent Street. Here Sir Joseph Banks was born, as already stated by us, in the reign of George II. Here, too, Northcote the painter lived and died. Of him Cyrus Redding writes in his "Recollections:"—"I used to visit Northcote before I went abroad, and often sat in Argyll Street talking to him about the West country, while he was painting. He was a vain man, of a contracted mind, an excellent small story-teller, not over good-natured. He owed to the assistance of others all the attempts he made in literature, and to no one was he so deeply in debt as to Hazlitt. His offence with that writer was pretended. When he died he left him a hundred pounds as a memento of their intimacy—rather an odd mode of exhibiting his wrath!"

In 1811 Madame de Staël, that brilliant and learned woman, was living in lodgings here; and here she put in force and exercised the prerogative of intellect, by actually making even the Prince Regent pay her a visit, before she would wait on him at Court. But we need not wonder at her boldness or her success, for she was the only human being before whom the great Napoleon quailed, and whom he owned that he could not conquer.

The house which was occupied by Madame de Staël is to be identified by the description of it in Mr. Cyrus Redding's "Fifty Years' Recollections." It was about the middle of the western side of the street, "nearly opposite to Lord Aberdeen's." Madame de Staël has been so often described, that it is difficult to say about her anything that is fresh. Redding records the fact that when he called, between one and two o'clock, he was long before her time of seeing visitors, as she spent her mornings in reading and writing in bed, and never left her room till after two o'clock. She was plain and unattractive in her appearance, and was so conscious of the fact, that she told him, as well as others, that "she would willingly exchange her literary reputation for personal beauty." And yet she was so far from aiming at what is generally thought a woman's empire, that she professed herself especially fond of men's society, on the ground of their being less disposed than women to frivolous conversation. She was seen, he tells us, at her best in a small circle, where her good sayings secured attention, though she was "fond of a large company in her drawing-room, on the ground, perhaps, that an actor likes to see a full house." He adds—"Madame de Staël's drawing-room in Argyll Street was a daily levée. All the world went to see her, and she to see all the world. If she had some little vanity, she had a just claim to be excused that fault. It would be difficult to find any female writer since to approach her in ability. She thus gained a precedence she never used ungracefully. Her critical remarks on Teutonic literature, her extensive acquirements and reading, and the aim she had in her writings of fiction, always elevated, and never downward or mean in tendency, showing the worthiest aspirations, made me, as I still am, one of the admirers of that renowned lady."

It is of Madame de Staël,—

"Necker's fair daughter, Staël the Epicene,"

that the story is told that, when she first came to London, she had hardly reached her lodgings when she inquired of the servant of the house if he could direct her to the tomb of Richardson. The man knew nothing of poems or comedies, and sent her to a tavern-keeper at Covent Garden, of that name, who had lately lost his father; but, of course, that was not the Richardson whom she wanted. At last, after sundry adventures, which took her to Cornhill and to Paternoster Row, she learned that Richardson lay buried in St. Clement Danes Churchyard. Off she packed at once, dark and drizzly as the evening was, in quest of the tomb of her favourite English writer, and, when she had found it, prostrated herself upon the cold and mud-sprinkled stone with such reverence and zeal that on returning to Argyll Street, it took her landlady and servant the whole evening to brush her dress, and make her presentable.

In this street lived George, Lord Lyttelton—the "good" Lord Lyttelton—the friend of Pope, Thomson, and Mallet. To him Pope alludes in these lines :—

"Sometimes a patriot, active in debate,
Mix with the world and battle for the State,
Free as young Lyttelton her cause pursue,
Still true to virtue, and as warm as true."

Lord Lyttelton's "Poems," "Dialogues of the Dead," "History of Henry II.," and "Dissertation on the Conversion of St. Paul," have given him a respectable rank in literature. It appears from his "Correspondence" that he wrote his treatise on St. Paul's conversion chiefly with a view to meet the case of Thomson, who, in that sceptical age, was troubled with doubts. Lyttelton was anxious that the amiable poet should unite the *faith* to the *heart* of a Christian, "for the latter he always had." The circumstance is highly honourable to Lyttelton, and is another instance of that warmth of friendship which Thomson inspired.

About the centre of this street, on the eastern side, there formerly stood a dull, heavy mansion of no architectural pretensions, called Argyll House, after the Dukes of Argyll, to whom it had originally belonged. It had a small paved court-yard before it, with a wall and gates of the approved pattern. Early in the present century it became the property of "the travell'd Thane, Athenian Aberdeen," as Lord Byron calls the late Earl of Aberdeen, who resided here both previously and whilst Premier

at the beginning of the Crimean war. His lordship was the last nobleman who lived on the eastern side of Regent Street, showing how thoroughly fashion's tide, like that of empire, sets to the westward amongst us. The house was pulled down about the year 1865, and the site was used for building. In its place arose an edifice which has been used for various purposes, being at one time the Corinthian Bazaar, and at another as Hengler's Circus.

At the corner of Little Argyll Street formerly stood the Argyll Rooms. The establishment was founded under the auspices of Colonel Greville, a noted sportsman and "man about town" under the Regency, who purchased a large house and turned it into a place of entertainment, as a rival to the Pantheon. The fashionable world worshipped at Colonel Greville's shrine, and its balls, masquerades, and amateur balls soon became part of the recognised amusements of West-end society.

In 1811 Lady Margaret Crawford, a lady of eccentric and individual character, gave a ball here "to all her friends, or rather her enemies." It is made a matter of complaint by a French gentleman of fashion in London, in 1823, addressing an English friend, "The wives and daughters of your most respectable country gentlemen no sooner arrive in London than, forgetting all high feelings of conscious virtue and hereditary pride, they seem anxious to purchase, at any price, the honour of belonging to 'The Argyll Street Rooms,' and of frequenting the Wednesday balls at 'Almack's.' Even mothers of families, who have gone through life with untainted reputation, if unable to gain the envied distinction themselves, will condescend to court the 'patronage' of women of very different characters, and to entrust their fair young daughters to the care of peeresses, whose 'indiscretions' would long since have banished them from all association with the best of their own sex, had not their lords been conveniently blind to their failings. No costs or pains are spared to propitiate these deities of fashion—the 'lady patronesses.'"

In 1818 the rooms were rebuilt in a handsome style, by Mr. John Nash, the architect. Here the *contralto* singer, Velluti, gave a concert in June, 1829. In the same year, M. Chabert, who rejoiced in the title of the "fire king," here exhibited his power of resisting the effects of poisons, and withstanding extreme heat. Among other things, we are told that he "swallowed forty grains of phosphorus, sipped oil at 333° with impunity, and rubbed a red-hot shovel over his tongue, hair, and face unharmed; that he swallowed a piece of a burning torch; and then, dressed in coarse woollen, entered an oven heated to 380°, sung a song, and cooked two dishes of beef-steaks!" "These performances," it is added, "were suspected of being a chemical juggle."

The building was burnt down in 1830. On this occasion, Mr. Braithwaite first publicly applied steam-power to the working of a fire-engine; and we are informed that "it required eighteen minutes to raise the water in the boiler to 212°, when the engine threw up from thirty to forty tons of water per hour to a height of ninety feet."

Adjoining the Argyll Rooms was a long range of buildings, formerly known as the "Harmonic Institution" of Messrs. Welsh and Hawes. It was originally a species of joint-stock company, associated for the publication of musical compositions, and other objects connected with that art. But from about the year 1828 it was conducted entirely by the two eminent musical professors whose name it bore. It had a portico, with capitals formed of female heads.

Oxford Street, the south side of which we now enter, has always been a street of shops, and for the most part of good shops also, as was eminently fitting for one of the two great westerly thoroughfares of the city of this "nation of shopkeepers." Less fashionable than Regent Street, because further from the court and courtly influences, and less devoted to pleasure than the Strand, owing to its greater distance from the theatres, it has always preserved the happy medium of respectability. It seems strange, indeed, now that we are bowled at the rate of nine or ten miles an hour in a hansom cab over the level pavement of Oxford Street, or at a slower rate in an omnibus, to learn that, within the memory of the antiquary Pennant (who died in 1798), it was little better than a quagmire, dangerous on account of its roughness, and on account of the "cut-throats" who frequented it, malgré the "Charlies" and the night-watch. But so it was. In spite of its containing the Oxford Music Hall, the Soho Bazaar, the Princess's Theatre, and the old Pantheon, it has, on the whole, steered clear of fashionable dissipation; and it now is content to be the chief thoroughfare in which the well-to-do, but not over-rich, classes purchase the necessaries and comforts of life, in the way of clothing, dresses, haberdashery, domestic wares, and generally those articles which form the delight and the comfort of the British matron.

Of the Soho Bazaar we have already spoken in the previous volume, and of the Oxford Music Hall we shall have to speak when describing the northern side of this great thoroughfare; but of the Pantheon, which may now (except in name) be reckoned among the places that have been, we may here state that it occupied a large space of ground between Argyll Street and Poland Street, and that it extended from Oxford Street back into Great Marlborough Street. The building, with a portico projecting over the pavement, is still called the "Pantheon," and was formerly known under that name as a bazaar. Its exterior has few pretensions to architectural beauty; but a guide-book of London, published in 1851, assures us that at that time "the interior, in point of extent, design, convenience of arrangement, and beauty of execution united," was "unequalled by anything of the kind in London, or even in Europe." Perhaps this may have been the case; but its interior beauty, and that of its fair bevy of *marchandes*, did not prevent it from running to the end of its career as a bazaar. About the year 1870 it was closed, and converted into wine stores.

The Pantheon, a century ago, was celebrated for its masquerades. In the *London Magazine* for 1773, we read: "The play-houses, the operas, the masquerades, the Pantheon, Vauxhall, Ranelagh, Mrs. Cornelys, the London Tavern, &c., are all crowded. . . . . The money squandered at the last masquerade was computed to be £20,000, though tradesmen go unpaid, and the industrious poor are starving." We are sorry to read this remark of a contemporary, who could scarcely be ignorant of facts, or have been allowed to pervert them uncontradicted; but hitherto we always supposed that such extravagances were defensible, mainly on the ground that they were "good for trade."

The Pantheon was originally built in 1770–1, as a place of public amusement, including concerts, balls, promenades, &c., with the view of cutting the wind out of the sails of Mrs. Cornelys, whose successes at Soho Square (as already recorded) roused feelings of jealousy in her rivals, the more strongly, perhaps, because she was a foreigner. The building was erected from the designs of James Wyatt, and was opened early in 1772. It was intended by its founders to be a sort of winter Ranelagh in London, and it cost £60,000. It was destroyed by fire in 1792; rebuilt on the same plan, and pulled down in 1812, the Oxford Street front being preserved from the original building. Having served as a place of amusement of various kinds, in 1834 it was remodelled, and made into a bazaar, similar to its rival in Soho Square.

The original Pantheon is immortalised by Sheridan, in one of his comedies, and is thus described by gossiping Horace Walpole, in May, 1770, in a letter to his friend, Sir Horace Mann:—"The new winter Ranelagh in the Oxford Road is nearly finished. It amazed me myself. Imagine Balbec in all its glory. The pillars are of artificial *giallo antico*. The ceilings even of the passages are of the most beautiful stuccos in the best taste of grotesque. The ceilings of the ball-rooms and the panels are painted like Raphael's *loggias* in the Vatican: a dome like the Pantheon glazed. It is to cost fifty thousand pounds."

In the year 1783, a masquerade took place here in honour of the coming of age of the Prince of Wales; it was got up by a noted clown of the period, named Delpini, and a charge of three guineas was made for each ticket. In the following year, a concert in commemoration of Handel was performed here, which was attended by the king, queen, and royal family.

Here, in September and October, 1784, was exhibited the balloon in which Lunardi had made his first successful ascent (September 15) from the Artillery Ground at Moorfields. He gained a large sum by the exhibition, and became the lion of the season, being presented at Court, to receive the king's and queen's congratulations on account of his achievement; although, if the truth must be told, the very first ascent in Great Britain had been made about three weeks before by a poor man at Edinburgh.

In 1788, after the destruction of the King's Theatre, the Pantheon was fitted up as an opera-house by Mr. O'Reilly, at a rent of £3,000. After that, in 1812, a lease of these premises was taken by Mr. Cundy, the builder, and some other persons, and the interior was reconstructed as a theatre, on a plan analogous to that of the Great Theatre at Milan, for the performance of Italian comic operas, burlettas, &c. The boxes, 171 in number, were disposed into four regular tiers, besides the upper or slip boxes. They were supported by gilt columns, furnished with curtains and chairs, and illuminated by chandeliers. The pit would accommodate about 1,200 and the gallery 500 persons. The stage was 56 feet wide and 90 feet deep. The devices and designs before the curtain were by Signio; the scene-painter was Marinari. A saloon, measuring 49 feet by 21 feet, was appropriated to the boxes, and a refreshment-room was attached to the pit. It was opened on the 25th of February, 1812, at opera prices, with T. Dibdin's opera of *The Cabinet*. In 1814 everything movable was sold, in which state it remained many years, only the bare walls being left. Several applications were made by Mr. Cundy for a renewal of a lease to open it again as a winter theatre, but failed.

In 1796-8 Miss Linwood's collection of needle-work was exhibited at the Pantheon, previous to its establishment at the Hanover Square Rooms. Miss Linwood died in 1845, at the age of ninety, seventy-six years after working the earliest of her pictures. "The designs," says Mr. Timbs, "were executed with five crewels, dyed expressly for her, on a thick tammy, and were entirely drawn and embroidered by her own hand."

The Pantheon has also its political recollections. Here, in 1806, Gale Jones, and other Radicals of the time of Pitt and Fox, used to meet and discuss the necessity of Parliamentary Reform, in spite of informers.

Close to the corner of Argyll Street, near Regent Circus, is a noted booking-office for heavy goods and parcels, called the "Green Man and Still." "This is," says Mr. Larwood, "a liberty taken with the arms of the distillers, the supporters of which are two Indians. The latter were transformed by the sign-painters into wild men, or green men, and the green men, again, into foresters; and then it was said that the sign arose from the partiality of foresters, as such, for the produce of the still!" In all probability, however, the reference is really to a "green man"—that is, a seller of green herbs and other produce of what used to be called a physic-garden, in which case the still would be easily understood as an adjunct.

The "Hog in the Pound" was the name of an inn in this street, commonly known as "The Gentleman in Trouble." It was a great starting-point for coaches to the western parts, and it gained notoriety by a murder committed by its landlady, Catherine Hayes. Having formed an improper acquaintance, she was induced by her paramour to murder her husband, after which she cut off his head, put it in a bag, and threw it into the Thames. It floated ashore; and being set up in the churchyard of St. Margaret's at Westminster, it was recognised, and by a train of events the murder was brought home to its perpetrators. The man was hanged, and Mrs. Hayes was burnt alive at Tyburn, in the year 1726.

The "North Pole" inn, which stands near Wardour Street, commemorates one of those expeditions which have been sent out to explore the Arctic regions, from the days of Frobisher to those of Franklin, M'Clintock, and Nares.

It may here be mentioned that a house in this street, near Soho Square, known as "the Balloon" fruit-shop, was the first in London to commemorate on its sign the conquest over nature which was thought to have been achieved in September, 1783, when the first "air-balloon" ascended at Versailles, in the presence of Louis XVI. and his family.

OLD STABLES IN SWALLOW STREET, 1820. (*See page 249.*)

CHAPTER XXI.

REGENT STREET AND PICCADILLY.

"Westward the tide of empire holds its way."

Westward Extension of the Metropolis—Albert Smith's and Horace Walpole's Remarks thereon—Origin of the Name of Piccadilly—Tradesmen's Tokens—Gradual Extension of Piccadilly—Appearance of the Site of Regent Street in the Last Century—The County Fire Office—The Quadrant—Regent Street—Archbishop Tenison's Chapel—Foubert's Riding Academy—*Fraser's Magazine* and its Early Contributors—A "Literary Duel"—Hanover Chapel—Anecdote of the Poet Campbell—Little Vine Street—The "Man in the Moon"—Swallow Street—Chapel of the Scotch Presbyterians—St. James's Hall—Piccadilly—Fore's Exhibition—M. Daguerre's Experiments—Lady Hamilton—Mr. Quaritch's Book-Store—The Genealogical and Historical Society—St. James's Church—Sir William Petty, the Political Economist—Eminent Publishers—Bullock's Museum—The Egyptian Hall—The Albany—"Dan" Lambert—Arlington Street—The Old "White Horse Cellar," and the Glories of Stage-coaching.

WHAT the poet has said so pithily about the tide of empire may be said also of the tide of fashion in this great metropolis, which for these two centuries and more past has set steadily westward. As Mr. Albert Smith remarks, in his "Sketches of London Life:"—"Proceeding in two parallel directions, divided by Oxford Street, Hanover Square gradually declined before that of Grosvenor, and Portman rose above that of Manchester. Still fashion kept marching on—the former division tending towards May Fair, and the latter to the Edgware Road; until the first, turned aside in its course by Hyde Park, reached the site of Belgravia, and the second, heedless of the associations connected with the gallows, and the decaying foliage of the Bayswater tea-gardens, colonised Tyburnia for its territory."

That old prince of gossips, Horace Walpole, writes thus to Miss Berry and her sister, in 1791:—"Though London increases every day, and Mr. Herschel* has just discovered a new square or circus somewhere by the New Road, in the 'Via Lactea,' where the cows used to be fed, I believe you will think the town cannot hold all its inhabitants, so prodigiously the population is augmented. I have twice been going to stop my coach in Piccadilly (and the same has happened to Lady Ailesbury), thinking there was a mob, and it was only nymphs and swains sauntering

* The great astronomer.

SWALLOW STREET DURING ITS DEMOLITION. (*See page* 249)

or trudging. T'other morning, *i.e.*, at two o'clock, I went to see Mrs. Garrick and Miss Hannah More at the Adelphi, and was stopped five times before I reached Northumberland House; for the tides of coaches, chariots, curricles, phaetons, &c., are endless. Indeed, the town is so extended, that the breed of chairs is almost lost; for Hercules and Atlas could not carry anybody from one end of the enormous capital to the other. How magnified would be the error of the young woman at St. Helena, who some years ago said to the captain of an Indiaman, 'I suppose London is very empty when the India ships come out.'"

And again, in the same letter: "There will soon be one street from London to Brentford—aye, and from London to every village within ten miles round. . . . London is, I am certain, much fuller than ever I saw it. I have twice this spring been going to stop my coach in Piccadilly, to inquire what was the matter, thinking there was a mob: not at all; it was only foot-passengers." He adds a few remarks, by way of consolation, to the effect that, in spite of the enormous increase of London, there was as yet no complaint that the country was coming to be depopulated, as Bath "shoots out into new crescents, circuses, and squares every year; while Birmingham, Manchester, Hull, and Liverpool would serve any king in England for a capital, and even make the Empress of Russia's mouth to water."

The origin of the name of Piccadilly is wrapped in obscurity, and has frequently been discussed in *Notes and Queries*, and in other quarters. Mr. Peter Cunningham and Mr. John Timbs, among modern antiquaries, have started the inquiry as to its derivation rather than solved it; and we must be content to believe, with them, that the street gradually took its name from a place of amusement, spoken of in the preceding chapter as formerly standing at its eastern or town end, styled Piccadilly Hall, which in its turn was so styled after the ruffs, called "pickadils," or "peccadillos," worn by the gallants of the reign of James I., the stiffened points of which, as Mr. Timbs observes, resembled spear-heads, or "picardills," a diminutive of the Spanish and Italian word *pica* (Latin *spica*) a spear. Ben Jonson writes, in his "Underwoods:"—

"And then leap mad on a neat pickardill."

To this line Mr. Robert Bell appends a note to the effect that the latter word is the name of "a stiff collar, or ruff, generally with sharp points, and derived from 'picca,' a spear-head. The ruff came into fashion, as we see by contemporary portraits, early in the reign of James I.; and, according to

some authorities, gave its name to the street of Piccadilly." But then, the further difficulty arises, how to connect Piccadilly Hall with so fanciful a word. Was it, as is sometimes said, because the man who built it—one Higgins, a draper—made his fortune by the sale of "pickadils" when they were the height of fashion? or was the Hall itself originally a way-side inn, so named by chance or caprice? or does some subtle and fanciful analogy underlie the name? and are we to suppose that it was so styled by the Londoners, as being "the utmost or skirt house of the suburbs that way?" This supposition is too far-fetched, and savours too much of poetry, we think, to be ascribed to the ordinary and commonplace Londoners. Then, again, an old writer, Blount, in his "Glossographia," interprets the word as denoting "the round hem about the edge or skirt of a garment, or a stiff collar or band for the neck and shoulders;" whence Butler, in his "Hudibras," styles the collars in the pillory "peccadilloes." If so, may not the name have originated from the pillory having been often set up here in the good old Tudor times? Pennant, again, has another derivation to offer, suggesting that it comes from a sort of cakes or turnovers called "piccadillas," which were sold in the fields about here. Whatever the connecting link may be, however, it is clear that the name, as applied to these parts, dates from the sixteenth century; for Gerard, in his "Herbal," published in 1596, speaks of the small wild buglosse which grows upon the dry ditch-banks about "Pickadilla." D'Israeli, in his "Curiosities of Literature," tells us that Piccadilly "was named after Piccadilla Hall, a place of sale for piccadillies, or turnovers, a part of the fashionable dress which appeared about the year 1814. It has preserved its name uncorrupted; for Barnabe Rich, in his 'Honesty of the Age,' has this passage on 'the body-makers that do swarm through all parts, both of London and about London.' He says, 'The body is still pampered up in the very dropsy of excess.' He that some forty years sithence should have asked after a Pickadilly, I wonder who should have understood him, or could have told what a Pickadilly had been, either fish or flesh.'" So we must be content to leave the inquiry where we found it, and pass on.

The name Piccadilly is found written in a variety of ways. Mr. Akerman, in his work on "London Tradesmen's Tokens," enumerates eleven different specimens, in the shape of copper coins, which bear date, "Piccadily," between 1660 and 1670. Some of these are issued by grocers, some by "sea-coal" dealers, and others apparently by the keepers of forges. They do not agree in their orthography, for the name is spelt "Peckadille," "Pickedila," "Pickadilla," and other ways.

The first thoroughfare bearing the name of Piccadilly, says Mr. Peter Cunningham, was a very short line of road, running no further west than the foot of Sackville Street; and the name Piccadilly Street occurs, for the first time, in the rate-books of St. Martin's, under the year 1673. Between Sackville and Albemarle Streets, or, as some say, to Stratton Street, or even to Hyde Park, at different times, the thoroughfare was called Portugal Street, after Catherine of Braganza, Queen of Charles II.; all beyond that point being the great Bath Road, or, as it is called in Aggas's map (1560), "the way to Reding." The Queen, however, was never a favourite with the people, and gradually the name of Piccadilly displaced her memory altogether. "The north side," says Pennant in 1790, "consists of houses, most of them mean buildings; but it finishes handsomely with the magnificent new house of Lord Bathurst, at Hyde Park Corner." It is amusing to compare the state of the street at that date with what it is in the reign of Victoria. The Green Park, opposite, was shut in by a brick wall, in which, however, were inserted, here and there, some "benevolent" railings, to enable the passers-by to catch a glimpse of the trees inside.

The first mansion built along Piccadilly was Goring House, which stood on what is now Arlington Street; it was bought by Bennett, Lord Arlington, after whom both Bennett and Arlington Streets were named. Nearly opposite it, about 1688, rose Clarendon House, and Burlington House, built by Sir John Denham, and re-fronted by the celebrated amateur architect, Boyle, Earl of Burlington. This negatives the hackneyed story of Lord Burlington having chosen the site of his mansion so far out of town that no one could build beyond him. Immediately to the east were the house and garden of the Earl of Sunderland, the treacherous minister of James II.; the site is now occupied by the Albany.

"In 1711," according to Hunter's "History of London," "the town extended as far west as Devonshire House. Beyond Clifford Street was built Bond Street, which took its name from the family of a baronet, now extinct, who owned the ground. But New Bond Street was still an open field, called Conduit Mead, from one of the conduits which supplied that part of the town with water, and from which Conduit Street, adjoining, derived its name. All beyond was open ground, a receptacle for dunghills, and every kind of refuse . . . Oxford Street was then built on the south side, as far as Swallow

Street (now absorbed in Regent Street), but almost unbuilt on the north side. It was a deep hollow road, full of sloughs, with here and there a ragged house, the lurking-place of cut-throats."

The head-quarters of the fashionable world, as lately as the beginning of the reign of George IV., lay between Piccadilly and Oxford Street. Hence, a witty personage, when giving advice to a rich country friend as to how to make a good show in London, says—

"Hire a house in the purlieus of *ton*, and take care
    That it stands in a street near some smart-sounding square,
    Such as ' Hanover,' ' Grosvenor,' or ' Portman,' at least."

A better incidental proof could not well have been given that Belgrave and Eaton Squares were not as yet erected. In fact, at that date Belgravia was a swamp, and its squares were cabbage-gardens.

Near the eastern extremity of Piccadilly the thoroughfare is intersected by Regent Street, which commences at Waterloo Place, and proceeds northward for nearly a mile. It crosses Piccadilly, by a circus, to the County Fire Office, whence it passes to the north-west by a curved road, called the Quadrant, and then again in a direct line northward, crossing Oxford Street to Langham Place. On the whole, this street—at all events in its lower parts—follows the line of Swallow Street, which it superseded. To judge from its appearance, as preserved to us in the prints of the time, the latter was a long, ugly, and irregular thoroughfare. The tradition is that it bore a reputation by no means good, and contained, among its other houses, a certain livery-stable, which in the last century was a noted house-of-call for highwaymen.

Of the appearance of this district in the last year of the reign of Charles II., Lord Macaulay gives us the following picture:—"He who then rambled to what is now the gayest and most crowded part of Regent Street, found himself in a solitude, and was sometimes so fortunate as to have a shot at a woodcock.* On the north the Oxford road ran between hedges. Three or four hundred yards to the south were the garden-walls of a few great houses, which were considered as quite out of town. On the west was a meadow, renowned for a spring, from which, long afterwards, Conduit Street was named. On the east (near where now stands Golden Square) was a field not to be passed without a shudder by any Londoner of that age. There, as in a place far from the haunts of men, had been dug, twenty years before, when the great plague was raging, a pit into which the dead-carts had nightly shot

---

* General Oglethorpe, who died in 1785, used to boast that he had shot such birds here in Queen Anne's reign.

corpses by scores. It was popularly believed that the earth was deeply tainted with infection, and could not be disturbed without imminent risk to human life. No foundations were laid there till two generations had passed without any return of the pestilence, and till the ghastly spot had long been surrounded by buildings. It may be added, that the 'pest-field' may still be seen marked in maps of London as late as the end of the reign of George I."

The County Fire Office, which stands at the commencement of the Quadrant, was built from the designs of Mr. Abraham. It is a stately pile, of the Composite order, with a rustic basement and arcade, above which rise six three-quarter columns, and pilasters at the angles, supporting the entablature; the latter is surmounted by a balustrade and parapet, on the centre of which is a colossal figure of Britannia, standing with her spear and shield, and at her side the British lion couchant.

The Quadrant had, originally, a Doric colonnade on either side, projecting over the foot-pavements. The columns—some 270 in number—were of cast-iron, sixteen feet high, exclusive of the granite plinth, and supported a balustraded roof. The effect of this novel piece of street architecture was generally considered as very fine and picturesque. The colonnades, however, in consequence of the darkness which they imparted to the shops, were removed in 1848, at which time a balcony was added to the principal floor. In the centre of the Quadrant, on the south-west side, is one of the entrances to the St. James's Hall. Cyrus Redding fixes the Quadrant as the scene of the following incident. He writes in his "Recollections:"— "Campbell and myself set off one morning to walk to Dulwich College, to see the pictures and dine. We were passing along the Quadrant, when we met Sir James Mackintosh, looking serious. 'What a melancholy affair this is,' was his remark, without a 'good morning.' 'What affair?' 'The death of Sir Thomas Lawrence.' Campbell, who had been with Sir Thomas the evening but one before, was thunderstricken. When Sir James had passed on, I could not help remarking I thought he would be the next to depart—he looked so ill. My surmise was confirmed. It was not long before I visited his resting-place, with his daughter, in Hampstead churchyard. Campbell became too disturbed in his mind to proceed to Dulwich, and a walk we had often talked about was never taken."

The long vista of Regent Street, as seen from the Quadrant, is very fine, exhibiting, as it does, a remarkable variety of architectural features. It was erected principally from the designs of Mr. John Nash, who deserves to be remembered as the author of this great metropolitan improvement; and it was named from the architect's patron, the Prince Regent. The expenditure of the Office of Woods and Forests in its construction was a little in excess of a million and a half. Of course, being a thoroughfare of so recent a date, having been commenced in 1813, Regent Street has scarcely a back history for us to record here, like Pall Mall and St. James's Street. It belongs to "new," and not to "old" London.

In his design for Regent Street, Nash adopted the idea of uniting several dwellings into a *façade*, so as to preserve a degree of continuity essential to architectural importance; and it cannot be denied that he has produced a varied succession of architectural scenery, the effect of which is picturesque and imposing, superior to that of any other portion of the then existing metropolis, and far preferable to the naked brick walls at that time universally forming the sides of our streets. The plaster fronts of the houses have given rise to some severe criticism, and the perishable nature of the brick and composition of which the houses in this street are built, gave rise to the following epigram in the *Quarterly Review* for June, 1826:—

"Augustus at Rome was for building renown'd,
And of marble he left what of brick he had found;
But is not our Nash, too, a very great master?
He finds us all brick, and he leaves us all plaster."

Regent Street is full of handsome shops, and during the afternoon, in the height of the London season, is the very centre of fashion, and with its show of fine carriages, horses, and gay company, forms one of the most striking sights of the metropolis. At the close of the London season "everybody who pretends to be anybody" goes away from town, and the West-end becomes comparatively a desert. As Mr. Albert Smith remarks, in his "Sketches of London Life and Character"— "The thousands who leave London make no difference to the stream of life that daily flows along its business thoroughfares; but Regent Street assimilates to Pompeii in its loneliness. There are no more lines of carriages at the kerb; no concert programmes at the music-shops; nor bouquets and lap-dogs on the pavements. Men run in and out of their clubs in a shy and nervous manner, as though they were burrows; not caring to be seen, and inventing lame reasons for their continuance in London. You may wander all round Eaton Square without finding a single window lighted up, or meeting one carriage rolling along, with its lamps like two bright eyes, to a party. All have departed—the handsome girls to recruit their somewhat jaded strength, and recover from the pallor induced by late hours and the thousand fretting emotions of society; the men to shoot, and ride, and sail; the heads of the families to retain their caste, because it is proper to do so; but all to get away as soon and as fast as they can, when Parliament is prorogued, and the grouse are reported to be ready for slaughter."

On the east side, about half way up, near Chapel Court, stood "Archbishop Tenison's Chapel," so called after its founder, who conveyed this chapel, or "tabernacle," to certain trustees (one of whom was the great Sir Isaac Newton), as a chapel of ease, or "oratory," for the parish of St. James's. The archbishop added to it an endowment for two "preachers," as also for a "reader" or chaplain, to say prayers in it twice daily, and for a school-master to teach sundry poor boys of the parish to read, write, and cast accounts. The chapel was opened in 1702. It was re-fronted when Regent Street was built; but about the year 1860, its endowment not being adequate to its maintenance, the west end of the building was cut off and turned into shops.

Higher up, on the same side of the street, a certain M. Foubert had, in the reign of Charles II., a riding academy, and his name is still retained in Foubert's Passage. Evelyn writes in his "Diary," under date September 17, 1684, that M. Foubert had "lately come from Paris for his religion, and resolved to settle here." In the following December he was again here, and gives a list of the performances, and also the names of the principal of the nobility present. On the site of Foubert's academy had previously stood the mansion of the Countess of Bristol.

In this street was the publishing office of Mr. James Fraser, the starter and proprietor of *Fraser's Magazine*. In the January number of that magazine for 1835, we have, from the pencil of Maclise, a sketch of an editorial banquet at the residence of Mr. Fraser, at which some eminent men were present. Mr. Mahony, the "Father Prout" of the magazine, in his account of this banquet, written some years later, tells us that it was a reality, and not a fiction. In the chair appears Dr. Maginn in the act of making a speech; and around him are some of the contributors, including Bryan Waller Procter (better known then as "Barry Cornwall"), Robert Southey, William Harrison Ainsworth, Samuel Taylor Coleridge, James Hogg, John Galt, Fraser the publisher, having on his right Mr. J. G. Lockhart, Theodore Hook, Sir David Brewster,

Thomas Carlyle, Sir Egerton Brydges, the Rev. G. R. Gleig, Edward Irving, and William Makepeace Thackeray, the last-named being easily recognised by his double eye-glass, for he was short-sighted even as a young man. Alas! of that pleasant and distinguished party, how few survive! Whilst speaking of *Fraser's Magazine*, we may add that in the zenith of its popularity, in the year 1837, its pages, or rather the connection of Dr. Maginn with it as editor, led to a duel, happily a bloodless one. As usual, there was "a lady in the case;" and the Hon. Grantley Berkeley, then M.P. for West Gloucestershire, came forward to espouse the cause of the lady, who conceived that she had been injured by Maginn. Mr. Berkeley was warned by Lady Blessington that Maginn would be sure to look out for some opportunity of revenge. The opportunity came very soon afterwards; for Mr. Grantley Berkeley wrote and published a novel, which Dr. Maginn reviewed in *Fraser's Magazine*, not, however, confining himself to fair criticism, but using malignant insinuations against Lady Euston, a cousin of the author. Accordingly, Mr. Grantley Berkeley, accompanied by his brother Craven, called at Mr. Fraser's shop to demand the name of the writer, and not obtaining it, administered to the publisher a severe chastisement. This was made, very naturally, the subject of a civil action; but, meantime, it leaked out incidentally that Dr. Maginn was the writer. The consequence was a duel, which was fought with pistols. Three shots were fired, but without effect, Major Fancourt being Mr. Berkeley's second, whilst Mr. Fraser acted in that capacity for Dr. Maginn. The ridiculous nature of this "literary duel" and its bloodless termination, literally "in smoke," helped to seal the doom of the once fashionable practice of duelling; and the publicity gained for the transaction, to use the words of the *Times*, "put a wholesome restraint upon the herd of libellers who, in the *Age* and *Satirist* newspapers, and in *Fraser's Magazine*, had for years been recklessly trading upon scandals affecting families of distinction." The *Age* and the *Satirist* are both happily defunct; and *Fraser's Magazine* has long since abandoned bad habits of this kind.

At the junction of Regent Street with Oxford Street is another circus. Of the portion of the street lying beyond this point we shall speak in a future chapter.

On the west side of the way, between Hanover and Princes Streets, stands Hanover Chapel, which was built, in 1823, from the designs of the late Mr. Cockerell, R.A.; it is of the Ionic order, and in its internal arrangement somewhat resembles St.

Stephen's Church, Walbrook. The altar is enriched with carved work, and the fabric generally forms a fine architectural display, though utterly unsuited to a church.

Before resuming our account of Piccadilly, we may be pardoned for introducing the following anecdote of the poet Campbell, as narrated by Southey:—"Taking a walk with Campbell one day up Regent Street," he says, "we were accosted us he would turn us both out; that he believed we came there to kick up a row for some dishonest purpose. So here was a pretty dilemma. We defied him, but said we would go out instantly, on his apologising for his gross insult. All was uproar. Campbell called out—'Thrash the fellow! thrash him!' 'You will not go out, then?' said the mercer. 'No, never, till you apologise.' 'Well, we shall soon see. John, go to Vine Street, and

THE QUADRANT, REGENT STREET, BEFORE THE REMOVAL OF THE COLONNADE. (*See page 250.*)

by a wretched-looking woman, with a sick infant in her arms, and another starved little thing at her mother's side. The woman begged for a copper. I had no change, and Campbell had nothing but a sovereign. The woman stuck fast to the poet, as if she read his heart in his face, and I could feel his arm beginning to tremble. At length, saying something about it being his duty to assist poor creatures, he told the woman to wait; and, hastening into a mercer's shop, asked, rather impatiently, for change. You know what an excitable person he was, and how he fancied all business must give way till the change was supplied. The shopman thought otherwise; the poet insisted; an altercation ensued; and in a minute or two the master jumped over the counter and collared him, telling fetch the police.' In a few minutes two policemen appeared; one went close up to Mr. Campbell, the other to myself. The poet was now in such breathless indignation that he could not articulate a sentence. I told the policeman the object he had in asking change, and that the shopkeeper had most unwarrantably insulted us. 'This gentleman,' I added, by way of a climax, 'is Mr. Thomas Campbell, the distinguished poet, a man who would not hurt a fly, much less act with the dishonest intention that person has insinuated.' The moment I uttered the name the policeman backed away two or three paces, as if awe-struck, and said, 'Guidness, mon, is that Maister Cammell, the Lord Rector o' Glasgow?' 'Yes, my friend, he is, as this card may convince you,' handing it to him. 'All this commotion has been caused by a mistake.' By this time the mercer had cooled down to a moderate temperature, and in the end made every reparation in his power, saying he was very busy at the time, and had he but known the

to the day when a vineyard, belonging to the Abbey of Westminster or to some wealthy lord, flourished and yielded the fruit of the grape on a sunny slope. Here, in 1805, was living, in comparative obscurity, a young artist, who after-

SIR ISAAC NEWTON. (*See page 232.*)

gentleman, he would have changed fifty sovereigns for him. 'My dear fellow,' said the poet, who had recovered his speech, 'I am not at all offended;' and it was really laughable to see them shaking hands long and vigorously, each with perfect sincerity and mutual forgiveness.''

But we must proceed. Between Regent's Quadrant and Piccadilly runs Little Vine Street, a thoroughfare remarkable now-a-days mainly for its police station; but carrying back our memories

wards became known as Sir Francis Chantrey, the eminent sculptor.

In this street there is to be seen the sign of the " Man in the Moon "—a sign representing, as antiquaries tell us, either Cain, or Jacob, or the man who was stoned for gathering sticks on the Jewish Sabbath (Numbers xv. 22, &c.), and so old as to be alluded to by Shakespeare and Dante. There were other houses bearing this sign in Cheapside and other parts of London.

We have already stated that a considerable part of Swallow Street was absorbed in the formation of Regent Street; a small portion, however, is still left between the Quadrant and Piccadilly, and into that we now pass. Here there has been a chapel belonging to the Scotch Presbyterians since 1710, when it was bought by a Dr. James Anderson from the French Huguenots, who had used it as one of the principal churches of their worship not long after their arrival in England after the revocation of the Edict of Nantes. Mr. Smiles, in his work on the Huguenots, tells us that "the congregation had originally worshipped in the French Ambassador's chapel in Monmouth House, Soho Square, from which they removed to Swallow Street in 1690." The records of their church, which are still preserved at Somerset House, show that it was the principal place for receiving back into church membership such refugees as had lapsed from their first fervour.

St. James's Hall, which covers a large space of ground between the Quadrant and Piccadilly, and is almost wholly concealed by houses and shop-fronts, was built in 1857, from the designs of Mr. Owen Jones, in the Arabesque or Moorish Alhambra style. The building, which has entrances in both thoroughfares, consists of one large room and two smaller ones. The principal hall is beautifully decorated, and surrounded on three sides with a gallery; the western end is apsidally constructed, and is so arranged that concerts may be given on an extensive scale, a class of entertainment for which the Hall was originally intended. Among the principal concerts given here are those of the New Philharmonic Society, and those widely-celebrated chamber concerts known as the "Monday Popular Concerts." The first public dinner held here was on June 2, 1858, under the presidency of Mr. Robert Stephenson, M.P., when a testimonial of the value of more than £2,500 was presented to Sir F. P. Smith, in recognition of services in the introduction of the screw-propeller into our steam fleet. Here Charles Dickens gave the second series of his "Readings," in the spring of 1861. In one of the smaller apartments entertainments on a humbler scale—such as panoramas, &c.—are given. In 1875, handsome and spacious dining-rooms, &c., were added to the building. Adjoining each room is a small kitchen, communicating, by means of a lift, with the general kitchen upstairs; the general fittings and furniture are handsome throughout, and in good keeping, marble and glazed tiling being largely employed in the panelling of the walls.

At Fore's Exhibition, which, towards the end of the last century, was in a house near the eastern end of Piccadilly, was to be seen the largest collection of caricatures by Gilray, Rowlandson, and the elder Cruickshank, including many political squibs and songs.

At No. 7, close to Regent Circus, in August, 1839, were made the first experiments in this country with the newly-discovered process of M. Daguerre, in the presence of a large body of scientific persons.

At a short distance westward from the circus, probably in the house now occupied by Mr. Quaritch, the eminent second-hand bookseller, but what was at the time No. 23, resided, in 1805, Emma Lyon, afterwards Lady Hamilton. She was born in Cheshire, and came to London, while a girl, in 1777, and lived in several families as a nurse-maid. In 1791 she was married to Sir William Hamilton. She became acquainted with Lord Nelson at Naples, in 1799, and here the great naval hero used to visit her. By him she had a child, named Horatia, who afterwards married a clergyman. It has been remarked by a writer in *Blackwood*, that "of her virtues, unhappily, prudence was not one. After the death of Nelson, and the disgraceful disregard of her claims by the Government, her affairs became greatly embarrassed. Those who owed wealth and honour to Nelson, and who had sunned themselves in her prosperity, shrank away from her. In her distress she wrote a most touching letter to one who had courted her smiles in other days, the Duke of Queensberry, imploring him to buy the little estate at Merton, which had been left to her by Nelson, and thus to relieve her from the most pressing embarrassments. The cold-hearted old profligate turned a deaf ear to the request. In 1813 Emma Hamilton was a prisoner for debt in the King's Bench. Deserted by the great, the noble, and the wealthy, abandoned by the heir of his title and the recipient of his hard-earned rewards, she, whom Nelson had left as a legacy to his country, might have died in a gaol. From this fate she was saved by one whose name is not to be found in the brilliant circle who surrounded her but a few short years before. Alderman Joshua Jonathan Smith (let all honour be paid to his most plebeian name) redeemed his share of his country's debt and obtained her release. She fled to Calais, where she died in destitution, and was buried by the hands of charitable strangers."

Mr. Quaritch's establishment is by far the most extensive of the kind in London, and probably in the world; and his catalogue, a most voluminous production, larger and more varied than even that of Mr. H. G. Bohn, is of itself of such interest in the literary world as to have merited a long and elaborate notice in the *Times*.

On the southern side of Piccadilly, nearly opposite the entrance to St. James's Hall, is the Museum of Practical Geology, of which we have spoken in a previous chapter.

At No. 208, on this side of the street, between the Circus and St. James's Church, are the Rooms of the Genealogical and Historical Society of Great Britain, an association which, though it has been in existence for twenty years, has hitherto published no "Transactions" or records of its proceedings, nor even the names of its president and council, or a list of its members !

St. James's Church, which is separated from the roadway by a paved court and brick wall, with handsome iron gates, owes its erection to the great increase in the parish of St. Martin-in-the-Fields. It was originally a chapel of ease only, and was built at an expense of about £8,500, chiefly by Henry Jermyn, Earl of St. Albans, and the neighbouring inhabitants.

It is well known that Sir Christopher Wren always regarded this as one of the best of his churches. He is said to have taxed his powers to the utmost here to provide "a room so capacious as with pews and galleries to hold 2,000 persons, and all to hear the service and see the preacher." It is divided in the interior into a nave and side aisles. The principal merit is in the formation of the roof, which is described by the late Professor Cockerell as "singularly ingenious and economical ; its simplicity, strength, and beauty being a perfect study of construction and architectural economy." The writer of "A New Critical Review of the Public Buildings" draws attention to its beautiful and commanding situation, while he expresses his regret that the architect troubled himself but little about beauty in his design.

The walls of this church are of brick and stone, with rustic quoins, &c.; the roof is arched, and supported by Corinthian pillars. The interior of the roof is beautifully ornamented, and divided into panels of crotchet and fret-work. The galleries have very handsome fronts, and the door-cases are highly enriched; that fronting Jermyn Street (originally the principal one) has above it the arms of the Earl of St. Albans. The font was carved by Grinling Gibbons, and represents the Fall of Man, the Salvation of Noah, &c. In Brayley's "Londoniana" it is asserted that the cover of the font, which was held by a flying angel and a group of cherubim, was stolen about the beginning of the present century, and subsequently hung up as a sign at a spirit-shop in the neigh-bourhood. The great east window was filled with stained glass in 1846, the subjects represented being Christ's Agony in the Garden, Bearing the Cross, the Passion, the Burial, Resurrection, and the Ascension. Of the altar-piece, which is very spacious, and highly enriched with carved work, Evelyn, in his "Diary," under date December 16, 1684, gives us the following particulars :—"I went to see the new church of St. James's, elegantly built. The altar was especially adorned, the white marble inclosure curiously and richly carved, the flowers and garlands about the walls by Mr. Gibbons, in wood ; a pelican, with her young at her breast, just over the altar in the carved compartment, and border environing the purple velvet fringed with (black) I.H.S. richly embroidered, and most noble plate, were given by Sir R. Greere, to the value (as was said) of £200. There was no altar anywhere in England, nor has there been any abroad, more handsomely adorned." The organ, which is considered very good, was built for James II., and intended for his Roman Catholic Oratory at Whitehall, but it was given to this parish by Queen Mary in 1691. At the north-west corner of the church is a tower and spire, rising to the height of about 150 feet. The spire, says Mr. Timbs, was a later addition, planned by a carpenter, whose design was preferred to that of Wren, from motives of economy. In 1850, the spire was coated with lead, when the exterior of the church was repaired throughout.

The church was consecrated in 1684, and many of its rectors have become bishops and high dignitaries in the Church. One of the earliest was Dr. Hoadly, afterwards Bishop of Winchester. Dr. Tenison, vicar of St. Martin's, and subsequently Archbishop of Canterbury, was appointed the first rector. The third rector, Dr. Wake, and the seventh, Dr. Secker, likewise at a later date became Archbishops of Canterbury. One of the rectors of St. James's in the last century was Dr. Samuel Clarke, the well-known latitudinarian divine, whose writings were so severely censured by the Lower House of Convocation as to cause a breach with the Upper House, and eventually to suspend the sittings of both Houses for nearly a century. He was a great favourite of Queen Anne (who placed his bust in her Hermitage) and of Queen Caroline, though disliked by Bolingbroke and Pope. On the death of Sir Isaac Newton he was offered the Mastership of the Mint, but refused it as "inconsistent with his profession," though in all probability he would have been better placed there than in a Trinitarian pulpit. Another of its rectors was Dr. Gerrard Andrewes, some time Dean of Canterbury, who refused the Bishopric of Chester, which was offered to him by Lord Liverpool in 1812. Another rector was Dr. Ward, Dean of Lincoln, who was succeeded by Dr. Jackson, since Bishop of London.

In 1762, a fire broke out most unaccountably in the vaults of this church, and destroyed two hundred coffins and their contents.

In this parish lived and died, at the age of eighty-seven, the Hon. Frederick Byng, a well-known member of the world of fashion, both before and under the Regency. He was always known as "Poodle Byng," on account of his curly hair. Of late years he took an active interest in the parochial affairs of St. James's, having lived for sixty years in the region of the clubs and of St. James's Place, where he resided. He was the subject of sundry caricatures by Dighton, in 1817.

In St. James's Church is buried the learned anatomist, Mr. Joshua Brookes, F.R.S., whose lectures at his theatre in Blenheim Street are said to have been attended by seven thousand pupils. His museum was almost a rival of that belonging to John Hunter, of whom we have already spoken in our account of Leicester Square : its doors were always open to scientific men of this and other countries. It was, however, dispersed on his death, in 1833.

Here, too, is buried Sir John Malcolm, the distinguished Indian general, who died in 1833. James Dodsley, many years an eminent bookseller in Pall Mall, of whom we have already spoken, is likewise interred here. There is a monument to his memory near the communion-table. Here, too, lies Mary Delaney, niece of Granville, Lord Lansdowne. Benjamin Stillingfleet, the naturalist, Charles Cotton, the friend and companion of Izaak Walton, and Dr. Sydenham, are also buried here. The latter is commemorated by a marble tablet, erected by the College of Physicians. Among other notabilities interred in this church may be mentioned Hayman and Michael Dahl, the portrait painters; G. H. Harlow, the painter of " The Trial of Queen Katharine ; " Dr. Akenside, the author of the " Pleasures of the Imagination," and also the two Vanderveldes, the marine painters.

Here, as at St. Giles's-in-the-Fields, unfortunately, the earlier volumes of the parish rate-books have disappeared; so that it is impossible to glean the same accurate information as to its inhabitants in the reigns of the earlier Stuarts, which meets us at every turn in those of St. Martin's-in-the-Fields and of St. Paul's, Covent Garden.

With reference to this parish, and to the line of roadway running westward, it may be stated that in an Act of Parliament, in the reign of James II., mention is made of the " mansion-house of the Earl of Burlington, fronting Portugal Street ; " and a "toft of ground" in Piccadilly is assigned to the rector of St. James's parish.

In a house at the corner of Sackville Street, " over against St. James's Church," in the year 1687, died Sir William Petty, the eminent writer on political economy, and an ancestor of the Lansdowne family. The son of a clothier in humble circumstances, he was born at Romsey, in Hampshire, in 1623, and was educated at the grammar school of his native town. He afterwards determined to improve himself by study at the University of Caen, in Normandy. Whilst there, he contrived to support himself by carrying on a small pedlar's trade with a " little stock of merchandise." Wishing to return to England, he bound himself apprentice to a sea-captain, who beat him most unmercifully. Leaving the navy in disgust, he took to the study of medicine, and having studied at Leyden and Paris, he took his degree, and was subsequently made professor of anatomy. During this part of his life he was reduced to such poverty that he subsisted for two or three weeks entirely on walnuts. But again he began to trade in a small way, and, " turning an honest penny," returned to England with money in his pocket. Steadily applying himself to his profession, he then became a successful London physician, and was one of the first fellows of the Royal Society, to which he presented the model of a double-bottomed ship, to sail against wind and tide. In 1652 he was appointed physician to the army in Ireland, and secretary to Henry Cromwell, by whom he was employed in surveying the forfeited lands, for which charges were alleged against him in the House of Commons, and he was dismissed from his appointments. At the Restoration he was knighted, and made Surveyor-General of Ireland. Sir William suffered much by the Great Fire of London ; but by marriage and various speculations he recovered his losses, and died very rich, in the year 1687. In his will, which is a curious document, singularly illustrative of his character, he writes, with a certain amount of self-pride, " At the full age of fifteen, I had obtained the Latin, Greek, and French tongues," and at twenty years of age " had gotten up threescore pounds, with as much mathematics as any of my age was known to have had." Sir William was buried in the fine old Norman church of Romsey. A plain slab, cut by an illiterate workman, with the inscription, " Here layes Sir William Petty," covers his tomb.

Next door but one to Sir William Petty, Verrio,

the Italian painter, was residing in the reign of William and Mary ; the reader will not have forgotten the often-quoted line which records his decorations of the ceiling of Whitehall—

    " Where sprawl the saints of Verrio and Laguerre."

In a shop opposite St. James's Church there was, in 1819, a curious collection of live animals, which had a run of popularity, but was unable to stand as a rival against Exeter 'Change.

Continuing our walk along Piccadilly, we pass on our left the publishing-houses of Messrs. Chapman and Hall, Messrs. Hatchard, and others. From the first-named shop were issued the successive numbers of " Pickwick " and " Nicholas Nickleby," which electrified and amazed the world in 1837-9, and made the name of " Boz " a " household word." Messrs. Chapman and Hall were the publishers of Charles Dickens's serial works down to and inclusive of "Martin Chuzzlewit" and the "Christmas Carol," which appeared in 1843-4 ; from that date, however, Messrs. Bradbury and Evans became his publishers, and those relations lasted until 1858, when he started *All the Year Round* on his own account. The publication of Charles Dickens's works is now again in the hands of the house in connection with which he first " made his mark " with "Pickwick." At the shop of Mr. Hardwicke, No. 192, were issued for some time the publications of the Ray Society. This society, which was formed in 1844, takes its name from John Ray, the celebrated naturalist.

The booksellers' shops here, at the close of the last century, had not ceased to be what those of Tonson, in the Strand, and Dodsley, in Pall Mall, had been—the resort of literary characters. At this time, Mr. D'Israeli tells us that Debrett's was the chief haunt of the Whigs, and Hatchard's that of the Tories. It was at Hatchard's that the elder D'Israeli was first introduced to Mr. Pye, the Poet Laureate, who was then busy on his translation of Aristotle's Poetics, and who, in passing Debrett's door, requested his new friend, who was then unknown, to go in and buy a pamphlet which he dared not be seen going in to purchase for himself.

The house No. 169 is remarkable as having been not only the shop where the *Anti-Jacobin* was published, but also the house in which its editor (William Gifford) and its writers used to meet in council ; a fact worthy of note, when we add that among the contributors to its columns were the younger Pitt, George Canning, and John Hookham Frere. This shop, then kept by a Mr. Wright, was much frequented by the friends of Mr. Pitt's

ministry. It was here that Dr. Wolcott was severely " castigated " by Gifford. No. 117 was the shop of William Pickering, the eminent publisher. The Aldine anchor, revived by the late Mr. Pickering on his title-pages, gave a celebrity to the books, mostly reprints of the poets and prose writers of the past, and works in curious paths of literature, which he issued from his shop.

The Egyptian Hall, the front of which forms one of the most noticeable features on the southern side of Piccadilly, nearly opposite to Bond Street, was erected in the year 1812, from the designs of Mr. G. F. Robinson, at a cost of £16,000, for a museum of natural history, the objects of which were in part collected by William Bullock, F.L.S., during his thirty years' travel in Central America. The edifice was so named from its being in the Egyptian style of architecture and ornament, the inclined pilasters and sides being covered with hieroglyphics ; and the hall is now used principally for popular entertainments, lectures, and exhibitions. Bullock's Museum was at one time one of the most popular exhibitions in the metropolis. It comprised curiosities from the South Sea, Africa, and North and South America ; works of art ; armoury, and the travelling carriage of Bonaparte. The collection, which was made up to a very great extent out of the Lichfield Museum and that of Sir Ashton Lever, was sold off by auction, and dispersed in lots, in 1819.

Here, in 1825, was exhibited a curious phenomenon, known as " the Living Skeleton," or " the Anatomic Vivante," of whom a short account will be found in Hone's " Every-Day Book." His name was Claude Amboise Seurat, and he was born in Champagne, in April, 1798. His height was 5 feet 7½ inches, and as he consisted literally of nothing but skin and bone, he weighed only 77¾ lbs. He (or another living skeleton) was shown subsequently—in 1830, we believe—at " Bartlemy Fair," but died shortly afterwards. There is extant a portrait of M. Seurat, published by John Williams, of 13, Paternoster Row, which quite enables us to identify in him the perfect French native.

Of the various entertainments and exhibitions that have found a home here, it would, perhaps, be needless to attempt to give a complete catalogue ; but we may, at least, mention a few of the most successful. In 1829, the Siamese Twins made their first appearance here, and were described at the time as " two youths of eighteen, natives of Siam, united by a short band at the pit of the stomach—two perfect bodies, bound together by an inseparable link." They died in America in the early part of the year 1874. The American dwarf, Charles S. Stratton, "Tom Thumb," was exhibited here in 1844; and subsequently, Mr. Albert Smith gave the narrative of his ascent of Mont Blanc, his lecture being illustrated by some cleverly-painted dioramic views of the perils and sublimities of the Alpine regions. Latterly, the Egyptian Hall has been almost continually used for the exhibition of feats of legerdemain, the most successful of these—if one may judge from the

owner, exchanged it with the Duke of York and Albany for his mansion in Whitehall, now Dover House. Near or on this site, says Pennant, stood the house of "that monster of treachery, that profligate minister, Charles Spencer, Earl of Sunderland, who, by his destructive advice, premeditatedly brought ruin on his unsuspecting master, James II. . . . . At the very time that he sold him to the Prince of Orange, he encouraged his Majesty

THE ALBANY, IN 1805.

"run" which the entertainment has enjoyed— being the extraordinary performances of Messrs. Maskelyne and Cooke.

In 1819, there was, adjoining Bullock's Museum, the Pantherion, a separate exhibition, "intended to display quadrupeds in such a manner as to convey a correct notion of their haunts and habits. In one orange-tree were disposed sixty species of the genus *Simia*, or monkeys. Besides animal nature, Mr. Bullock exhibited, in connection with it, many exotic trees."

Nearly opposite the Egyptian Hall is "The Albany." This building, which is separated from the main thoroughfare by a small paved court-yard, was known in the last century as Melbourne House. Lord Melbourne, however, the then

in every step which was certain of involving him and his family in utter ruin."

The present central building, designed by Sir William Chambers, was sold by Lord Holland, in 1770, to the first Lord Melbourne. In 1804 the mansion was altered and enlarged, and first let in chambers, and named the Albany, after the second title of the Duke of York. It extends in the rear as far as Burlington Gardens, having a porter's lodge and entrance at either end. It is entirely occupied by bachelors (or widowers), and comprises sixty sets of apartments, each staircase being marked by one of the letters of the alphabet. Most of the occupants of these suites are members of one or other of the Houses of Parliament, or naval or military officers. Among those who have occupied chambers here in their day were Lord Byron, George Canning, Lord Macaulay (who here wrote the greater part of his " History of England "), Lord Lytton, Lord Glenelg, and Sir John C. Hobhouse. Here, too, as we learn from his Autobiography, Lord Brougham was living in bachelor chambers

Clarges' house, which is described, in the year 1675, as being "near Burlington House, above Piccadilly."

In 1806, the house adjoining the Albany was occupied, for the purposes of exhibition, by Daniel Lambert, a Leicestershire man, who bore the repu-

THE NEW "WHITE HORSE CELLAR." (*See page* 261.)

from 1806, when studying for the Bar, down to 1808, when he removed to chambers in the Middle Temple. It is said that no person who carries on a trade or commercial occupation is allowed to reside on the premises ; and that, as a rule, " ladies are not admitted," excepting the mothers, sisters, grandmothers, and aunts of the occupants of the chambers; but this rule, we fancy, is not very strictly adhered to.

The Albany adjoins the site of Sir Thomas

tation of being the " heaviest man that ever lived." His weight, at the age of thirty-six, was upwards of eighty-seven stone. It is stated that, although in most instances, when the body exceeds the usual proportions, the strength correspondingly diminishes, this was not the case with Lambert, for it is recorded that, notwithstanding his excessive corpulency, he tested his ability by carrying more than four hundredweight and a half—a feat that many a sinewy athlete would fail to accomplish. During his stay here, "Dan" Lambert was as fashionable a celebrity as Albert Smith or "General" Tom Thumb became in later years, at the Egyptian Hall opposite. Thousands went to see him daily, and from morning till night his reception-room was thronged with men in cocked hats and ladies in furbelows, coming alike from Kensington and Cheapside.

On the opposite side of the road, between St. James's Street and the Green Park, is Arlington Street, of which we have already spoken.* The exact date of building this street is not known, but it must have been between 1680 and 1690. The street stands partly on the site of Goring House. Evelyn, in his "Diary," under date of 29th March, 1665, tells us how that he "went to Goring House, now Mr. Secretary Bennet's; ill built, but the place capable of being made a pretty villa." The same diarist records its destruction by fire, November 21, 1674, when a fine collection of pictures, as well as much handsome plate, hangings, and furniture, perished; and he elsewhere describes the appointments of the house as "princely." From Pepys we learn that a sister of John Milton was married here in July, 1660.

We might add here, as one of the residents of this street in former times, the name of Lady Mary Wortley Montagu, who, before her marriage, was living here in the house of her father, the Marquis of Dorchester, afterwards Duke of Kingston. She was the author of those charming, lively, and witty letters, written at Constantinople, and addressed by Lady Mary to friends at home, descriptive of Turkish life and society, and in which, it has been said, she displays "the epistolary talents of a female Horace Walpole." She was very eccentric in her attire; indeed, Horace Walpole once described her dress as consisting of "a groundwork of dirt, with an embroidery of filthiness."

Horace Walpole himself resided in this street for many years, before removing further west into Berkeley Square (where he died); and from Arlington Street are dated many of his letters to Lady Ossory. At Horace Walpole's house, on one occasion, there was a large party present at dinner, when Bruce, the celebrated African traveller, was talking in his usual style of exaggeration. Some one asked him what musical instruments were used in Abyssinia. Bruce hesitated, not being prepared for the question, and at last said, "I think I saw a lyre there." George Selwyn, who was one of the party, whispered to his next man, "Yes, there is one less since he left the country." Admiral Lord

Nelson, too, was living in this street when his wife separated from him, in 1801.

Close by Arlington Street was a well-known hostelry, the old "White Horse Cellar." In the "good old days," before the power of steam had been developed, or railways planned, even Londoners rejoiced, on summer evenings, to lounge about this noted house, and watch the mails drive down Piccadilly, *en route* for the West of England. On the king's birthday, especially, the scene was picturesque, and of special interest. The exterior of the "Cellar" was studded over with oil lights of many colours, arranged in tasty lines and capital letters. The sleek-coated horses stepped along as if they were proud of their new harness, and the bright brass ornaments on their trappings glittered in the light. The coachmen and guards, too, were dressed in unsullied scarlet coats, which they wore for the first time on that day—woe for them if it was wet—and there were gay rosettes of ribbons and bunches of bright flowers at each of the horses' heads, as well as in the coachman's button-hole. The coaches themselves were, if not newly painted, at all events, freshly "touched-up" with the brush, and the post-horn sounded pleasantly as the ostlers cried, "All right; off they go!" In the reign of George IV., many of the coaches which left London were driven by gentlemen, and in some cases the reins were handled by peers of the realm. Sir St. Vincent Cotton drove the Brighton "Age;" another coach on the same road was horsed and driven by the Marquis of Worcester, afterwards Duke of Beaufort; Sir Thomas Tyrrwhitt Jones drove the "Pearl;" and the Reading coach was driven by Captain Probyn.

Hazlitt has thus described, in his own graphic manner, the scene presented on the starting of the old mail-coaches:—"The finest sight in the metropolis," he writes, "is the setting off of the mail-coaches from Piccadilly. The horses paw the ground and are impatient to be gone, as if conscious of the precious burden they convey. There is a peculiar secrecy and dispatch, significant and full of meaning, in all the proceedings concerning them. Even the outside passengers have an erect and supercilious air, as if proof against the accidents of the journey; in fact, it seems indifferent whether they are to encounter the summer's heat or the winter's cold, since they are borne through the air on a winged chariot. The mail-carts drive up and the transfer of packages is made, and at a given signal off they start, bearing the irrevocable scrolls that give wings to thought, and that bind or sever hearts for ever. How we hate the Putney and Brentford stages that draw up when they are

* See p. 169, ante.

gone! Some persons think the sublimest object in nature is a ship launched on the bosom of the ocean; but give me for my private satisfaction the mail-coaches that pour down Piccadilly of an evening, tear up the pavement, and devour the way before them to the Land's End." Poor Hazlitt! in the fall of the mail-coach he sees a type of the rapid changes to which all mortal inventions and fashions are subject. In Cowper's day the mail-coach had scarcely superseded the post-boy and stage; and in Hazlitt's time they had entered on their decline and fall; and we have lived to see the Putney and Brentford stages superseded by omnibuses!

At the old "White Horse Cellar," when it served as the head-quarters of the departure of the passengers by the country coaches, there used to stand a small confraternity of Jews, who sold oranges, pencils, sponges, brushes, and other small wares; but these, of course, disappeared when the system of travelling was changed, and the old house came, in the end, to be converted into a railway booking-office for luggage.

A new house on the opposite side of the way, it is true, rejoices in the sign of the "White Horse Cellar;" and at Hatchett's Hotel, which adjoins it, an attempt has been made, within the last few years, to revive the taste for coaching, and, with this aim in view, stage-coaches have been run daily during the summer to Sevenoaks, Tunbridge Wells, Windsor, Brighton, Dorking, &c. The history of this movement is worth epitomising, in the words of a well-known writer on sporting subjects:—

"The Brighton road was the last to give up the old-fashioned stage-coach, and the first selected by the amateurs who are the stage-coach owners of to-day. Up to about 1862, the 'Age,' the property of and driven by 'Old Clark,' ran during the summer, *viâ* Kingston and Dorking (where the 'coach' dined), to Brighton. In its latter days the Duke of Beaufort and Mr. Charles Lawrie, of Bexley, Kent, helped the proprietor in a substantial and practical manner, but the 'Age' was like any other business speculation, and soon after it ceased to pay it stopped. In the year 1866, and chiefly through the exertions of Mr. Lawrie, a little yellow coach, called the 'Old Times,' was subscribed for in shares of £10 each, and made its appearance on the 'Brighton' road, the Duke of Beaufort, Mr. Chandos Pole, Lord H. Thynne, and Mr. C. Lawrie being among the shareholders. The success was so considerable, that in the April of the following year the Brighton was 'doubled,' and two new coaches built especially for the work, and horsed by the Duke of Beaufort and his friends, ran during

that summer. Alfred Tedder and Pratt were the coachmen, and the lunching-place (where the coaches met) was the 'Chequers,' at Horley, an inn now kept by Mr. Tedder (the driver of the Brighton coach of to-day). At the close of the season of 1867, Mr. Chandos Pole determined to carry on one coach by himself. This he did through the entire winter; and further, with his brother's (Mr. Pole-Gell's) aid (the latter found twelve of the horses), 'doubled' the coach in the succeeding summer. At the season's close, after the horses had been dispersed by the auctioneer's hammer at Aldridge's, a few lovers of the road gave 'the Squire' (Mr. Chandos Pole) a dinner at 'Hatchett's,' Piccadilly, and presented him with a handsome silver flagon (value £50) to commemorate his plucky behaviour, and in admiration of his wonderful ability as a 'whip.' At a later date there was presented to Tedder, the coachman, a smaller flagon (value £20), as a token of the appreciation of his friends of his ability on the 'bench' (*i.e.*, the driving-seat). In 1869, Mr. A. G. Scott first took the position of honorary secretary to the Brighton coach, which then made the 'Ship' at Charing Cross its starting-place. This was the best year the coach has known, as it never once had a clean bill up or down. The proprietors were Lord Londesborough, Colonel Stracey-Clitheroe, Mr. Pole-Gell, and Mr. G. Meek, who each provided the horses for one stage; while Mr. Chandos Pole again took the largest responsibility by providing the horses for two stages. But the example of the Brighton coach was followed. Towards the end of the season of 1867, Mr. Charles Hoare started a coach between Beckenham and Sevenoaks. This developed the following year into the Sevenoaks coach, starting from Hatchett's, and this carried such good loads, that in 1868 its proprietor carried it on to Tunbridge Wells, to the delight of thousands who have since enjoyed the exquisite scenery it has introduced them to. Since 1868 the Brighton has continued a single coach, but several new candidates for public favour have appeared."

Apropos of the subject of coaching, we may add that Mr. Larwood tells us in his "History of Sign-boards," that there is still (1866) a sign of the "Coach and Six" to be seen in Westminster; but he does not specify the exact spot. It does not appear, however, in the "Post Office Directory" for 1876. The sign, however, speaks of the day when the roads even near London were so bad in the winter time that four horses were not enough to carry a coach safe out of the deep and miry ruts. Mr. Larwood also tells us, that in 1866 there were still no less than fifty-two public-houses, exclusive of beer-houses, coffee-houses, &c., which rejoiced in the sign of the "Coach and Horses," in spite of the progress made by railways.

While on the subject of sign-boards, we may state that Piccadilly was the place in which the "Cat and Fiddle" first appeared as a public-house sign. The story is that a Frenchwoman, a small shopkeeper at the eastern end, soon after it was first built, had a very faithful and favourite cat, and that, in lack of any other sign, she put up over her door the words, "Voici une Chat fidèle." From some cause or other the "Chat Fidèle" soon became a popular sign in France, and was speedily Anglicised into the "Cat and Fiddle," because the words form part of one of our most popular nursery rhymes. We do not pledge ourselves for the correctness of the derivation, but simply tell the story as told to us.

It has often been observed that while the fashionable world flitting westwards occupied the streets to the north and south of Piccadilly—its tributaries —the great thoroughfare itself was given up to tradesmen and shopkeepers, with the exception of two or three great mansions, which, though *in* it, were scarcely *of* it.

CHAPTER XXII.

PICCADILLY.—BURLINGTON HOUSE.

" Burlington's fair palace still remains :
Beauty within—without, proportion reigns ;
There Handel strikes the strings, the melting strain
Transports the soul, and thrills through every vein ;
There oft I enter, but with cleaner shoes,
For Burlington's beloved by every muse."—*Gay's "Trivia."*

The Earl of Burlington's Taste for Classical Architecture—Walpole's First Visit to Burlington House—A Critical Reviewer's Opinion of the Old Entrance and Colonnade—Pope lampooned by Hogarth—Anecdotes of Pope and Dean Swift—Burlington House under the Regency— Visit of the Allied Sovereigns—The Elgin Marbles—The Mansion purchased by Government—Various Plans drawn up for rebuilding it— Description of the New Buildings—The Royal Society—Charles II. and his Piscatorial Query—Scientific Experiments under the Auspices of the Royal Society—How Sir Isaac Newton became a Member—Remarkable Events connected with the Royal Society—Principal Presidents, Secretaries, and Fellows of the Society—Society of Antiquaries of London—The Linnæan Society—The Geological Society— The Royal Astronomical Society—The Chemical Society—The Royal Academy—Burlington Arcade.

THIS splendid mansion, now the home of the Royal Academy, the Royal Society, and other learned and scientific associations, dates its existence from the time of Charles II., having been erected by Richard Boyle, third Earl of Burlington, on the site of a house built by Sir John Denham, the poet, whose wife was the mistress of James II. when Duke of York, and is said to have been poisoned. Lord Burlington was a man actuated by a fine public spirit. He was at the expense of repairing St. Paul's Church, Covent Garden, the work of Inigo Jones ; and by his publication of the "Designs" of that great architect, and of the " Antiquities of Rome " by Palladio, he contributed to form a taste for classical architecture in England. To this Pope alludes in his fourth Epistle, at the same time expressing his fear that the public will be slow to profit by such works :—

" You show us Rome was glorious, not profuse,
And pompous buildings once were things of use :
Yet shall, my lord, your just and noble rules
Fill half the land with imitating fools,
Who random drawings from your sheets shall take,
And of one beauty many blunders make."

Lord Burlington also deserves to be held in honour for having helped that pure and simple-minded philosopher, Dr. Berkeley, by his powerful recommendation, to attain the dignity of an Irish bishopric.

It is to this Lord Burlington that the author of the " New Critical Review of the Public Buildings, &c., in and about London and Westminster, in 1736," most appropriately dedicated his work, as one of those few persons who " have the talent of laying out their own fortunes with propriety, and of making their own private judgment contribute to the public ornament." We have already mentioned one instance of this public spirit in the part which he took towards the rebuilding of the great dormitory at Westminster School.*

At the time when Pope dedicated his " Epistle on Taste" to Lord Burlington, his lordship was in his thirty-sixth year. He was then engaged in ornamenting his gardens, and building his villa at Chiswick. The celebrated front and colonnade at Burlington House had been erected some years before, in 1718. There is reason to believe that, in this splendid improvement, his lordship, then very young, had the assistance of a practical architect, Colin Campbell, though Walpole considers that the

* See Vol. III., p. 469.

design is too good for the latter. The same lively and picturesque writer thus describes the effect which the Burlington colonnade had upon him when he first beheld it:—"Soon after my return from Italy, I was invited to a ball at Burlington House. As I passed under the gate by night it could not strike me. At daybreak, looking out of the window to see the sun rise, I was surprised with the vision of the colonnade that fronted me. It seemed one of those edifices in fairy tales that are raised by genii in a night-time."

The author of the "Critical Review," above mentioned, observes that "in this street we are entertained with a sight of the most expensive wall in England, namely, that before Burlington House." This he criticises, and, on the whole, favourably. "The grand entrance," he says, "is august and beautiful, and by covering the house entirely from the eye, gives pleasure and surprise at the opening of the whole front, with the area before it, at once." He complains, however, of the columns of the gate, as "merely ornamental, and supporting nothing." The colonnade remained till the last, but the dead wall in front concealed from the public all view of the fine architecture within.

During the life of Lord Burlington, the town mansion which bore his name was the haunt of all the wits, poets, and learned men of his day. Pope was a frequent visitor; and it was in allusion to his noble host's talents as an architect that he wrote—

"Who plants like Bathurst, or who builds like Boyle?"

In satire of Pope's adulation of Lord Burlington, and his fierce onslaught on the "princely" Duke of Chandos, under the character of "Timon," Hogarth made a humorous design, in which the poet was represented as standing on a builder's stage or platform, engaged in whitewashing the gate of Burlington House, and at the same time bespattering the coach of the duke as it passed by along Piccadilly.

Dr. King, in his "Anecdotes of his Own Times," tells a story about Pope, which shows that, at all events, he was not a teetotaler, and had no idea of sinking down into one of those water-drinkers whose poems, according to Horace, have no chance of immortality. He writes: "Pope and I, with my Lord Orrery, and Sir Harry Bedingfield, dined with the late Earl of Burlington. After the first course Pope grew sick, and went out of the room. When dinner was ended, and the cloth was removed, my Lord Burlington said he would go out, and see what was become of Pope. And soon after they returned together. But Pope, who had been casting up his dinner, looked very

pale, and complained much. My lord asked him if he would have some mulled wine, or a glass of old sack, which Pope refused. I told my Lord Burlington that he wanted a dram. Upon which the little man expressed some resentment against me, and said he would not taste any spirits, and that he abhorred drams as much as I did. However, I persisted, and assured my Lord Burlington that he could not oblige our friend more at that instant than by ordering a large glass of cherry-brandy to be set before him. This was done, and in less than half an hour, while my lord was acquainting us with an affair which engaged our attention, Pope had sipped up all the brandy. Pope's frame of body did not promise long life; but he certainly hastened his death by feeding much on highly-seasoned dishes, and drinking spirits."

Sir John Hawkins tells us, in his "History of Music," that Handel lived for three years an honoured guest here.

Swift also was a frequent guest here, and he did not always carry to the table of its hospitable owner the manners of a gentleman. For instance, in Scott's "Life of Swift" an anecdote is related, to the effect, that on the last occasion of the Dean being in London, he went to dine with the Earl of Burlington, then recently married. The earl, it is supposed, being willing to have a little diversion, did not introduce him to his lady, nor mention his name. After dinner, said the Dean, "Lady Burlington, I hear you can sing; sing me a song." The lady looked on this unceremonious manner of asking a favour with distaste, and positively refused. He said "she should sing, or he would make her. Why, madam, I suppose you take me for one of your poor English hedge-parsons; sing when I bid you." As the earl did nothing but laugh at this freedom, the lady was so vexed that she burst into tears, and retired. His first compliment to her when he saw her again was, "Pray, madam, are you as proud and ill-natured now as when I saw you last?" To which she answered, with great good-humour, "No, Mr. Dean, I'll sing for you if you please." From which time he conceived a great esteem for her ladyship.

Lord Burlington died in the year 1753, and with his demise a title honoured and ennobled through three generations by genius, virtue, and public spirit, became extinct. It was afterwards revived in the person of a member of the ducal house of Cavendish, who had inherited part of his fortune. Nightingale says that the mansion was left to the Cavendishes on the express condition that it should not be pulled down, but the statement is questioned.

BURLINGTON HOUSE, ABOUT 1700.

Pennant says, that long after the year 1700, Burlington House was the last house westwards in Piccadilly; but the statement may be questioned. It will be remembered that the nobleman who had built the mansion in the seventeenth century, had placed it there, "because he was certain that no one would build beyond him." This aim, however, if it was ever true in fact, was speedily frustrated, for shortly afterwards we read that to the west of

House, and of building a crescent of houses on its site. "I do not know," she writes, "why the plan fell to the ground; but in 1814, the great *fêtes* in honour of the Allied Sovereigns were given in these gardens, which were enclosed for the purpose; and now," she adds, "in 1868, the site is likely to be applied to still better purposes"— alluding, probably, to the University of London. "The whole garden of Burlington House was

BURLINGTON HOUSE, 1875.   (*See page* 266.)

Burlington House rose Clarges House, named after Sir Thomas Clarges, and two others, inhabited, according to Strype, by "Lord Sherbourne and the Countess of Denby" (*sic*).

Burlington House, in 1811, was tenanted by the Earl of Harrington, who gave there a grand ball. Under the Regency and in the reign of George IV., the mansion became occasionally the rallying-point of the Liberal party. In 1817, as Lord Russell tells us in his "Recollections," there was held here a meeting, at which Lord Grey, as the leader of the party, sketched out the policy of Lord Liverpool's ministry, and his own plan of opposition tactics. The Honourable Miss Amelia Murray tells us in her "Recollections," that about the year 1812 there was an intention of pulling down Burlington

enclosed by tents and temporary rooms. I did not think the Emperor of Russia a handsome man; he looked red, and stiff, and square: but Nicholas, the future Emperor, was a magnificent young prince. Among the numerous followers of the Emperor of Russia, there were the 'Hetman' Platoff, and twelve of his Cossacks, who were lodged by Lord James Murray, in Cumberland Place."

At Burlington House were exhibited the Elgin marbles, on their first arrival from the East, till they could find a permanent home at the British Museum. Cyrus Redding, in his "Fifty Years' Recollections," records his first visit to them here, in company with Haydon the painter.

In 1854, the mansion was purchased by the Government, and some five years later Lord John

Manners (then First Commissioner of Works) instructed Messrs. Banks and Barry to prepare a plan for buildings covering the entire site, which were then intended to comprise " a new Royal Academy, the University of London, and a Patent Office much enlarged, and to be connected with an extensive museum of patented invention for public reference, and also accommodation for at least six of the principal learned and scientific societies, who, it was considered, by past usage had acquired claims to be lodged at the public expense." The design consisted of two spacious quadrangles, each communicating with the other, and having arched gateways in the centre of the façades to Piccadilly and Burlington Gardens, thus connecting all together internally, and giving a thoroughfare through the building from the one part to the other. By this arrangement the Royal Academy would have had allotted to it nearly the whole of the Piccadilly façade, and the whole side of the first quadrangle on the west. This appropriation of the site, however, involved the removal of Old Burlington House, and, as the *Builder* remarks, " the sentimental ideas of its architectural importance and beauty were allowed to set aside this arrangement."

It was subsequently proposed by the Government to remove the national collection of pictures from Trafalgar Square, giving up the whole building there to the Royal Academy only, and to construct a National Gallery on the Burlington House lands. Accordingly, in 1863, fresh plans were prepared to meet this arrangement, by which the old mansion was to remain, the screen-wall in Piccadilly was to be replaced by a handsome open railing, the colonnades being retained, and, with the old building, being made to furnish the access to the new galleries. Again their plans met with the approval of the trustees of the National Gallery, after most careful deliberation, and also of the Government; but the vote for carrying this scheme into effect was refused by Parliament, partly on the same grounds as before—namely, the much-feared interference with the architectural glories of Old Burlington House.

" At last," says the *Builder*, " in the year 1866, it was proposed to reverse the above scheme, and that the National Gallery should remain in Trafalgar Square, and the Royal Academy should have a lease for 999 years, at a nominal rent, of the centre portion of Old Burlington House, with about half the garden in the rear, on which latter area they should erect new galleries and schools at their own cost, and under the direction of one of their members, Mr. Sydney Smirke; the access

to the same being through the old building, which was to accommodate the administration."

The grounds in the rear, extending to Burlington Gardens, were to be given as a site for the University of London, and their new edifice has been erected accordingly, under the direction of Sir James (then Mr.) Pennethorne. The wing-buildings, the colonnades, and the wall to Piccadilly were to be removed, and Messrs. Banks and Barry were again called upon to prepare designs for the erection of the new buildings, which were to accommodate six of the learned and scientific societies, namely, the Royal Society, the Linnæan Society, and the Chemical Society, who had hitherto occupied Old Burlington House, and the Society of Antiquaries, the Geological Society, and the Astronomical Society, who at that time were occupying parts of Somerset House. Arrangements having once more been made with the governing bodies of each society, as to the accommodation which they considered would be necessary for them respectively, and the plans having been finally approved by the then Government and by Parliament, and obtaining the Royal assent, the foundations for the present buildings were commenced in November, 1868.

The space now occupied by Burlington House extends from Piccadilly northwards into Burlington Gardens, having a frontage to each of about 200 feet, and a depth between them of nearly 600 feet. The old mansion, which still remains, stands at a distance of about 225 feet back from Piccadilly. The site of the south wall and the colonnades and wings is now covered with lofty and spacious buildings, forming three sides of a quadrangle, which, in the shape of an oblong square, has replaced the old court-yard. In the new façade towards Piccadilly, the most peculiar feature is the grand central archway leading into the court-yard; it is probably the largest archway of the sort in London, being 20 feet clear in width and about 32 feet in height. The façade of Burlington House (now the Royal Academy of Arts) is fully seen from Piccadilly through this archway. The colonnade mentioned above was removed in 1868-9, and has found a temporary resting-place in Battersea Park.

The style of architecture adopted by Messrs. Banks and Barry is pure Italian; and, as the authority above quoted observes, "taking as the key-note the general features and proportions of the façade of Old Burlington House, which was to form one side of the quadrangle, the architects have endeavoured to blend it with their new composition, with sufficient similarity of design to effect this, but with more finished details."

On the completion of the new building intended for the learned societies, those which at that time occupied the old mansion vacated their apartments, and that building was wholly made over to the Royal Academy, with the proviso that the Academy should, at their own expense, heighten their building by the addition of an upper storey. The portions of the buildings occupied by the members of the several societies are arranged on two floors, on the upper of which are situated the libraries—with the exception of that of the Geological Society, which is on the ground floor—each fitted with galleries, and lighted from the roof as well as at the sides. The Geological Society has its museum on the first floor, and this is fitted with two tiers of galleries.

The Royal Society has on the first floor a noble suite of reception-rooms, available for the annual *soirées* of the president, and a library which it is computed will give room for nearly 35,000 volumes, enabling it to continue what it now is, one of the most perfect scientific libraries in the world. The libraries of the Linnæan and Antiquarian Societies are very spacious, and all of them two storeys in height, with internal galleries.

The resident officers of the various societies located here have their apartments on the first and second floors of the building, in positions convenient to the scene of their daily labours. Dispersed throughout the rooms occupied by the Royal Society are the portraits of the presidents, distinguished Fellows, and other great luminaries of science, painted by Van Somer, Sir Peter Lely, Sir Godfrey Kneller, Sir Joshua Reynolds, Sir Thomas Lawrence, and other great artists.

It will not be out of place to introduce in this place a brief mention of some of our chief learned societies which have the advantage of free quarters here.

First and foremost, of course, stands the Royal Society. This is the oldest scientific society, with a consecutive history, in Europe, and stands with the French Institute at the head of the science of the world. As stated already (Vol. I., page 104), it dates its existence from the year 1645, and its early meetings were held sometimes at the lodgings of Dr. Goddard (one of its originators) in Wood Street, sometimes in Cheapside, and on other occasions in Gresham College. In 1648 and the following year, some of the supporters of these meetings became connected with the University of Oxford, and instituted a similar society in that city. Ten years later, several of the members of this philosophical society came to London, and held their meetings at Gresham College, where they were joined by Lord Brouncker, John Evelyn, and others; but owing to the political troubles of the times, their meetings were not long continued. In 1660, it was agreed to constitute a society for the study of science, when, in accordance with this resolve, a president, secretary, and registrar were elected; the president was Sir Robert Moray.

During the two centuries of the society's life it has occupied several dwellings. First at Gresham College; then at Arundel House, which was lent by Henry Howard, afterwards Duke of Norfolk; and again at Gresham College, where the society remained until 1710, when it removed to Crane Court. It continued here, in its own house, until 1780, when apartments in Somerset House were provided for it; and in these it remained till its removal to Burlington House, but its annual dinners were held at the "Thatched House Tavern" until the latter was taken down.

In 1859, the dinner party of the Royal Society would appear to have been remarkably cosmopolitan; the Electric Telegraph having been represented by Professor Wheatstone, the Railway System by Mr. Robert Stephenson, the Penny Post by Rowland Hill, and Astronomy by Sir Thomas Maclear, now Astronomer Royal at the Cape of Good Hope.

Charles II. presented the society with a silver-gilt mace, which is still placed on the table whenever the council or society meets, and without which no meeting can be legally held. This mace was for long supposed to be the "bauble" that Cromwell so unceremoniously ordered to be taken away from the table of the House of Commons, but Mr. Weld unluckily proved that it was made expressly for the society by command of the king. Another benefactor was Henry Howard, who presented the Arundel Library, which is still in the possession of the society; but the collection of antiquities and curiosities was presented to the British Museum when the apartments at Somerset House were found to be too contracted for its reception. The society still possesses several relics of Newton; as the sun-dial which he cut in the wall of his father's house when he was a boy; the first reflecting telescope, made, in 1671, with his own hands; and the original mask of his face, taken by Roubiliac.

The meetings of the society take place once a week, from the third Thursday in November to the third Thursday in June. A record of these meetings is published in the octavo "Proceedings," and a selection of the best papers is printed in the quarto "Transactions." These last were first printed in 1665, under the title of "Philosophical Transactions, giving some Account of the present Undertakings, Studies, and Labours of the Ingenious in many considerable Parts of the World;" and the series now extends to upwards of 160 volumes.

The society has at its disposal four medals, in the distribution of which it is able to mark its appreciation of scientific investigations and distinguished discoveries. The first award of the Copley medal was made in 1731, and of the Rumford medal in 1800 to the founder himself (Benjamin, Count Rumford) for his various discoveries respecting light and heat. In the year 1825, George IV. communicated through Sir Robert Peel his intention "to found two gold medals of the value of fifty guineas each, to be awarded as honorary premiums under the direction of the president and council of the Royal Society in such manner as shall by the excitement of competition among men of science seem best calculated to promote the objects for which the Royal Society was instituted." These medals were first awarded, in the year 1826, to John Dalton and James Ivory. William IV. and Queen Victoria have continued the gift of these royal medals, and they are, therefore, annually awarded. Besides these, the society undertakes the distribution of the annual grant of £1,000, which is voted by Parliament to be employed in aiding the promotion of science in the United Kingdom; and it also performs the office of scientific adviser to the Government on the difficult questions that arise in the various public departments. Through a committee of its Fellows, the Royal Society has made itself gratuitously useful to Her Majesty's Government for many years by directing the business of the Meteorological Department, which was formerly part of the duty of the Board of Trade.

In 1874, an attempt was made, though unsuccessfully, to limit the number of fellows to be e ected in each year to fifteen. The proposal was carefully considered by a committee, to whom it was referred; but after a long discussion, a resolution was passed by the Council not to make any change in the existing rules.

Many particulars about the society and its convivial meetings, &c., may be learnt from a privately printed history of the club by the late Admiral Smyth, one of its most active and zealous members.

The following story of the merry monarch and of the learned society, though often told before, will bear being told again in the present chapter:— When King Charles II. dined with the members on the occasion of constituting them a Royal Society, towards the close of the evening he expressed his satisfaction at being the first English monarch who had laid a foundation for a society which proposed that their whole studies should be directed to the investigation of the arcana of nature, and added, with that peculiar gravity of countenance he usually wore on such occasions, that among such learned men he now hoped for a solution to a question which had long puzzled him. The case he thus stated:—Suppose two pails of water were fixed in two different scales that were equally poised, and which weighed equally alike, and two live bream, or small fish, were put into either of the pails; he wanted to know the reason why that pail, with such addition, should not weigh more than the other pail which was against it. Every one was ready to set at quiet the royal curiosity; but it appeared that every one was giving a different opinion. One at length offered so ridiculous a solution, that another of the members could not refrain from a loud laugh; when the king, turning to him, insisted that he should give his sentiments as well as the rest. This he did without hesitation; and told his Majesty, in plain terms, that he denied the fact; on which the king, in high mirth, exclaimed: "Odds fish, brother, you are in the right!" The jest was not ill designed, and the story is often useful to cool the enthusiasm of the scientific visionary, who is apt to account for what never existed.

All sorts of scientific experiments have been made from time to time under the auspices of the Royal Society. The following may be taken as a specimen:—In 1667, the Royal Society successfully performed the experiment of transfusing the blood of a sheep into a man in perfect health. The subject of the experiment was Arthur Coga, who, as Pepys says, was a kind of minister, and, being in want of money, hired himself for a guinea. Drs. Lower and King performed the experiment, injecting twelve ounces of sheep's blood, without producing any inconvenience. The patient drank a glass or two of canary, took a pipe of tobacco, and went home with a stronger and fuller pulse than before. The experiment was in a day or two afterwards repeated on Coga, when fourteen ounces of sheep's blood was substituted for eight ounces of his own. Pepys went to see him, and tells us that he heard him give an account in Latin of the operation and its effects.

The following is Sir David Brewster's account, in the *North British Review*, of the circumstances under which the great Sir Isaac Newton became a member of the society:—"Mr. Isaac Newton, Professor of Mathematics at Cambridge, was proposed as a Fellow by Dr. Seth Ward, Bishop of Sarum. Newton, then in his thirtieth year, had made several of his greatest discoveries. He had discovered the different refrangibility of light; he had invented the reflecting telescope; he had deduced the law of gravity from Kepler's theorem; and he had discovered the method of fluxions. When he heard of his being proposed as a Fellow, he expressed to Oldenburg, the secretary, his hope that he would be elected, and added, that he would endeavour to testify his gratitude by communicating what his poor and solitary endeavours could effect towards the promoting their philosophical design. The communications which Newton made to the society excited the deepest interest in every part of Europe. His little reflecting telescope, the germ of the colossal instruments of Herschel and Lord Rosse, was deemed one of the wonders of the age."

The most remarkable events connected with the society during the last century were the bequest of £100 by Sir George Copley in 1709, which resulted in the institution of the Copley medal; the measures taken for observing the transit of Venus, which, according to Halley, was to occur in 1761 and 1769, and the grand discovery of the composition of water in 1784, by some attributed to Cavendish, by others to Watt. In the early part of the present century Sir Humphry Davy commenced his well-known scientific career, and after having had all the honours of the Royal Society showered upon him, in 1820 took his seat as president in the chair previously occupied by Wren, Sir Isaac Newton, Sloane, and Banks.

The first list of Fellows includes such names as Sir Kenelm Digby, Sir William Petty (of whom we have spoken in the preceding chapter *), Matthew Wren, Robert Boyle, John Dryden, and Isaac Barrow. The signatures of all the Fellows, from the time of Charles II., when the society received the royal charter, down to the latest elected, are preserved in a vellum charter-book, which is a treasure of the highest interest. The number of presidents of the society, from Lord Brouncker—the first after its incorporation—down to Dr. Hooker, who was chosen in 1874—is thirty-two, among whom have been Sir Christopher Wren, Sir Hans Sloane, Sir Isaac Newton, Samuel Pepys, Lord Chancellor Somers, Sir John Pringle, Sir Joseph Banks, Sir Humphry Davy, Sir Benjamin Brodie, the Duke of Sussex, and the Earl of Rosse. The list of secretaries is specially rich in great names, such as John Evelyn, Dr. Halley, Sir John Herschel, Bishop Wilkins, Robert Hooke, Sir Humphry Davy, and many others.

The Society of Antiquaries of London, already mentioned in our account of Somerset House,† was founded by Archbishop Parker, in 1572. The members assembled at the house of Sir Robert Cotton, near Westminster Abbey, for twenty years. They applied to Elizabeth for a charter and a public building; but their hopes were frustrated by the queen's death. James I. took umbrage at some of the society's proceedings, and dissolved it. It would appear, however, to have existed privately during the seventeenth century, for in Ashmole's "Diary" we read of the "Antiquaries' feast on July 2, 1659," probably their annual dinner, which has now fallen into desuetude.

In 1707, we hear of their resuming their meetings in a more public form, and under the presidency of Le Neve. With him were associated Dr. William Stukeley, Humphrey Wanley, Roger Gale, Vertue, Browne Willis, and many others well known to fame. The minutes of the society commence in 1717, and in the same year they resolved to issue the first of that great series of prints which grew up into the work known as the "Vetusta Monumenta." We may here mention that the society has recently (1875) issued some *fasciculi* of great interest in completion of the sixth volume of this valuable collection.

In 1751, a royal charter of incorporation was granted to the society. In 1776, the king gave orders, when Somerset House was rebuilt, that the society should be accommodated with apartments in the new building. The whole of the fittings were put up at the expense of the Government, and in 1781 the society was formally inducted into possession of their new apartments.

The Society of Antiquaries was no favourite, strange to say, in spite of his antiquarian tastes, with Horace Walpole, who writes: "I dropped my attendance there four or five years ago, being sick of their ignorance and stupidity, and have not been three times amongst them since."

When the Royal Society removed to Burlington House, some changes were effected as to the rooms occupied by this society. In 1866, a scheme was submitted to the society by Her Majesty's Government for accommodating the society in Burlington House. To this scheme the society acceded, not without some reluctance, and only on the understanding that adequate accommodation should be provided, and that the expense of the fittings should be borne by the Government.

The services which the society has rendered are patent to the world. Its "Transactions" can only

* See *ante*, p. 256.   † See Vol. III., page 94.

be compared with the "Memoirs" of the Académie des Inscriptions et Belles Lettres for range and depth. Among the more recent and public services rendered by the society may be mentioned the restoration of the Chapter House at Westminster, which was undertaken mainly at the instance and through the zeal of its council. The late Lord Stanhope, better known by his former title of Lord Mahon, held the presidential chair of the Society

the Royal Society, Sir Joseph Banks, to whom it was indebted for pecuniary assistance, and for large additions to its library and collections.

From an early period of its existence, the Linnæan Society took a high station in the world of science, and it stands now, as it always has done, at the head of the natural history societies of the United Kingdom, and on a level with the most distinguished of similar societies abroad.

CLARENDON HOUSE, IN 1666. (*See page* 273.)

of Antiquaries from 1846 down to his death at the close of 1875.

The Linnæan Society, so called after the great naturalist, Linnæus, was founded, as stated in our account of Soho Square,* in 1788, for the study of natural history, more especially that of the British Islands, and was incorporated by royal charter in 1802. It was the earliest offset of the Royal Society, the separation taking place with the ready assent and concurrence of the parent body, it being felt that natural history was a science of sufficient extent and importance to demand the entire attention of a distinct society. The infant society was warmly aided by the then president of

Its "Transactions" now include about thirty copiously-illustrated quarto volumes, and form, unquestionably, the most important series of memoirs on natural history which this country has produced. In addition, it has now for many years published an octavo journal in two sections, Zoology and Botany, where those papers appear which have less need of illustration.

The library and collections of the society are very extensive, including those of Linnæus (invaluable in themselves, and in illustration of the works of the great Swedish naturalist), which, together with the additions made by its founder, Sir J. E. Smith, were purchased by the society, in 1829, for £3,000, and the extensive herbarium of Indian plants, munificently presented by the

* See Vol. III., p. 191.

Court of Directors of the East India Company in 1832.

The funds of the society, with the exception of a very small return, in proportion to the outlay, from the sale of its publications, are wholly derived from the contributions of its Fellows, to whom the "Transactions" and "Journal" are distributed without further payment.

By the cost of printing and illustrating these

1828, the late Sir Robert Peel, then Secretary of the Treasury, assigned to it the apartments in Somerset House which it continued to occupy till its removal to Burlington House in 1874. Previously it had occupied a house in Bedford Street, Strand. The charter says: "Whereas the Reverend William Buckland, B.D., Arthur Aikin, esquire, John Bostock, M.D., George Bellas Greenough, esquire, Henry Warburton, esquire, and several

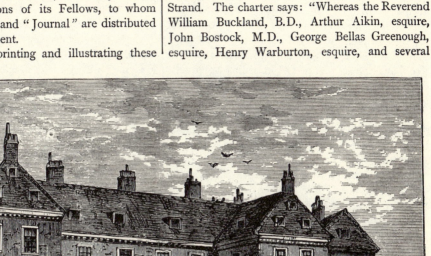

CLARGES HOUSE, PICCADILLY. (*From Mr. Crace's Collection.*)

publications, and in other necessary expenses, the society was, for a long period, seriously cramped in its operations. When, therefore, in 1856, the Government offered to put the Royal Society in possession of the main building of Burlington House, on the understanding that suitable accommodation therein should be assigned to the Linnæan and Chemical Societies, the Linnæan, although it had recently renewed, for a long term, its lease of the house in Soho Square, availed itself of the proposal, which, in the first place, promised to place its library and collections out of danger from fire, and would relieve the funds of the society from the outlay for rent.

The Geological Society was established in 1807, and incorporated by royal charter in 1826. In

others of our loving subjects, being desirous of forming a society for investigating the mineral structure of the earth, and having for promoting such investigation expended considerable sums of money in the collection and purchase of books, maps, specimens, and other objects, and in the publication of various works, the said William Buckland, Arthur Aikin, John Bostock, George Bellas Greenough, and Henry Warburton have humbly besought us to grant unto them and unto such other persons as shall be appointed and elected Fellows of the Society, as hereinafter is mentioned, our Royal Charter of Incorporation, for the better carrying on the purposes aforesaid." A charter was accordingly granted, Dr. Buckland being appointed first president. The early publications of the society consisted of "Proceedings" in octavo, and "Transactions" in quarto : of the former, four volumes were published ; and of the latter, twelve volumes in two series (of five and seven). The "Transactions" ceased in 1856, but in 1845 a quarterly journal was started, and has been carried on ever since in their place. The society also publishes Mr. Greenough's Geological Map of England. The society possesses an extensive library, and a museum consisting of fossils, minerals, &c.; the collection of foreign fossils being particularly interesting.

The Royal Astronomical Society was founded in the year 1820 by the exertions of the Rev. Dr. Pearson, Mr. Francis Baily, and other gentlemen at that time eminent in the science of astronomy, its objects being "the encouragement and promotion of astronomy." We need scarcely add that it has been eminently successful in carrying out these objects, having published thirty-eight volumes of "Memoirs," and thirty volumes of "Monthly Notices," which are held in much estimation both by English and foreign astronomers.

The only remaining learned body located here is the Chemical Society. This was founded in 1841, and incorporated under royal charter in 1848. Its objects are defined to be "the promotion of chemistry and of those branches of science immediately connected with it, by the reading, discussion, and subsequent publication of original communications." The society holds fortnightly meetings during eight months of the year, and publishes a journal in monthly numbers. Its management is vested in a president and a council, chosen, for the most part, annually by ballot.

Of the rise and progress of the Royal Academy we have already spoken in our notice of the National Gallery, Trafalgar Square.* It only remains to add that, since the removal hither, the exhibitions of the Royal Academy have gone on steadily increasing in popularity, and that during "the season" not only are the spacious apartments here crowded with the *élite* of society, but the exhibitions have become sufficiently attractive to induce artisans and others belonging more to the working classes to flock thither, and in such numbers as to warrant the council in allowing the works of art annually brought together to be exhibited during the evening by gas-light. *Apropos* of the good work achieved by the Royal Academy, it may be stated that the choice of Angelica Kauffmann and Mrs. Montague among its first members

gave an impetus to female education, and helped to keep alive till a more enlightened period the claims of women to take their place side by side with men in the battle of life, and in following the professions. As a proof that their example was not without effect, we may add that, in the year 1778, the publisher of "The Ladies' Pocket-book" gave, as a frontispiece, a group of nine ladies celebrated in art or in literature, namely, Miss Carter, Mrs. Barbauld, Angelica Kauffmann, Mrs. Sheridan, Mrs. Lennox, Mrs. Montague, Miss Moore, Mrs. Macaulay, and Miss Griffith, each lady in the fanciful character of one of the nine Muses.

On the west side of Burlington House is the Burlington Arcade, which was built as a bazaar by Lord George Cavendish, afterwards Earl of Burlington, in 1819. This arcade, upwards of 200 yards in length, forms a covered pathway between Piccadilly and Burlington Gardens ; it has shops on each side for the sale of millinery, jewellery, and, in fact, almost every article of fashionable demand. It is closed at night by gates at each end under the charge of a beadle in livery. It is stated by Mr. Peter Cunningham that the rents of the shops in this arcade amount to upwards of £8,000 a year, only about half of which finds its way into the pockets of its owners, the Cavendishes.

We have given on page 264 a view of the original Burlington House, with its gardens in the rear, laid out on the square formal French fashion. It shows the little temporary church or chapel in Conduit Street, standing quite isolated from every other building. There is also a view, by Kip, of the first Burlington House, built by Sir John Denham, the author of the poem called "Cooper's Hill," and also Surveyor of Buildings under the Crown.

With reference to the old court-yard and colonnade, of which we have already spoken, we may add that it is represented in the first of the above-mentioned views, and that to it Sir William Chambers thus alludes :—"In London, many of our noblemen's palaces towards the street look like convents. Nothing appears but a high wall, with one or two large gates, in which there is a hole for those who are privileged to go in and out. If a coach arrives, the whole gate is indeed opened ; but this is an operation that requires time, and the porter is very careful to shut it up again immediately, for reasons to him very weighty. Few in this vast city, I suspect, believe that behind an old brick wall in Piccadilly there is one of the finest pieces of architecture in Europe."

---

* See Vol. III., pp. 146—149.

CHAPTER XXIII.

NOBLE MANSIONS IN PICCADILLY.

" Est via declivis."—Ovid.

Clarendon House—Lord Clarendon incurs the Displeasure of the Populace—Extracts from the Diaries of Evelyn and Pepys referring to Clarendon House—The Name of " Dunkirk House " given to the Mansion—Its Demolition—Berkeley House : Descriptions of the Building—Devon-shire House : Description of the Building—The Picture Galleries and Library—The Earl of Devonshire, and the Murder of Mr. Thynne of Longleat—Anecdote of the First Duke of Devonshire—Devonshire House as a " Pouting Place of Princes "—The Mansion as a Rendezvous of the Whig Party—Georgiana, Duchess of Devonshire—Walpole's Compliment to the House and its Owner—Fashionable Entertainments and Dramatic Performances at Devonshire House—Stratton Street—Mrs. Coutts, afterwards Duchess of St. Albans—Sir Francis Burdett : his Seizure, and Committal to the Tower—Pulteney Hotel—Bath House—Anecdotes of Lord Orford and Lord Bath—Watier's Club—The Dilettanti Society—Grafton House, now the Turf Club—Egremont House, now the Naval and Military Club—Hertford House—Coventry House, now the St. James's Club—The Rothschilds—Viscountess Keith—Hope House, now the Junior Athenæum Club—John, Earl of Eldon—Gloucester House—The Duke of Queensberry, " Old Q."—Lord Byron's Residence—Lord Palmerston's House—The " Hercules Pillars "—The " Triumphal Chariot "—Historical Remarks.

ALONG the line of Piccadilly, when the district was more or less open country, besides Burlington House, stood some of the mansions of the nobility of the seventeenth century.

Westward of Burlington House, facing the top of St. James's Street, and on the site of what is now Bond Street, Stafford Street, and Albemarle Street, formerly stood Clarendon House. Pennant places the mansion as far to the north as Grafton Street ; but the existing maps would seem to show that Stafford Street would mark more precisely the spot on which it stood. In a plan of London etched by Hollar, in 1686, it is evident that the centre of Clarendon House must have occupied the whole of the site of Stafford Street. No. 74, in Piccadilly, the publishing house of the late Mr. J. C. Hotten—now Messrs. Chatto and Windus—is said to be built of the old materials of the mansion. It was a heavy, high-roofed house, standing a little back from the street, with projecting wings; it had square-headed windows, including a row of attic windows which pierced the roof. A flight of stone steps led up to the door, which was in the centre.

Lord Clarendon, when Lord Chancellor under Charles II., having built his magnificent house soon after the sale of Dunkirk to Louis XIV., about the year 1664, found that he had incurred in the eyes of the people the full blame of the transaction, and that his mansion was called by the public not Clarendon but Dunkirk House, on the supposition that it had been built with French money. No sane person can doubt the fact of Charles II. having received large sums from the Court of Versailles for purposes hostile to the interests of his people ; but there is no proof what-ever that Lord Clarendon was privy to such trans-actions, much less that he derived any personal profit from them. It was, in his case, the old story repeated—

" Delirant reges, plectuntur Achivi."

A view of Lord Clarendon's house as it appeared during its brief decade of existence, may be found in the first volume of Charles Knight's " London," and there is also an engraving of it in the *Gentle-man's Magazine* for August, 1789.

From the Diaries of Evelyn and Pepys we learn something of the varying fortunes of Clarendon House during its brief existence. Under date 15th October, 1664, Evelyn writes : " After dinner, my Lord Chancellor and his lady carried me in their coach to see their palace now building at the upper end of St. James's Street, and to project the garden." Pepys, in January, 1665-6, makes this entry in his Diary : " To my Lord Chancellor's new house which he is building, only to view it, hearing so much from Mr. Evelyn of it ; and indeed it is the finest pile I ever did see in my life, and will be a glorious house." Evelyn, about the same time, wrote to Lord Cornbury, the Chancellor's eldest son : " I have never seen a nobler pile . . . Here is state, use, solidity, and beauty, most symmetrically combined together. Nothing abroad pleases me better, nothing at home approaches to it." Besides the laying out of the gardens, Evelyn appears to have contributed to the internal adornment of this magnificent mansion, for in March, 1666-7, he sent the Chancellor a list of " pictures that might be added to the assembly of the learned and heroic persons of England which your lordship has already collected ;" and on a subsequent occasion, in recording the fact of his dining here with Lord Cornbury, after the Chancellor's flight, Evelyn remarks that it is " now bravely furnished, especi-ally with the pictures of most of our ancient and modern wits, poets, philosophers, famous and learned Englishmen, which collection I much commended, and gave a catalogue of more to be added." Pennant says it was built with the stones intended for the rebuilding of St. Paul's.

The whole place, according to Charles Knight, " would seem to have resembled in stately dignity the style of the ' History of the Great Rebellion.' " " The plague, the Great Fire, and the disgraceful war with Holland," says the above authority, " had goaded the public mind into a temper of savage mutiny; and the 'wits and misses,' to aid their court intrigues against the Chancellor, had done what in them lay to direct the storm against his head. The marriage of the Chancellor's daughter to the Duke of York and the barrenness of the Queen were represented as the results of a plot; the situation of Clarendon House, looking down on St. James's, and the employment of stones collected with a view to repair St. Paul's, were tortured into crimes." At length the storm of public wrath fairly burst over Clarendon House, as the following entry in Pepys's "Diary" will show. Under date 14th of June, 1667, he writes :—" Mr. Harter tells me, at noon, that some rude people have been, as he hears, at my Lord Chancellor's, where they have cut down the trees before his house, and broke his windows; and a gibbet either set up before or painted upon his gate, and these words writ, 'Three sights to be seen—Dunkirk, Tangier, and a barren Queen.'"

In a volume of rare London ballads and broadsides in the British Museum is one entitled, "A Hue and Cry after the Earl of Clarendon," dated in 1667. Our readers may gather how strong was the popular feeling against him on account of the sale of Dunkirk from the opening lines :—

" From Dunkirk House there lately ran away
    A traitor whom you are desired to slay.
    You by these marks and signs may th' traitor know,
    He's troubled with the gout in feet below.

*   *   *   *   *   *   *   *   *

    This hopeful blade being conscious of his crimes,
    And smelling how the current of the times
    Ran cross, forsakes his palace and the town
    Like some presaging rat ere th' house fall down."

Evelyn mentions, in the following terms, a journey made by him in June, 1683, along Piccadilly, doubtless on the way to his residence in Dover Street :— " I returned to town in a coach with the Earle of Clarendon, when, passing by the glorious palace his father had built but few years before, which they were now demolishing, being sold to certain undertakers [contractors], I turned my head the contrary way till the coach was gone past it, lest I might minister occasion of speaking of it, which must needs have grieved him that in so short a time their pomp was so sadly fallen."

"The sumptuous palace," writes Macaulay, "to which the populace of London gave the name of Dunkirk House, is among the many signs which indicate the shortest road to boundless wealth in the days of Charles II." The enormous gains then made by prime ministers, partly by salaries, and partly by the sale of posts and places, were the real secret of the tenacity with which men clung to office in those days.

Lord Clarendon seems to have been particularly fond of this mansion, though it was so offensive to the public. The day before his lordship's flight, Evelyn " found him in his garden at his new-built palace, sitting in his gowte wheel-chaire, and seeing the gates setting up towards the north and the fields. He looked and spake very disconsolately. Next morning I heard he was gone." His lordship, even in his exile, after writing that " his weakness and vanity " in the outlay he made upon it, " more contributed to that gust of envy that had so violently shaken him than any misdemeanour that he was thought to have been guilty of," confesses that, when it was proposed to sell it, in order to pay his debts and to make some provision for his younger children, " he remained so infatuated with the delight he had enjoyed, that, though he was deprived of it, he hearkened very unwillingly to the advice."

Under date of September, 1683, Evelyn thus writes in his " Diary :"—" I went to survey the sad demolition of Clarendon House, that costly and only sumptuous palace of the late Lord Chancellor Hyde, where I have often been so cheerful with him, and sometimes so sad. . . . The Chancellor gone and dying in exile," he continues, " the earl, his successor, sold the building, which cost £50,000, to the young Duke of Albemarle for £25,000 to pay debts, which how contracted remains yet a mystery, his son being no way a prodigal. . . . However it were, this stately palace is decreed to ruin, to support the prodigious waste the Duke of Albemarle had made of his estate since the old man died. He sold it to the highest bidder, and it fell to certain rich bankers and mechanics, who gave for it and the ground about £35,000; they design a new town, as it were, and a most magnificent piazza. . . . See the vicissitude of earthly things! I was astonished at the demolition, nor less at the little army of labourers and artificers levelling the ground, laying foundations, and contriving great buildings, at an expense of £200,000, if they perfect their design."

In Smith's " Streets of London " it is stated that "the earliest date now to be found upon the site of Clarendon House is cut in stone and let into the south wall of a public-house, the sign of ' The Duke of Albemarle' in Dover Street, thus : ' This is Stafford Street, 1686.'"

It is said by Isaac D'Israeli, in his " Curiosities of Literature," that the two Corinthian pilasters on either side of the gateway of the " Three

Kings," on the north side of Piccadilly, are the only remains of the house built by the great Earl of Clarendon, whose name, however, has been perpetuated, at all events, down to the year 1870, in the Clarendon Hotel hard by.

Berkeley House, a little further to the west, according to Pepys, was built about the same time as Clarendon House. It was so called because it was built for Lord Berkeley, of Stratton, an able officer in the Royal army under Charles I., and whose name is still commemorated in the neighbourhood, by Berkeley Square and by Berkeley and Stratton Streets. Slightly at the rear, as it would seem, was a farm-house, from which Hay Hill, possibly, derives its name.

"Before the date of Burlington House," writes Pennant, "there was built here a fine mansion belonging to the Berkeleys, Lord Berkeley (of Stratton). It stood between the south end of Berkeley Square and Piccadilly, and gave the name to the square and an adjacent street (Berkeley Street). The misery and disgrace which the profligacy of one of the daughters brought on the house, by an intrigue with her brother-in-law, Lord Grey (afterwards engaged in the Monmouth Rebellion), is too lastingly recorded in our State Trials ever to be buried in oblivion."

Evelyn tells us that the mansion was "very well built," and that it had "many noble rooms; but," he adds, "they are not very convenient, consisting but of one *corps de logis*. They are all rooms of state, without closets. The staircase is of cedar; the furniture is princely; the kitchen and stables are ill placed, and the corridor worse, having no respect to the wings they join to. For the rest, the fore-court is noble, so are the stables, and, above all, the gardens, which are incomparable, by reason of the inequality of the ground, and a pretty *piscina* [a fish-pond]. The holly hedges on the terrace I advised the planting of. The porticos are in imitation of a house described by Palladio, but it happens to be the worst in his book, though my good friend, Mr. Hugh May, his lordship's architect, affected it."

In the "New View of London," published in 1708, Berkeley House is described as "a spacious building on the north side of Portugal Street, near Piccadilly, with a pleasant, large court, now in the occupation of the Duke of Devonshire. The house," it is added, "is built of brick, adorned with stone pilasters, and an entablature and pitched pediment, all of the Corinthian order, under which is a figure of Britannia carved in stone. At some distance on the east side is the kitchen and laundry; and on the west side stables and lodg-

ing-rooms, which adjoin to the mansion by brick walls, and two circular galleries, each elevated on columns of the Corinthian order, where are two ambulatories."

Independently of the beauties of the mansion and gardens, there is but little interest attaching to Berkeley House. Its founder is represented by Pepys as "a passionate and but weak man as to policy; but, as a kinsman, brought in and promoted by my Lord St. Albans." It was destroyed by fire on the 16th of October, 1733, soon after it had passed into the hands of William, first Duke of Devonshire.

"On the site of the house," continues Pennant, "fronting Piccadilly, stands Devonshire House. Long after the year 1700 it was the last house in this street, at that time the portion (sic) of Piccadilly." He means, no doubt, that the Piccadilly of that day formed only a portion of the present long street.

The old house, according to Pennant, was frequented by Waller, Denham, and many others of the wits and poets of the reign of Charles II.; and he speaks of it as containing, in his own time, an excellent library and a very fine collection of medals. He also enumerates the pictures, which are very much the same as now, adding, that the collection of specimens by the great Italian masters "is by far the finest private collection now in England."

The author of the "New Critical Review of the Public Buildings" speaks in very high terms of the former Devonshire House, the ruins of which were still standing in 1736, when he wrote. He attributes its destruction to the carelessness of the duke's servants, and their disregard of the family motto, "Cavendo tutus." He describes it as simple in plan, yet very elegant, and quite worthy of the master hand of Inigo Jones, its only fault being the great number of its chimneys, which he calls "a heavy Gothic incumbrance to the whole." He laments the loss of a fine statue of Britannia, which, having escaped the flames, was accidentally destroyed by a second act of carelessness.

The present Devonshire House is briefly dismissed by Mr. J. H. Jesse with the curt remark that, "except during the brief period when the beautiful Georgiana, Duchess of Devonshire, held her court within its walls, and when Fox, Burke, Windham, Fitzpatrick, and Sheridan did homage at her feet, little interest attaches to the present edifice." But we think that this remark is scarcely just; for the court of Georgiana, the beautiful duchess (of whom we have made mention in our account of the Westminster election at Covent

Garden), was not a very "brief" one, nor does it deserve to be put aside out of memory after so summary a fashion.

The mansion, which for more than a century has divided with Holland House the reputation of being the head-quarters of the leaders of the great Whig party, was built about the year 1737, by William, third Duke of Devonshire, on the site of part of the property of Lord Berkeley of Stratton.

on the north side, of marble and alabaster, with rails of solid crystal, was erected by the late duke. The ornamentation of the great staircase, and of most of the rooms in the house, is by Mr. Crace.

The picture-galleries in this house are scattered through the long range of rooms which passes all round it on the first floor. It would be impossible, in this work, to give a complete list of the art treasures that are to be found here, but we may

DEVONSHIRE HOUSE, ABOUT 1800.

The design of the house was by Kent; and it cost upwards of £20,000. The house recedes a little from the rest of the houses in this street. It has little or nothing in its exterior appearance to recommend it to particular notice, but its interior is richly stored with some of the finest works of art in any private collection.

The entrance to the house was originally up a double flight of stone steps, arranged as an external staircase, in the front, and leading straight into the reception-rooms on the first floor; but this arrangement was done away by the late duke, who made the entrance on the ground level into a hall of low elevation, beyond which he threw out on the north or garden side a semi-circular apse, containing a new staircase. The interior staircase

mention a few of the most important. In the large north room hang "The Madonna and Child and St. Elizabeth," by Rubens; "The Prince and Princess of Orange," by Jacob Jordaens; and also "a Portrait," unknown, by Titian. In the green-room adjoining is "Jacob's Dream," by Salvator Rosa, and "Samson and Delilah," by Tintoretto. In the blue drawing-room is "Moses in the Bulrushes," by Murillo. A small room on the north side is hung almost entirely with specimens of Van Dyke, including a noble portrait of the great Lord Strafford; in the same room is Lord Richard Cavendish, by Sir Joshua Reynolds. In addition to the portraits mentioned above, the list also comprises John Hampden's friend, Arthur Goodwin, by Van Dyke, and his daughter Jane, wife of

Philip, Lord Wharton; a head of the virtuous and accomplished Lord Falkland; Sir Thomas Browne (author of the "Religio Medici"), his wife, and daughters; a Jewish Rabbi, by Rembrandt; a head of Titian, by himself; Philip II., by the same; and the old Countess of Desmond. A list

laid down in turf as lawns, and contain some fine elm-trees.

But to pass from the bricks and mortar of the house to the personal history of its owners. We have already mentioned the murder in Pall Mall of Mr. Thynne, of Longleat. The then Earl of

SIR FRANCIS BURDETT. (*See page* 281.)

of some of the finest pictures to be seen in this mansion is printed in Dr. Waagen's work on "Art and Artists in England."

In the library here is kept John Philip Kemble's celebrated collection of old English plays, probably the finest in existence. It was made at the cost of £2,000, and was purchased by the sixth duke, after the collector's death. The library is very rich also in other departments of early English literature. The gardens in the rear of the house are mostly

Devonshire, as friend of Mr. Thynne, desired to avenge his death, and challenged the dastardly foreigner, who had plotted his assassination, to meet him in a duel. The Count (says Pennant) accepted the challenge, but afterwards his conscience (!) prevented him from meeting the Earl. It is some comfort to know that on returning to his own country the Count met with that fate which he so richly deserved here.

A good story is told in the "Apology for the

Life of Colley Cibber" respecting the Earl of Devonshire, who was raised to the dukedom in reward for the leading part which he took in the Revolution of 1688. Being one day in the Royal Presence Chamber shortly before that event, and being known to be no friend of the Court or the Ministry, he was insulted by a person who trod purposely on his foot. The insult was returned on the spot by a blow, which brought the offender to his senses. But as the act was committed within the king's court, the striker was sentenced to a fine of thirty thousand pounds. Having, however, time allowed for paying it, he retired to Chatsworth, whither King James sent a messenger to him with offers to mitigate the fine if he would pay it promptly. The earl, knowing the "lie of the land," replied, that if his Majesty would allow him a little time longer, he would rather choose to play "double or quits" with him. The Revolution being near at hand, there was no time for any further parley; and the king speedily found himself in a position in which he might inflict, but could not enforce, the fine.

It is stated of the above nobleman, by Dr. W. King, in "Anecdotes of his Own Times," that he received, after the accession of George I., more than £200,000 in places and pensions, without having done any service to his country or his sovereign. Let us hope that this censure was not well deserved, or else that the money has since been recouped to the country by the services of his descendants.

Like Leicester House, already mentioned,* Devonshire House played for two years the part of a "pouting place of princes." From 1692 to the death of her sister Mary, Anne, Princess of Denmark, and her husband lived here, not being on the best of terms with their then Majesties.

For a century and a half this house has been one of the special rendezvous of the Whig party. "Three palaces in the year 1784," writes Sir N. W. Wraxall, "the gates of which were constantly thrown open to every supporter of the 'Coalition' (against Pitt), formed rallying-points of union." One of these was Burlington House, then tenanted by the Duke of Portland; the second was Carlton House, the residence of George, Prince of Wales; the third was Devonshire House, which, "placed on a commanding eminence opposite to the Green Park, seemed to look down upon the Queen's House, constructed by Sheffield, Duke of Buckingham, in a situation much less favoured by nature."

At this time its leading spirit was Georgiana, Duchess of Devonshire, a lady whose character

formed a perfect contrast to the indolence of her husband, and who, in respect of her beauty, her accomplishments, and the part which she played in the world of politics, may be compared with Anne Genevieve de Bourbon, Duchesse de Longueville, in the French annals. She is described by Sir N. W. Wraxall as "one of the most distinguished ladies of high rank whom the last century produced. Her personal charms," he adds, "constituted her smallest pretension to universal admiration; nor did her beauty consist, like that of the Gunnings, in regularity of features and faultless formation of limbs and shape; it lay rather in the graces of her deportment, in her irresistible manners, and the seduction of her society. Her hair was not without a tinge of red, and her face, though pleasing, had it not been illumined by her mind, might have been considered an ordinary countenance. Descended, in the fourth degree, lineally from Sarah Jennings, the wife of John Churchill, Duke of Marlborough, she resembled the portraits of that celebrated woman. In addition to the external advantages which she received from nature and fortune, she possessed an ardent temper, susceptible of deep as well as strong impressions, a cultivated understanding, illumined by a taste for poetry and the fine arts, and much sensibility, not exempt, perhaps, from vanity and coquetry."

In our account of Covent Garden,† and the scenes witnessed there in former times in connection with the elections for Westminster, we had occasion to speak of the part taken by the Duchess of Devonshire in securing the return of Mr. Fox in 1784. The following lines were written in consequence of her Grace's canvass on his behalf :—

"Arrayed in matchless beauty, Devon's fair
In Fox's favour takes a zealous part ;
But oh ! where'er the pilferer comes—beware !
She supplicates a vote, and steals a heart."

The lines quoted above were, no doubt, intended as complimentary to the duchess; she had, however, a more elegant compliment paid to her one day at Chatsworth by a gentleman who, after viewing the garden and the library, applied to her the words of Cowley :—

"The fairest garden in her looks,
And in her mind the choicest books."

Towards the close of her life, however, the beautiful duchess would often say "that of all the compliments paid her, the drunken Irishman, who asked to light his pipe by the fire of her beautiful eyes, paid her the highest."

It was at Devonshire House, however, and not at

Carlton Palace, that the procession of the multitude was brought to an end on the occasion of Fox's election to which we refer ; and so great was the excitement that, according to Sir N. W. Wraxall, " on the procession entering the great court in front of the house, the Prince of Wales, who had already saluted the successful candidate from the garden wall on the side of Berkeley Street, appeared within the balustrade before the mansion, accompanied by the most eminent members of the Whig Coalition, both male and female, Fox dismissing the assembled mob with a brief harangue."

The Duke of Devonshire, if not a man of very great abilities, was a man of his word and the soul of honour. Dr. Johnson said of him that he was " a man of such ' dogged veracity,' that if he had promised an acorn, and not one had grown in his woods that year, he would have sent to Denmark for one !" A strong testimony to a Whig nobleman's honour from so staunch a Tory as the learned doctor.

William, the third duke, who is satirised by Pope for his meanness, as " dirty D——," was a staunch Whig, like the rest of his family. Horace Walpole said of him, that " his outside was unpolished and his inside unpolishable."

It is said that one day, not long after the erection of the present mansion, the great Sir Robert Walpole looked in to make a morning call on its owner, and not finding him at home, left on his table the following Latin epigram :—

" Ut dominus domus est ; non extra fulta columnis
    Marmoreis splendet : quod tenet, intus habet."

A higher or more graceful compliment could hardly be paid to either the house or its owner, than to say that they were both " all glorious within."

George IV., as Prince of Wales, was a constant frequenter of the coteries and parties of Devonshire House, which was at that time the resort, not only of the Whig Opposition, but of all the wits and *beaux esprits* of the time. Among the rest were Sheridan, Grey, Whitbread, Lord Robert Spencer, Fox, Hare, Fitz-Patrick, and George Selwyn, all members of the society of *bon ton* in their day.

Mr. T. Raikes thus mentions Devonshire House in his " Journal:"—" In these entertainments, which many years ago engrossed all the wit and fashion of London society for a long period, since quoted as the era of refinement and pleasure, Lady Bessborough was a leading character. Even Lady Grenville now, when she meets an ancient votary of those days, illustrated by her mother, will say, ' He, too, remembers Devonshire House.' "

Here, in 1814, William, the sixth Duke of Devonshire, gave several splendid entertainments

to the Emperor of Russia, the King of Prussia, and the other military personages who accompanied the Allied Sovereigns to England. Here the Prince of Orange was present at a grand ball on the evening before he returned to the Continent in the character of the discarded lover of the Princess Charlotte. Shortly before, Lady Brownlow tells us in her " Reminiscences," she had seen the royal affianced pair at a party given by the Prince Regent at Carlton House, when the Emperor of Russia and the King of Prussia were present. " At this party I well remember seeing the Princess Charlotte and the Prince of Orange sitting together and walking about arm-in-arm, looking perfectly happy and lover-like. What were the intrigues and influences that changed the princess's feelings and caused her to break off the marriage is a mystery, known, I believe, to few. There were many rumours—many stories afloat, but none to be relied on ; the only thing positive being the fact that the prince was dismissed."

The entertainments at Devonshire House have not been confined to balls and such-like aristocratic amusements, but have had a much wider range. Here the celebrated dwarf, Count Boruwlaski, was received by the Duke and the Duchess at one of their entertainments and presented by their Graces to the King, the Queen, and the Prince of Wales, and the rest of the nobility, with whom he became a " lion," and by whom he was *fêted* and caressed to an extent which would strike us as absurd and incredible if we did not remember the more recent visit of " Tom Thumb " to this metropolis and the fuss that was made with him.

But Devonshire House has its literary as well as its fashionable and political associations. As very many of our readers will remember, it was more than once, in the time of the late duke, the scene of amateur private theatricals given on a scale of magnificence which reminds us of the days when English actors were " the king's " and the duke's " servants." When, in 1850, Charles Dickens, in concert with Sir E. Bulwer Lytton, was endeavouring to set afloat the " Guild of Literature and Art " by the proceeds of a farce written by the former, and a comedy by the latter, the Duke of Devonshire, as Mr. Forster tells us in his " Life of Dickens," " offered the use of his house in Piccadilly for their first representations, and in his princely way discharged all the expenses attending them. A movable theatre was built and set up in the great drawing-room, and the library was turned into a green-room. *Not so Bad as we Seem* was played for the first time at Devonshire House on the 27th of May, 1851, before the Queen and the Prince

Consort, and as large an audience as could be found room for. *Mr. Nightingale's Diary* was the name of the farce." The representation was a great success. It was repeated several times over at the Hanover Square Rooms, and continued at intervals both in London and in the country during that and the following year. Among the distinguished authors and artists who took part in the performance at Devonshire House, besides Lord Lytton and Dickens, were Douglas Jerrold, John Leech, and Mr. Maclise.

The western side of Devonshire House is bounded by a street without a thoroughfare, called Stratton Street, after Lord Berkeley of Stratton, by whom it was built in the year 1694. At No. 12 the gallant Lord Lynedoch died, at the age of ninety-four, in 1843. This street, and also Berkeley Street, on the east side of Devonshire House, it would seem, were laid out after a design of John Evelyn, who thus writes under date June, 1684 :—
"I went to advise and give directions about building two streets in Berkeley Gardens, reserving the house and as much of the garden as the breadth of the house. In the meantime I could not but deplore that sweet place (by far the most noble gardens, courts, and accommodations, stately porticos, &c., anywhere about town) should be so much straitened and turned into tenements. But that magnificent pile and gardens contiguous to it, built by the late Lord Chancellor Clarendon, being all demolished and designed for piazzas and buildings, was some excuse for Lady Berkeley's resolution of letting out her gardens, also for so excessive a price as was offered, advancing near £1,000 per annum, in mere ground rents ; to such a mad intemperance was the age come of building about a city by far too disproportionate already to the nation."

In the corner house of Piccadilly and Stratton Street, noticeable for its fine bow windows, overlooking the Green Park, lived for many years the rich and benevolent Mrs. Coutts, widow of Thomas Coutts, the banker, originally Miss Harriet Mellon, the actress, and afterwards Duchess of St. Albans. As an instance of her benevolence, it is recorded that, in the year 1836, when a fund was set on foot for the relief of the Spitalfields weavers, she not only sent a subscription equal in amount to that of royalty, but also gave the weavers an order for a suite of damask curtains for her drawing-rooms, at the price of a guinea a yard, an example which was followed by other wealthy families.

Captain Gronow tells us, in his "Anecdotes and Reminiscences," an amusing story connected with this house. On the day after the coronation of George IV., Mr. Hamlet, the jeweller, came to the house, expressing a wish to see the wealthy banker. It was during dinner ; but owing, no doubt, to a previous arrangement, he was at once admitted, when he placed before Mr. Coutts a magnificent diamond cross which had been worn the previous day by the Duke of York. It at once attracted the admiration of Mrs. Coutts, who loudly exclaimed, "How happy I should be with such a splendid specimen of jewellery !" "What is it worth ?" immediately exclaimed Mr. Coutts. "I could not allow it to pass out of my possession for less than £15,000," said the wary tradesman. "Bring me a pen and ink," was the only answer made by the doting husband, and he at once drew a cheque for that amount upon the bank in the Strand ; and with much delight the worthy old gentleman placed the jewel upon the fair bosom of the lady.

"Upon her breast a sparkling cross she wore,
  Which Jews might kiss, and infidels adore."

The following anecdote of the early life of this lady, as related by herself, may be of interest :—
"When I was a poor girl," she used to say, "working very hard for my thirty shillings a week, I went down to Liverpool during the holidays, where I was always kindly received. I was to perform in a new piece, something like those pretty little affecting dramas they get up now at our minor theatres, and in my character I represented a poor, friendless orphan girl, reduced to the most wretched poverty. A heartless tradesman prosecutes the sad heroine for a heavy debt, and insists on putting her in prison unless some one will be bail for her. The girl replies, 'Then I have no hope—I have not a friend in the world.' 'What ! will no one be bail for you, to save you from prison ?' asks the stern creditor. 'I have told you I have not a friend on earth,' was my reply. But just as I was uttering the words I saw a sailor in the upper gallery springing over the railing, letting himself down from one tier to another, until he bounded clear over the orchestra and footlights, and placed himself beside me in a moment. 'Yes, you shall have *one* friend at least, my poor young woman,' said he, with the greatest expression in his honest sunburnt countenance ; 'I will go bail for you to any amount. And as for *you*,' turning to the frightened actor, 'if you don't bear a hand, and shift your moorings, you lubber, it will be worse for you when I come athwart your bows.' Every creature in the house rose ; the uproar was perfectly indescribable ; peals of laughter, screams of terror, cheers from his tawny messmates in the gallery, preparatory scrapings of violins from the

orchestra; and amidst the universal din there stood the unconscious cause of it, sheltering me, 'the poor, distressed young woman,' and breathing defiance and destruction against my mimic persecutor. He was only persuaded to relinquish his care of me by the manager pretending to arrive and rescue me with a profusion of theatrical banknotes."

The Duchess of St. Albans, who died in 1837, left her immense fortune, amounting, it is said, to £1,800,000, to Miss Angela Burdett, who thereupon assumed the additional name of Coutts. It was stated in the newspapers at the time, that the weight of this enormous sum in gold, reckoning sixty sovereigns to the pound, is 13 tons 7 cwt. 3 qrs. 12 lbs., and would require 107 men to carry it, supposing that each of them carried 298 lbs., equivalent to the weight of a sack of flour. This large sum may be partially guessed, by knowing also that, counting at the rate of sixty sovereigns a minute for eight hours a day, and six days, of course, in the week, it would take ten weeks, two days, and four hours to accomplish the task. In sovereigns, by the most exact computation (each measuring in diameter $\frac{17}{20}$ of an inch, and placed to touch each other), it would extend to the length of 24 miles and 260 yards, or about the distance between Merthyr and Cardiff; and in crown pieces, to 113½ miles and 280 yards. It may be noted that £1,800,000 was the exact sum also left by old Jemmy Wood, the banker and millionaire of Gloucester, who died in 1836. After inheriting the property in question, Miss Burdett-Coutts distinguished herself by furthering works of charity and benevolence, and in recognition of her largeheartedness she was, in the year 1871, raised to the peerage as Baroness Burdett-Coutts.

Close by, during his demagogue days, lived Sir Francis Burdett, the father of Lady Burdett-Coutts. The old baronet enjoyed the distinction of being the last political or state prisoner who was confined in the Tower of London. On April 6, 1810, a vote passed the House of Commons for his committal to the Tower, on account of a letter written and published by him in *Cobbett's Register* of a week or two previously, which was considered to be "libellous and scandalous, and a breach of privilege." Sir Francis resisted the Speaker's warrant for his committal "upon principle," wishing, of course, to make political capital out of the affair, and to be regarded by the mob as a patriot. Accordingly that part of Piccadilly which lay opposite his house was blocked up by a mob from Westminster and the southern suburbs, who kept on shouting "Burdett for ever!" till the Guards were

called out and rode up to the spot. They were received on their arrival with a volley of stones. The Guards charged the mob, whence they were nicknamed the "Piccadilly Butchers." The whole of the West-end of London was in uproar and confusion, and the windows of the chiefs of the party who had procured the warrant for his arrest were smashed. At length, on the third day, Sir Francis Burdett, believing further resistance vain, was taken prisoner in the king's name, and carried off in a glass coach; but, in spite of this being done with all possible privacy, the mob tried to stop the carriage on Tower Hill, and a conflict ensued between the soldiers and the people, in which one rioter lost his life, and others were wounded.

The riot arose out of the following circumstances, the account of which we abridge from Hughson:—"On the 21st of February, a Mr. John Gale Jones, a well-known orator at various debating societies in the metropolis, was committed to Newgate by an order of the House of Commons for a gross breach of the privileges of that House. The breach complained of was contained in a bill issued from a debating society, called the 'British Forum,' of which Jones was president. The question in the bill was, 'Which was a greater outrage on the public feeling, Mr. Yorke's enforcement of the standing order to exclude strangers from the House of Commons, or Mr. Windham's recent attack on the liberty of the press?'

"On the 12th of March, Sir Francis Burdett moved in the House of Commons that John Gale Jones should be discharged on the ground of the illegality of the measure. This motion, however, was lost; and on the 24th of March there appeared in *Cobbett's Political Register* a letter inscribed, 'Sir Francis Burdett to his constituents, denying the power of the House of Commons to imprison the people of England,' accompanied with the arguments by which he had endeavoured to convince the gentlemen of the House of Commons that their acts in the case of Mr. Jones were illegal. On the 26th, the publication was brought before the House of Commons by Mr. Lethbridge, who desired the Speaker to ask Sir Francis Burdett whether he acknowledged himself to be the author of the letter, which Sir Francis did. The next day Mr. Lethbridge resumed the subject, and laid the number of *Cobbett's Register* before the House. Sir Francis Burdett made a short but very able defence; and after some further discussion the House adjourned till next day, March the 28th, and then to the 5th of April, when the resumed debate was continued till half-past seven in the morning;

the House then voted that Sir Francis Burdett should be committed to the Tower, the letter in question being a libellous and scandalous paper, reflecting upon the just rights and privileges of that House. The sergeant-at-arms found great difficulty in serving his warrant; and it was not until the fourth day after he had received it from the Speaker, that Sir Francis was conveyed to the Tower, and only then by means of breaking into his house, attended by a posse of constables and soldiers."

door east from the corner of Bolton Street, as that from which Sir Francis was carried a state prisoner to the Tower, and he quotes the following *jeu d'esprit* on the arrest :—

> " The lady she sat and she played on the lute,
>   And she sang, ' Will you come to my bower ?'
> The sergeant-at-arms had stood hitherto mute,
> But now he advanced, like an impudent brute,
>   And said, ' Will you come to the Tower ?' "

The house was subsequently occupied by the Duke

CAMBRIDGE HOUSE, IN 1854. (*See page* 285.)

On the prorogation of Parliament, June 21st, the captive was set free, but he did not care to return home with the same demonstrations. The populace had planned a triumphal procession from the Tower to Piccadilly; but Sir Francis contrived to give his friends the slip, crossed the river in a boat, and drove off in a carriage. which was waiting for him on the south side of London Bridge, for his country residence at Wimbledon. The story of his committal to the Tower narrated above stands out in strong contrast to the staunch Conservatism which marked his later years; nevertheless he was

> " Through good and ill report, through calm and storm,
>   For forty years the pilot of reform."

Mr. J. H. Jesse identifies the house No. 80, one

of St. Albans, who, however, migrated two or three doors more to the east when he married the widow of Thomas Coutts, of whom we have spoken above.

Late in life Sir Francis Burdett, who was known among his constituents at Westminster as "Old Glory," changed his colours, abandoned his Radical allies, and died a most loyal and peaceable Conservative. About the year 1820 he had removed to St. James's Place, where he died, and as we have already seen in a previous chapter,* his death was as pathetic as his parliamentary life had been famous.

At the western corner of Bolton Street, facing Piccadilly, stands Bath House, the residence of

---

* See *ante*, p. 171.

OLD HYDE PARK CORNER IN 1820. *From Mr. Crace's Collection.* (*See page 290.*)

Lord Ashburton. It contains a fine collection of pictures, chiefly of the Dutch and Flemish schools, formed by the builder of the mansion, Mr. Alexander Baring, afterwards the first Lord Ashburton of the present creation. Dr. Waagen gives a list of the pictures to be seen here, in his work on "Art and Artists in England." The house occupies the site of the Pulteney Hotel, where many royal personages were lodged during their visits to London; among others the Emperor Alexander of Russia, during the sojourn of the Allied Sovereigns in 1814. It was so called because it had been formerly the residence of Pulteney, Earl of Bath, the great rival and antagonist of Sir Robert Walpole. Pulteney, who up to about 1741 had been, as a commoner, the most violent and popular patriot of his day, dwindled down, in 1742, into the Earl of Bath. Sir Robert Walpole, when forced, about the same time, to retire into the peerage, had laid this trap for his antagonist, who readily fell into it. On their first meeting, after what one of them called their respective "falls up-stairs," Lord Orford said to Lord Bath, with malicious good humour, "My lord, you and I are now the most insignificant fellows in England." A coronet, in fact, as well as a mitre, has often proved an extinguisher, and this fact well illustrates Pope's line with reference to William Pulteney :—

"He foams a patriot to subside a peer."

Walpole relates the following story concerning the earl, which appears almost too amusing to be true :—"Lord Bath once owed a tradesman eight hundred pounds, and would never pay him. The man determined to persecute him till he did; and one morning followed him to Lord Winchilsea's, and sent up word that he wanted to speak with him. Lord Bath came down, and said, 'Fellow, what do you want with me?' 'My money,' said the man, as loud as ever he could bawl, before all the servants. He bade him come next morning, and then would not see him. The next Sunday the man followed him to church, and got into the next pew; he leaned over, and said, 'My money; give me my money.' My lord went to the end of the pew; the man too—'Give me my money.' The sermon was on avarice, and the text, 'Cursed are they that heap up riches.' The man groaned out, 'O Lord!' and pointed to my Lord Bath; in short, he persisted so much, and drew the eyes of all the congregation, that my Lord Bath went out and paid him directly." Lord Bath died not long after the accession of George III.

At the opposite corner of Bolton Street stood, from 1807 to 1819, Watier's Gambling Club. Con-

cerning the origin of this club—or rather, gaming-house, for it was nothing more—the following anecdote is told by Captain Gronow:—"Upon one occasion, some gentlemen of both 'White's' and 'Brooks's' had the honour to dine with the Prince Regent, and during the conversation the Prince inquired what sort of dinners they got at their clubs; upon which Sir Thomas Stepney, one of the guests, observed that their dinners were always the same, the eternal joints or beef-steaks, the boiled fowl with oyster sauce, and an apple tart. 'That is what we have at our clubs, and very monotonous fare it is.' The Prince, without further remark, rang the bell for his cook, Watier, and in the presence of those who dined at the royal table, asked him whether he would take a house and organise a dinner-club. Watier assented, and named the Prince's page, Madison, as manager, and Labourie, from the royal kitchen, as cook. The club flourished only a few years, owing to the night-play that was carried on there. The favourite game played there was 'Macao.'" The Duke of York patronised it, and was a member. Tom Moore also tells us that he belonged to it. The dinners were exquisite; the best Parisian cooks could not beat Labourie.

Mr. John Timbs, in his account of this club, remarks, with sly humour, "In the old days, when gaming was in fashion, at Watier's Club both princes and nobles lost or gained fortunes between themselves;" and by all accounts "Macao" seems to have been a far more effective instrument in the losing of fortunes than either "Whist" or "Loo."

Mr. Raikes, in his "Journal," says that Watier's Club, which had originally been established for harmonic meetings, became, in the time of "Beau" Brummell, the resort of nearly all the fine gentlemen of the day. "The dinners," he adds, "were superlative, and high play at 'Macao' was generally introduced. It was this game, or rather losses which arose out of it, that first led the 'Beau' into difficulties." Mr. Raikes further remarks, with reference to this club, that its pace was "too quick to last," and that its records show that none of its members at his death had reached the average age of man. The club was closed in 1819, when the house was taken by a set of "black-legs" who instituted a common bank for gambling. This caused the ruin of several fortunes, and it was suppressed in its turn, or died a natural death.

At the end of the last or early in the present century it was proposed that the Dilettanti Society, already mentioned by us in our account of the "Thatched House Tavern," should erect a permanent home for itself in Piccadilly, either near the

Pulteney Hotel, or else near the foot of the descent, opposite the Ranger's Lodge; but the proposal was never carried out.

At the south-west corner of Clarges Street is the Turf Club. This club was originally established in Grafton Street. The former building, known as Grafton House, was dull, heavy, and ugly, probably the *ugliest* house in London. It was built, says Charles Knight, by the father of Mr. Michael Angelo Taylor, M.P., but others say by the duke himself, who forgot to insert a door, and who therefore had to buy the adjoining house in Clarges Street to make an entrance. The house was taken by the Turf Club in 1875, and a noble new club-house has since been erected.

Passing along Piccadilly, we soon arrive at No. 94, the Naval and Military Club. The building, the site of which was once occupied by an inn, was originally erected for the Earl of Egremont, and called Egremont and afterwards Cholmondeley House. The house has a noble appearance; it is fronted with stone, and overlooks the Green Park. It has a small court-yard in front of it. For many years it was the residence of Adolphus, late Duke of Cambridge, who died here in 1850, and whose name it bore also when occupied by Lord Palmerston, whose body was brought hither from Brockett Hall, where he died, in 1865, the day before it was deposited in Westminster Abbey. Shortly after his lordship's death the house was purchased by the Naval and Military Club, who have greatly improved and enlarged it.

Between White Horse and Engine Streets (No. 105) is a noble Italian mansion, called Hertford House, after the late Marquis of Hertford, who built it about the year 1850, from the designs of a Polish or Russian architect, named Novosielski. It was left by Lord Hertford to his natural son, Sir Richard Wallace, who sold it to one of the family of the Goldsmids. Though his lordship built the house, he chose, with his usual eccentricity, never to reside in it, because the parishioners of St. James's refused to allow him to pave the street in front of it after a fashion of his own. The house contained a very fine collection of works of art, purchased by Lord Hertford from the galleries of Cardinal Fesch, the late King of Holland, and Lord Ashburnham, and many others from the Salt-marshe collection.

The next house westward, at the opposite side of Engine Street, is Coventry House, now the St. James's Club. It was for a century the residence of the Earls of Coventry, one of whom procured, by his influence, the abolition of the "May Fair" in the rear of his mansion. It occupies the site of the old "Greyhound Inn," and, as Mr. John Timbs informs us, it was bought by the Earl of Coventry of Sir Hugh Hunlocke, in 1764, for 10,000 guineas.

The house adjoining the St. James's Club is the residence of the Baroness Meyer de Rothschild, widow of Baron Meyer Amschel de Rothschild, of Mentmore, Buckinghamshire, who was many years M.P. for Hythe, and who died in 1874. The house of another member of this wealthy family is situated further westward, next to Apsley House. The Rothschilds, who began by sweeping out a small shop in the Jews' quarter of the city of Frankfort, over which hung suspended the sign of the "Red Shield," whence they derive their name, have become the metallic sovereigns of Europe. From their different establishments in Paris, London, Vienna, Frankfort, St. Petersburg, and Naples they have obtained a control over the European exchanges which no party ever before could accomplish, and they now seem to hold the strings of the public purse. No sovereign without their assistance now could raise a loan. When the first Baron Rothschild was at Vienna, having contracted for the Austrian loan, the emperor sent for him to express his satisfaction at the manner in which the bargain had been concluded. The Israelite replied, "Je peut assurer votre Majesté que la maison de Rothschild sera toujours enchantée de faire tout ce qui pourra être agréable à la maison d'Autriche."

Nathan Meyer de Rothschild, the father of the two sons mentioned above, and himself the third son of the founder of the wealth and influence of this great commercial family, was a native of Frankfort; he was naturalised as a British subject by royal letters patent in the reign of George III., and subsequently was advanced to the dignity of a Baron of the Austrian Empire. He died in 1836, leaving a family of four sons, all Austrian barons. Ten years later, in 1846, an English baronetcy was conferred on his second son, Anthony, with remainder, failing his own male issue, to the sons of his elder brother Lionel. Sir Anthony died in January, 1876, when his English title accordingly passed to his nephew, Mr. Nathan Meyer de Rothschild, M.P. for Aylesbury.

A few doors westward, at No. 110, lived for many years Hester Maria, Viscountess Keith. She was the last remaining link between the present generation and that brilliant literary circle which congregated around Johnson at "the Club," and which thronged the hospitable mansion of her mother, Mrs. Thrale, at Streatham. During the first eighteen years of her life she was surrounded

by Johnson, Reynolds, Garrick, Boswell, Beauclerk, and Bennet Langton. Johnson was her
tutor, and Baretti her language-master. From
her mother she learnt to value and to cultivate
intellectual pursuits, while from her excellent father
she derived those solid and sterling qualities which
belong more especially to the true English character.
On the death of Mr. Thrale, and the re-marriage of
her mother to Signore Piozzi—a marriage highly
disapproved by the Leviathan of literature—Miss
Thrale retired to her late father's house at Brighton,
where she applied her mind to several courses of
severe study, and acquired a knowledge of many
subjects rare in a woman at all times, and especially so in the less cultivated days of the last
century. Here she remained until the time arrived
for her to take possession of the fortune left her by
her father, when she settled herself in a handsome
mansion in London. In the meantime she had
the misfortune to lose her valued friend and pre-
ceptor, the illustrious Johnson, whose death-bed
she assiduously attended. A few days before his
death the venerable philosopher addressed Miss
Thrale in these words :—" My dear child, we part
for ever in this world ; let us part as Christians
should : let us pray together." He then uttered a
prayer of fervent piety and deep affection, invoking
the blessing of Heaven on his pupil. In 1808,
Miss Thrale became the wife of George Keith
Elphinstone, Admiral Viscount Keith, one of the
most distinguished commanders by whom the naval
honour of Great Britain was so greatly exalted
during the war against the great Napoleon. Lady
Keith was left a widow in 1823. For several years
she held a distinguished position in the highest
circles of the fashionable world in London, and
was one of the original patronesses of " Almack's."
Having lived to the advanced age of ninety-five,
Lady Keith died in March, 1857.

The house standing at the south-east corner of
Down Street is the Junior Athenæum Club. This
splendid mansion was built for the late Mr. Henry
Thomas Hope, M.P., in 1849–50, from the designs
of M. Dusillon and Professor Donaldson. The
building has some remarkably handsome external
decorations in stone and metal, in the modern
French style. The decorations were executed
chiefly by French artists, and the iron railing is
particularly fine, both with regard to design and
workmanship. The mansion was for some years
known as Hope House, and during the time of
Mr. Hope's occupation it was noted as containing
one of the finest picture-galleries in London. The
pictures were chiefly of the Dutch and Flemish
masters, and of the very highest quality of art in

these schools ; they were obtained by Mr. Hope's
ancestors (bankers at Amsterdam) principally from
the painters themselves. A list of the principal of
them is given in Dr. Waagen's " Art and Artists
in England." Mr. Hope had also here a fine
collection of ancient Greek sculpture. Mr. Hope,
who was the owner of Deepdene, in Surrey, and
was many years M.P. for Gloucester, &c., died in
1861, leaving an only daughter, who was married
in the same year to Alexander, sixth Duke of New-
castle. Shortly after Mr. Hope's death his house
was sold, and converted into a club.

The house at the corner of Hamilton Place,
facing Piccadilly, was for many years the town
residence of John, Earl of Eldon, the distinguished
Chief Justice of the Court of Common Pleas, and
Lord Chancellor of England, during the early part
of the present century. He died in 1838.

Gloucester House, at the corner of Park Lane,
now the residence of the Duke of Cambridge, was
formerly that of William Henry, the last Duke of
Gloucester, who purchased it on his marriage, and
who died in 1834. In spite of being Chancellor of
Cambridge, he was called "Silly Billy." Mr. Raikes
describes him as "a quiet, inoffensive character,
rather tenacious of the respect due to his rank, and
strongly attached to the ultra-Tory party." The
mansion was previously the residence of the Earl of
Elgin, at which time it was known as Elgin House.
Here, on their first arrival in this country, were
deposited the Elgin Marbles, previous to their
removal to Burlington House, whence they were
taken to the British Museum in 1816. It is in
allusion to this fact that Lord Byron, in his
" English Bards and Scotch Reviewers," calls Elgin
House a " stone shop," and

> " General mart
> For all the mutilated blocks of art."

The houses now numbered 138 and 139, between
Park Lane and Hamilton Place, were, at the beginning of the present century, one mansion, remarkable for its large bow window, and occupied by
the eccentric and licentious Duke of Queensberry,
better known to society by his nickname of " Old
Q." In his old age, when sated with pleasures of
the grossest kind, he would sit in sunny weather
in his balcony, with an umbrella or parasol over
his head, and amuse himself with watching the
female passers-by, ogling every pretty woman, and
sending out his minions to fetch them in, as a spider
will draw flies into his web. The duke had an
exterior flight of steps built to aid him in this sport.
These steps were removed long subsequently to
his death, in 1810.

Mr. T. Raikes, in his " Journal," under date of

1840, writes :—"The late Duke of Queensberry, whom I remember in my early days, called 'Old Q.,' was of the same school as the Marshal Duc de Richelieu in France, and as great a profligate. He lived at the bow-window house in Piccadilly, where he was latterly always seen looking at the people who passed by ; a groom on horseback, known as Jack Radford, always stood under the window to carry about his messages to any one whom he remarked in the street. He kept a physician in the house, and, to ensure attention to his health, his terms were that he should have so much per day while he lived, but not a shilling at his death. When he drove out he was always alone in a dark-green vis-à-vis, with long-tailed black horses ; and during winter, with a muff, two servants behind in undress, and his groom following the carriage, to execute his commissions. He was a little, sharp-looking man, very irritable, and swore like ten thousand troopers : enormously rich and selfish."

The duke was one of the three individuals who were said to be the fathers of Maria Fagniani, afterwards Marchioness of Hertford, to whom he left a very large portion of his property ; the title passing to a distant relative, the Duke of Buccleuch.

Of the two houses above mentioned, that numbered 139 maintained its celebrity by being at one time the residence of Lord Byron. Here he was living when the separation between himself and Lady Byron took place a year after their ill-starred marriage ; and here he wrote "Parisina" and the "Siege of Corinth." It was also from this house that Lady Byron left the poet, carrying with her his infant child, whom he commemorates so touchingly as "Ada, sole daughter of my house and heart." "The moment that my wife left me," he writes, "I was assailed by all the falsehoods that malice could invent or slander publish ; . . . . there was no crime too dark to be attributed to me by the moral (?) English, to account for so common an occurrence as a 'separation in high life.' I was thought a devil, because Lady Byron was allowed to be an angel !" Poor man ! bad as he may have been, he deserved to have met with a creature endowed with some small store of sympathy, and at least some little feminine weakness, in the woman whom he made his wife.

At No. 144, one of the mansions between Hamilton Place and Apsley House, Lord Palmerston was living about the time of the Crimean War, and shortly before his acceptance of the Premiership. His lordship removed thence to Cambridge House, of which we have already spoken as being now the Naval and Military Club.

Where Apsley House now stands, if we may accept the statement of Charles Knight, was the tavern called the "Hercules' Pillars," "the same at which the redoubted Squire Western, with his clerical satellite, is represented as taking up his abode on his arrival in London, and conveying the fair Sophia." The sign of the "Hercules' Pillars" was given to the tavern probably as marking, at that time, the extreme "west-end" of London. Its name is recorded by Wycherley, in his *Plain Dealer*, and is said to have been a haunt of the Marquis of Granby, and of other members of the titled classes. The character of the house in Fielding's time may be gathered from the following quotation from "Tom Jones," touching Squire Western's arrival in London :—"The squire sat down to regale himself over a bottle of wine, with his parson and the landlord of the 'Hercules' Pillars,' who, as the squire said, would make an excellent third-man, and would inform them of the news of the town ; for, to be sure, says he, he knows a good deal, since the horses of many of 'the quality' stand at his door."

Mr. J. H. Jesse tells us that the tavern in question stood *between* Apsley House and Hamilton Place, and that, on account of its situation, it was much frequented by gentlemen from the West of England. Wherever may have been the exact spot on which the house stood, it seems at best to have been a comfortable but low inn on the outskirts of the town, where gentlemen's horses and grooms were put up, and farmers and graziers resorted.

In the reign of George II. all the ground to the west of Devonshire House up to Hyde Park Corner was covered by a row of small shops and yards of the statuaries ; nor were the latter of the best and purest kind, if we may judge by the loud complaints against their design and execution uttered by the author of "A New Critical Review of the Public Buildings, &c.," at that date. In fact, the tasteless atrocities in sculpture there perpetrated could not well be exceeded now-a-days by the artists of the "figure-yards" of the Euston Road. On the site of the last remaining "figure-yard" in this neighbourhood was built, in the early part of the reign of George III., a house for the eccentric and notorious Lord Barrymore, but it was burnt down before it had been many years in his occupation.

Between the "Hercules' Pillars" and what now is Hamilton Place, instead of the magnificent houses of the Marquis of Northampton, and Barons Lionel and Ferdinand de Rothschild and others, long known collectively as Piccadilly Terrace, was a row of low and mean tenements, one of which bore conspicuously in the street before it the grand sign of the "Triumphal Chariot." Mr. J. H. Jesse suggests that "this was, in all probability, the 'pretty tavern' to which the unfortunate Richard Savage was conducted by Sir Richard Steele on the occasion of their being closeted together for a whole day, busy in composing a hurried pamphlet which they had to sell for two guineas before they could pay for their dinner," as Johnson tells us in his "Life of Savage." The tavern is stated to have

review-days, when long wooden seats were fixed in the street before the doors for the accommodation of as many barbers, all busily employed in powdering the hair of these sons of Mars !"

Near the "Hercules' Pillars" and "Triumphal Chariot," there would appear to have been quite a cluster of other small inns, "convenient" to the wayfarer as he entered London from the western counties. Mr. Larwood enumerates among these

HAMILTON PLACE IN 1802. *From a Drawing in the Guildhall Library.* (*See page* 291.)

been a "watering-house" for hackney-coaches, &c. Charles Knight says that "by the kerbstone in front of it there was a bench for the porters, and a board over it for depositing their loads ; " and he gives a view of just such another "watering-house" still standing at Knightsbridge in 1841, answering in every minute detail to the above, except in the sign, for it is not the "Triumphal Chariot," nor a "chariot" at all, but "The White Hart."

The sign of the "Triumphal Chariot" was probably an allusion to the soldiery from the barracks, who were its chief supporters. Mr. J. T. Smith, in his "Antiquarian Rambles in the London Streets," tells us that, "in the middle of the last century, this and other public-houses were much resorted to by the red-coats on Sundays and

the "Red and the Golden Lion," the "Swan," the "Horse Shoe," the "Running Horse," the "Barley Mow," the "White Horse," and the "Half Moon," of which the last has left the trace of its being in the name of a street running out of Piccadilly.

Thoughtful observers will note the slight but graceful bend of the roadway of Piccadilly, and will see in it with us a proof that the road itself was of ancient date. Modern streets are almost always driven straight ; but the earliest roads follow the tracks of cart-wheels and pack-horses ; and probably it was by the pack-horses or market-carts of five centuries ago that this road was first gradually worn. The only proof of its existence in the days of antiquity is to be found in the map of Ralph Aggas, where it forms but a continuation of the line marked out at the top of the Haymarket as "the way to Reading," just as what now is Oxford Street is marked "the way to Uxbridge." We find, however, a corroboration of the map in the narrative of the rebellion raised by Sir Thomas Wyatt and his Kentish followers on the unpopular marriage of Queen Mary with Philip of Spain, when it would seem that, in addition to a lower way running past the front of St. James's Palace

that it was upon a hill beyond St. James's, "almost over against the Park Corner, on the hill in the highway, above the new bridge over against St. James's."

How Wyatt passed on first to Charing Cross and then to Ludgate, how he was there captured, and how he was beheaded and afterwards quartered on Tower Hill, are matters well known to nearly every reader of English history. His head as

THE ROYAL INSTITUTION. (See page 296.)

to Charing Cross, there was also a "highway on the hill," along which some of the rebel forces and ammunition were brought up. This event is, indeed, the earliest matter of historical interest connected with Piccadilly. We read that, unable to effect the passage of London Bridge, Wyatt marched to Kingston, where he crossed the Thames, and so forced his way to Knightsbridge. In our account of Charing Cross* we have already given the narrative of Wyatt's advance on London, as told by honest John Stow, and therefore we need not repeat it here, further than to say that, in all probability, it was in Piccadilly that he "planted his ordenance," for the old chronicler tells us

Stow further informs us, was set up on the gallows at Hay Hill, at that time almost if not quite in sight of the spot where he had left his "ordenance." The "new bridge" spoken of in Stow's narrative probably spanned the brook which ran in this direction down from Tyburn, giving its appellation to the Brook Fields, whence "Brook Street" derives its name, as we shall see in a future chapter.

It was near the western extremity of Piccadilly that the citizens of London fortified themselves against the threatened approach of Charles I. and his army in 1642, when the citizens of the West-end, aided by the female population, and, indeed, even ladies of high birth and blood, lent a helping hand in the trenches, and in throwing up earthworks

* See Vol. III., p. 125.

In this emergency, men, women, and even children, assisted in hundreds and thousands, and speedily a rampart of earth was raised, with batteries and redoubts at intervals. The fort here was armed with four bastions. The active part taken by the women in this undertaking is described with much graphic humour by Butler, in his "Hudibras." He writes that they

> "Marched rank and file, with drum and ensign,
> T' entrench the city for defence in ;
> Raised ramparts with their own soft hands,
> To put the enemy to stand ;
> From ladies down to oyster-wenches
> Laboured like pioneers in trenches,
> Fall'n to their pickaxes and tools,
> And helped the men to dig like moles."

In spite of its proximity to the Court suburb, it would appear that Piccadilly was not a very secure thoroughfare, even during the reigns of the first Hanoverian kings. For instance, it is on record, that in 1726 the Earl of Harborough was stopped here, whilst being carried in his sedan chair, during broad daylight ; we read that "one of the chairmen pulled a pole out of the chair and knocked down one of the villains, while the earl came out, drew his sword, and put the others to flight, but not before they had raised their wounded companion, whom they took off with them." Indeed, even a quarter of a century later, the neighbourhood of Piccadilly, and, in fact, all the western and northern suburbs of London, were infested with footpads and highwaymen ; and, under cover of the darkness, favoured by the ill-lighted and ill-protected state of the streets, highway robberies continued to be committed with impunity, in the heart of London, up to a much more recent period than is generally supposed. Mr. Jesse tells us that about the year 1810 a near relative of his own, accompanied by a friend, was forcibly stopped in a hackney-coach in Piccadilly, opposite to St. James's Church, by ruffians, who presented their pistols, and forced them to give up their money and watches. He adds, that in this case the driver, in all probability, was in league with the highwaymen.

The modern history of Piccadilly may be soon told. In process of time the thoroughfare has undergone great alteration since buildings were first erected on its northern side. Bath House, of which we have spoken above, was the first mansion of any pretension erected to the west of Devonshire House ; and down to about the year 1770, with the exception of the one just named, there were no houses more than one or two storeys high. Many years ago the pavement on the north side of all the middle portion was raised, and formed a terrace ; and when the name of the terrace ceased to be used in this part of the street, it came to be applied to the larger mansions further westward and lying between Down Street and Apsley House. Now, however, it is restricted to the row of houses situated to the west of Hamilton Place.

About the end of the year 1825 the toll-gate at Hyde Park Corner, which narrowed the thoroughfare, interrupted the traffic, and gave a confined appearance to the street, was removed. Mr. Hone, in his "Every Day Book," published in the year 1826, thus records the sale by auction of this toll-gate :—"The sale by auction of the 'toll-houses' on the north and south side of the road, with the 'weighing-machine' and lamp-posts at Hyde Park Corner, was effected by Mr. Abbott, the estate agent and appraiser, by order of the trustees of the roads. They were sold for building materials ; the north toll-house was in five lots, the south in five other lots ; the gates, rails, posts, and inscription boards, were in five more lots ; and the engine-house was also in five lots." It is not stated what amount was realised by the sale, but Hone gives a graphic illustration representing the auctioneer raising his hammer and calling out, "Going, going, gone !" He adds, "The whole are entirely cleared away, to the great relief of thousands of persons resident in this neighbourhood," and then he moralises as follows : "It is too much to expect everything vexatious to disappear at once ; this is a good beginning, and, if there be truth in the old saying, we may expect a good ending." At the same sale were put up and knocked down the weighing-machine and toll-house at "Jenny's Whim," of which we shall have more to say when we come to Knightsbridge, and also the toll-house near the "Original Bun-house" at Chelsea, with the lamp-posts on the road.

Thanks to the iron roads out of London, which steam has opened of late years, Piccadilly is no longer the great "coaching" thoroughfare which it was in the days "when George III. was King ;" but still, "in the season," it is always lively and well filled, and there is no street in London where the miscellaneous character of London conveyances and "carriage folk," from the outside passengers on a lordly "drag," down to the city clerks on the knifeboards of omnibuses, and even to the donkey-driving costermongers, may be seen in greater variety. All ranks are jostled together in Piccadilly, if anywhere in this great metropolis.

CHAPTER XXIV.

PICCADILLY : NORTHERN TRIBUTARIES.

"Intervalla vides humanè commoda ; verum
Puræ sunt plateæ."—*Horace, " Satires."*

Hamilton Place and its Noted Residents—White Horse Street—Halfmoon Street—Boswell's Lodgings—Clarges Street—Bolton Street—Berkeley Street—Dover Street—Dr. John Arbuthnot—Residence of the Bishops of Ely—Albemarle Street—Grillon's Hotel and Club—Hotels, Clubs, and Scientific Societies in Albemarle Street—Royal Institution—Professor Faraday—St. George's Chapel—Stafford Street—"Street Clubs"—Grafton Street—Old and New Bond Street—Clifford Street—Burlington Gardens—The London University—Old Burlington Street—Boyle Street—Uxbridge House—Queensberry House—Vigo Street—Sackville Street—Air Street—Cork Street—Savile Row—New Burlington Street.

HAVING already dealt with the various streets abutting on the south side of Piccadilly, and in the preceding chapters described the principal buildings and objects of interest to be met with along the route from the southern Regent Circus to Hyde Park Corner, we now retrace our steps, noting on the way the several streets and outlets on its northern side, or, at least, such as have anything worthy of remark appertaining to them in the way of history and personal associations.

Hamilton Place, the first turning on our way back eastward from Apsley House, brings down to our own times the memory of Colonel James Hamilton, a boon companion of Charles II., who gave him the Rangership of Hyde Park. He was a brother of Anthony Hamilton, the witty chronicler of the Court of Charles II., but perhaps better known to the world in general as the same " Beare" Hamilton who was so amusingly duped by the Countess of Chesterfield at Bretby Park. " Being considerably in the king's favour," writes Mr. J. Larwood, in his "Story of the London Parks," " Hamilton received some grants in connection with the park. One of these was the triangular piece of ground between the lodge (which stood on the site of Apsley House) and the present Park Lane ; during the Commonwealth a fort and various houses had been built upon it. This was now granted to Hamilton, with the covenant that he should make leases to purchasers to be appointed at half the improved rents. Of course, it is from him that this site still bears the name of Hamilton Place. He was shot in an engagement with the Dutch in 1673, on which occasion the king renewed the lease for ninety-nine years to his widow."

The Duke of Wellington was living in Hamilton Place in 1814, during the interval of peace consequent on the abdication of Napoleon and his retirement to Elba ; and here he received a deputation of the House of Commons sent to present him with an address of thanks for his services in the field in Spain. Of No. 1 we have already spoken, as the house of old Lord Eldon. No. 2 was the town residence of the Duchess-Countess of Sutherland, who, by her marriage with the Marquis of Stafford, put the coping-stone to the fortunes of the now ducal house of Leveson-Gower. Hamilton Place, too, was the last residence of Mr. H. A. J. Munro, of Novar, N.B., who was the owner of a fine gallery of paintings, and also of a valuable library.

Park Lane, in the reign of Queen Anne, was a desolate by-road, generally spoken of as " the lane leading from Piccadilly to Tyburn." It is now a noble thoroughfare, built only on the eastern side, the other being open to Hyde Park. We shall have more to say of it in a future chapter when making our way to Oxford Street.

Passing Down Street (which leads to Mayfair, and in which D'Israeli lived in his bachelor days), we arrive at White Horse Street. " The bay-fronted house at the west corner of this street," says Mr. Peter Cunningham, " was the residence of Mr. Charles Dumergue, the friend of Sir Walter Scott ; until a child of his own was established in London, this was Scott's head-quarters when in town."

Halfmoon Street, the next turning eastward, took its name from an inn which stood at the corner, facing Piccadilly. The sign was not an uncommon one ; and it may be well here to remind the reader that the lower half of Bedford Street, Strand, was formerly called Halfmoon Street, and for the same reason. The half-moon or crescent, according to Mr. Larwood, was the emblem of the temporal, as the sun was that of the spiritual power. There was another " Half Moon " tavern at Upper Holloway, famous for its cheese-cakes, which were hawked about London by a man on horseback, and at one time formed one of the established " cries of London." Another " Half Moon " in Aldersgate Street, was connected with the name of Ben Jonson. But our business is with the street bearing the name of the Half-moon. The street may be speedily dismissed, for it has but few literary reminiscences, and has for several generations consisted of respectable houses of the middle class, let out in apartments to members of Parliament and others. The east corner house was formerly the residence of Madame d'Arblay. In this street Boswell, as he tells us in his " Life of Johnson," was lodging in May, 1768, when he was visited by the great lexicographer, who, having expressed a dislike of the publication of a portion of one of his letters, on being asked by his future biographer whether he forbade his letters to be published after his decease, gave the bluff reply, " Nay, sir, when I am dead you may do as you will "—a reply to which posterity is deeply indebted.   Here, too, died, in 1797, the celebrated actress, Mrs. Pope ; she was buried in the cloisters of Westminster Abbey.

According to the " New View of London," published in 1708, the Lady Clarges was the owner of a stately new building on the north side of Piccadilly, then in the occupation of the Venetian Ambassador.   Its site is now covered by Clarges Street, which was named after Sir Walter Clarges, and was built about the year 1717.   At No. 12 in this street Edmund Kean, the tragedian, lived for some few years, and it is said that, in the adjoining house (No. 11) Lady Hamilton was residing at the time of Lord Nelson's death.   If this statement be correct, she must have removed to this street only a few days before from Piccadilly.   In the year 1826, No. 14 was the residence of William Mitford, the historian of Greece, brother of Lord Redesdale.   His opinions disqualified him from appreciating the Athenian constitution, and his work has ceased to be valued.   He died in the year 1827.

It was not till many mansions had been built further west that the ground about May Fair came to be utilised.   Towards the end of the seventeenth century, indeed, a considerable plot of ground adjoining Clarges Street was leased by Sir Thomas Clarges (whose wife was a Berkeley) to one Thomas Neale, Groom-Porter to his Majesty (of whom Charles Knight tells us that he was the introducer of lotteries on the Venetian plan, and the builder of the Seven Dials, in St. Giles's), on the condition that he should lay out £10,000 in building on it, but the agreement was never carried out, and the lease was forfeited or cancelled.   After his son obtained back the lease granted to Neale by Sir Thomas Clarges, the grounds on the slope of the hill in Piccadilly westward, toward Park Lane, were, as we have already stated, soon covered with buildings.

Bolton Street is a dull, narrow, and heavy thoroughfare, with no great interest attaching to its houses.   In it, however, lived, in the time of Queen Anne and George I., the celebrated Earl of Peterborough, who, as Mr. John Timbs tells us, " in his biography (fortunately never printed), confesses having committed three capital crimes before he was twenty years of age."   Pope, however, did

not, on this account, object to stay with him here as a guest.   The Hon. Mrs. Norton was living here in 1841, before settling in Chesterfield Street. Hatton, in 1708, speaks of Bolton Street as being " the most westerly street in London, between the road to Knightsbridge south and the fields north." But almost every street in this neighbourhood, at one time or other, might have had the same thing said of it.

Of Stratton Street, which forms a *cul de sac*, we have already spoken ; and of Berkeley Street, which is opposite the north-east corner of the Green Park, we have but little to say, beyond the fact that it dates from the year 1642, at which it was the western extremity of Piccadilly, or, as it was then called, Portugal Street, and that it was named from Berkeley House, which it bounded on the east.   In this street was the last town apartment occupied by Pope, who came to live here in order to be near his friend, Lord Burlington.   One side of the street is now occupied entirely by the wall of Devonshire House, and the other by a few respectable houses and the stables belonging to the mansions in Dover Street.

Dover Street, which was built in the year 1642, was so called after Henry Jermyn, Lord Dover, the " little Jermyn " of De Grammont's Memoirs ; he resided on the east side of the street, and died in 1782.   The street stands on a part of the ground that had been for a few years occupied by Clarendon House, the " Dunkirk House " of the populace, and the princely mansion of Lord Chancellor Clarendon.   John Evelyn, who had been " oftentimes so cheerful, and sometimes so sad, with Chancellor Hyde " on that very ground, lived for some time close by Lord Dover's house.

On the west side of this street lived Dr. John Arbuthnot, " Martinus Scriblerus," physician to Queen Anne, and the friend of Pope and other literary celebrities of his time.   On the death of the queen, Arbuthnot, like the other attendants at Court, was displaced, and had to leave his apartments at St. James's.   He removed into Dover Street, " hoping still," as he said, " to keep a little habitation warm in town, and to afford half a pint of claret to his old friends."   It is to this " displacement " that Pope alludes in his well-known apostrophe to Arbuthnot :—

" O friend ! may each domestic bliss be thine !
 Be no unpleasing melancholy mine :
 Me let the tender office long engage,
 To rock the cradle of reposing age,
 With lenient arts extend a mother's breath,
 Make languor smile, and smooth the bed of death ;
 Explore the thought, explain the asking eye,
 And keep awhile one parent from the sky !

On cares like these if length of days attend,
May Heaven, to bless those days, preserve my friend;
Preserve him social, cheerful, and serene,
And just as rich as when he served a queen."

Dr. Arbuthnot, the son of a nonjuring clergyman in Scotland, was born at Arbuthnot, in Kincardineshire, about the period of the Restoration. Early in life he settled in London, and for some time gained his livelihood as a teacher of mathematics. He had studied medicine in his native country, but a fortunate accident brought him into practice here as a physician. He happened to be at Epsom on one occasion, when Prince George, who was also there, was suddenly taken ill. Arbuthnot was called in, and having effected a cure, was soon afterwards appointed one of the physicians in ordinary to the queen. He continued to practise, enjoying considerable professional distinction, till his death, in 1735.

No. 37 in this street is the town residence of the Bishops of Ely. It was purchased or built in the year 1772, out of the proceeds of the sale of the ancient Palace of the Bishops of Ely, in Ely Place, Holborn. On the front of the house is a mitre, sculptured in stone. In the adjoining house (No. 38) resided Lord King, the "bishop hater," who wrote a life of his kinsman, John Locke. This work was published in 1829. In 1841, No. 23 was the residence of Lady Byron, widow of the poet.

In this street also was the gun-shop of the celebrated "Joe Manton," who was a favourite with almost all the aristocratic sportsmen of his day. He patented his principal improvements in the manufacture of guns in 1792.

Here, too, for many years, was the publishing house of Mr. Edward Moxon, who continued to surround himself as a publisher with such a host of poetical clients, that his shop may be said to have become a modern temple of the Muses. From this shop were issued the successive volumes of Barry Cornwall, Wordsworth, Tennyson, &c. But this passed away about the year 1870, when the business was transferred elsewhere, and the poetic halo disappeared from Dover Street.

Albemarle Street was so called after Christopher Monk, second Duke of Albemarle, who purchased the mansion of the Earl of Clarendon which stood partly on its site. The street was built towards the close of the seventeenth or beginning of the eighteenth century by Sir Thomas Bond, of Peckham, Comptroller of the Household to Henrietta Maria, the Queen of Charles II., and a loyal friend of James II., whom he accompanied in his exile to St. Germains. Evelyn tells us, in his "Memoirs," that this Sir Thomas Bond bought part of the grounds of Clarendon House, "in order to build a street of tenements to his undoing." Clarendon House was sold by the Duke of Albemarle, when in difficulties, soon after he had purchased it. Hatton, in 1708, describes Albemarle Street as "a street of excellent new buildings, inhabited by persons of quality, between the fields and Portugal Street."

At No. 50A, on the west side of this street, is the shop of John Murray, publisher. It is scarcely necessary here to do more than just remind our readers of the connection of this house with Lord Byron, whose poems were first issued hence to the public, as they came fresh from the anvil of his brain, between 1807 and his death in 1822. Nor will they forget how the poet's fondness for his publisher stands recorded in his lordship's verses and letters. With Byron he was "my Murray." In 1812 appeared the first two cantos of "Childe Harold's Pilgrimage," and so eminently successful were they, that, as Byron himself briefly described in his memoranda, he awoke one morning and found himself famous. The copyright money paid by Mr. Murray, £600, his lordship presented to his friend, Mr. Robert C. Dallas, saying, that he never would receive money for his writings,* "a resolution," as Moore tells us in his "Life of Byron," "he afterwards wisely abandoned." We learn from Alibone, that Mr. Murray paid, at different times, for copyrights of his lordship's poems, certainly over £15,000. As we have already mentioned in another place,† the publishing business was first established in Fleet Street by the grandfather of the present head of the house, Mr. John McMurray, a Scotchman, who came to London after the Jacobite troubles to push his fortunes. It was a bold step of John Murray the elder to venture so far west, and so far not only from Paternoster Row, but from that highway of literature, Fleet Street and the Strand; but it was amply justified by the result.

The elder Mr. John Murray died in 1793, and was succeeded by his son of the same name, one of whose earliest "hits" was Mrs. Rundell's "Cookery-book," the sale of which, we are told, proved even more remunerative, perhaps, than "Childe Harold." Becoming connected with Thomas Campbell and Sir Walter Scott, in 1809 Mr. Murray projected the *Quarterly Review*, as the recognised organ of the Tory party. The new review soon acquired a hold on the mind of the educated classes, which it had hardly lost at the end of half a century, in spite of the progress made by the cheaper monthly, weekly, and now daily press. The first editor

---

* See Dallas's "Recollections of Lord Byron."
† See Vol. I., p. 46.

of the *Quarterly* was William Gifford ; and among its earliest contributors were George Canning, John Hookham Frere, Sir Walter Scott, Byron, Dean Milman, and Jonathan Croker. "Some of the scholarship notices," says Mr. Cyrus Redding, in his "Fifty Years' Recollections," "are excellent. A selection of these, in three or four volumes, from the mass of high-flown rubbish and falsified pro-phecies of national ruin would be most useful. In in Albemarle Street. Byron himself has thus de-scribed the scene :—

> "The room's so full of wits and bards,
> Crabbes, Campbells, Crokers, Freres, and Wards."

Mr. Murray's dinner-parties included politicians and statesmen, as well as authors and artists. The second Mr. John Murray died in 1843, and was succeeded by his son, John Murray the third. Under his *régime* the house has published many

LONG'S HOTEL, BOND STREET. (*See page* 302.)

its classical articles, the *Review* as far outshone the *Edinburgh* as the *Edinburgh* outshone the *Quarterly* in the truth of its political predictions and that advocacy of improvement and reform for which its reputation is imperishable." Gifford, like many others who have risen in life, was extremely vain ; he would even go so far as to boast that he had the power of distributing literary reputations. "Yes," observed Sheridan, "and you deal them out so largely that you have left none for your-self !"

It was in Mr. Murray's establishment in Albe-marle Street that Byron and Scott first met, and here Southey made the acquaintance of Crabbe ; indeed, it has been said that almost all the literary magnates of the day were "four o'clock visitors" of the greatest works in history, travel, biography, art, and science of the present age, among which may be mentioned Dr. Livingstone's "Travels," Smiles's "Life of George Stephenson," and Darwin's "Origin of Species by Natural Selection ;" and the Handbooks of English Counties and Continental travel of late years brought out by this firm owe much to the personal assistance and superinten-dence of the head of the house. Mr. Murray has counted among his clients, besides the writers named above, Colonel Leake, Dean Milman, Sir Henry Holland, Henry Hallam, George Grote, Mrs. Somerville, Dean Stanley, and nearly all the most distinguished authors of the present century. We may add that the sign-board of Mr. MacMurray, or Murray, in Fleet Street, was the "Ship in full sail," a sign probably assumed by him in opposition to that of Messrs. Longman, a "Ship at anchor."

No. 7, on the opposite side of the street, now the Royal Thames Yacht Club, was formerly Grillon's Hotel. Here Louis XVIII. of France stayed in 1814, on his journey from Hartwell to France, to take his seat on the throne of the

do with politics. To it belonged most of the distinguished public men of the Regency, and of the reigns of George IV. and William IV. Here, every Wednesday during the Parliamentary season, its members dined together, "the feuds of the previous day being forgotten, or made the theme of pleasantry and genial humour at a table where all

PROFESSOR FARADAY. (*See page* 297.)

Bourbons, to which he had been restored mainly by the intervention of England. He was escorted from London to Dover by the Prince Regent himself. Out of this hotel grew a private club, called "Grillon's Club," which used to hold its meetings here. It was formed in 1813 by some members of both Houses of Parliament, who wished for some neutral ground on which they might meet, politics being strictly excluded. "Grillon's" differed from most of the other clubs of the first half of the present century in having nothing to

sets of opinions had their representatives. To this club belonged George Canning, Lord Dudley and Ward, Lord F. Leveson-Gower (afterwards better known as Lord Francis Egerton), Lord Harrowby, Lord Wharncliffe, Lord Clare, Sir Robert Harry Inglis, Mr. G. Agar-Ellis, Sir R. Wilmot-Horton, and Sir James Graham.

Here, and at the Clarendon Hotel, in New Bond Street, were held for many years the Roxburghe Club Dinners. In 1860, there was sold at the rooms of Messrs. Puttick and Simpson a collection of nearly eighty portraits of members of Grillon's Club, almost all of them members of Parliament and of various Governments, mostly engravings from private plates, after drawings by Slater, George Richmond, and other artists.

In this street are several large hotels, such as the Pulteney, the York, the St. George's, and the Albemarle. In the days of the Regency, when the club system was as yet in its infancy, the hotels at the West-end were much more frequented than now-a-days is the case. There was then a very large class of men, including Wellington, Nelson, Collingwood, Sir John Moore, and some few others, who seldom frequented the clubs. The persons to whom we refer, and amongst whom were many members of the sporting world, used to congregate at a few hotels, of which the "Clarendon," "Limmer's," "Ibbetson's," "Fladong's," "Stephens's," and "Grillon's" were the most fashionable. The "Clarendon," mentioned above, was at that time kept by a French cook, Jacquiers, who contrived to amass a large sum of money in the service of Louis XVIII. in England, and subsequently with Lord Darnley. This was the only public hotel where a genuine French dinner could be obtained, but the sum charged seldom amounted to less than three or four pounds ; a bottle of champagne or of claret in the year 1814 usually cost a guinea.

No. 23 has been for many years the home of different clubs, more or less successful. In 1808 the "Alfred" was established here ; it is described by Lord Dudley in his time, as "the dullest place in existence, the asylum of doting Tories and drivelling quidnuncs." Lord Byron was a member of this club, and he tells us that "it was pleasant, a little too sober and literary, and bored with Sotheby and Francis d'Ivernois ; but one met Rich, and Ward, and Valentia, and many other pleasant or known people." On the break-up of the "Alfred," another club was started here, called the "Westminster ;" but its career does not appear to have been altogether a flourishing one. At the Albemarle Hotel, at the junction of the street with Piccadilly, another club was inaugurated towards the close of 1875, and called "The Albemarle." It was established for the accommodation of both gentlemen and ladies. "This," observes one of the daily papers, "is a noble experiment, and upon its success depends the settlement of the question whether women as a body are feræ naturâ, or social and clubable animals."

At No. 22 are the rooms of the Royal Asiatic Society, the London Mathematical Society, and the British Association for the Advancement of Science. The first-mentioned of these societies was founded in 1823, for the investigation and encouragement of arts, science, and literature in connection with Asia. Its museum contains, inter alia, a choice collection of Persian, Chinese, and Sanskrit MSS., with Oriental arms and armour, and various other illustrations of the history, arts, and antiquities of the Eastern world. The British Association was established in 1831, for the purpose of affording scientific men, both of this and other countries, an opportunity of assembling together and discussing on scientific subjects, and for which purpose meetings of a week's duration are held annually in different parts of England.

The Royal Institution, near the north-east corner of this street, was established in 1799, mainly through the exertions of Count Rumford, the most able practical philosopher of the day, for the purpose of encouraging improvements in arts and manufactures. Its meetings were commenced in 1800, shortly before which time the proprietors of the original shares obtained a charter of incorporation for the purpose of helping on the introduction of useful and mechanical inventions and improvements, and for teaching, by courses of philosophical lectures and experiments, the application of science to the common purposes of life, whence the motto of the institution—"Illustrans commoda vitæ." The building is spacious and well adapted for the purposes to which it is applied ; it originally consisted of five private houses, which having been purchased by the institution, an imposing architectural front was added, from the designs of Mr. L. Vulliamy, consisting of fourteen fluted half-columns, of the Corinthian order, placed upon a stylobate ; and occupying the height of three floors, support an entablature and the attic storey. On the fascia is inscribed, "The Royal Institution of Great Britain." The lectures delivered here are of a very popular class, and are well attended. In the reading-room are deposited choice or rare specimens of art, taste, and virtu.

The institution has, since its foundation, undergone a very considerable change in constitution. Some years ago, in consequence of the low state of the funds, the majority of proprietors relinquished their proprietary claim, and became shareholders for life only ; the dissentients from such terms selling their respective shares to the institution for a stipulated sum. By this means and by some personal bequests, the funds were materially improved. About the year 1830 the Royal Institution acquired fresh fame as the scene of Professor Faraday's experimental researches in electricity, the success of which has few parallels in the records of modern science.

A native of Newington, Surrey, and the son of a working smith, Michael Faraday, as a boy, was apprenticed to a bookseller and bookbinder; and during his term of apprenticeship a few scientific works had occasionally fallen into his hands, among them being the treatise on "Electricity" in the "Encyclopædia Britannica," and Mrs. Marcet's "Conversations on Chemistry." The perusal of the first led to the construction of his first electrical machine with a glass phial, and this he speedily followed up by a variety of experiments. Through the kindness of Mr. Dance, a member of the Royal Institution and a customer of his master, young Faraday was enabled to attend the last four lectures delivered by Sir Humphry Davy, in the early part of 1812. In the following year he was appointed Chemical Assistant at the Royal Institution, under Sir Humphry as Honorary Professor, and Mr. Brande as Professor of Chemistry; and shortly afterwards he went abroad, as assistant and amanuensis to his patron, Sir Humphry Davy. On his return, after an absence of three years, Mr. Faraday resumed his duties, and took up his residence at the Royal Institution, where he remained almost till the day of his death. In 1827 he first appeared at the lecture-table in the great theatre, and he continued to deliver lectures on scientific subjects every year from that time. In 1831 he commenced the series of experimental researches in electricity which have been published from time to time in the "Transactions" of the Royal Society. In the year 1833, when Mr. Fuller founded the chair of chemistry called after his name in the Royal Institution, he nominated Mr. Faraday the first professor; and two years later Professor Faraday received from Lord Melbourne's Government a pension, as a recognition of the importance of his scientific discoveries. In 1836 he was appointed scientific adviser on lights at sea to the Trinity House, and in the same year became a member of the Senate of the University of London; and he was subsequently scientific adviser on the same subject to the Board of Trade. Professor Faraday was a corresponding member of the Academy of Sciences at Paris, a fellow of the Royal Society, and a member of several learned and scientific bodies, not only in this country, but also on the Continent, and in America. The University of Oxford conferred upon him the honorary degree of Doctor of Civil Laws. Late in life he settled down in retirement at Hampton Court Green, where he died in the year 1867. The *Athenæum*, in recording his death, observes that "nothing can be written about his career without entering upon the whole history of electricity in connection with

magnetism during the last fifty years;" and that his great talents were "overshadowed in private life by his singular modesty and gentleness."

Among the members of the scientific world who have lectured within the walls of the institution with which Faraday was so long and so honourably connected, have been Murchison, Lyell, Sedgwick, Whewell, Tyndall, and Huxley. The scientific world has likewise been benefited by a "Journal" published at the expense of the Royal Institution, in a less costly, and consequently more available, form than that of the average of "Transactions" and "Proceedings."

Opposite to the Royal Institution is St. George's Chapel, a private "chapel of ease"; it is a building with little or no architectural pretensions. In fact, the religious edifices in this neighbourhood take the shape of proprietary chapels rather than of parish churches. "In this enlightened age," says Pennant, with dry humour, "it was found that 'godliness was profitable to many.' Accordingly the projector, the architect, the mason, the carpenter, and the plasterer united their powers. A chapel was erected, well pewed, well warmed, dedicated and consecrated. A captivating preacher is next provided, the pews are filled, and the good undertakers amply repaid by the pious tenantry."

Lord Orkney and Lord Paulet were living in Albemarle Street in 1708. Here, too, in 1785, died Richard Glover, the poet, the author of "Leonidas" and "Admiral Hosier's Ghost."

In 1852 the Roman Catholics established, at Crawley's Hotel, in Albemarle Street, a club, which they called the "Stafford-Street Club," from its entrance being in that thoroughfare, which crosses Albemarle Street about midway. This was the first and only instance of a London club named from a street, though such a practice is common in Dublin; but, according to Mr. John Timbs, it was common in the last century, in the early part of which many "street clubs" were formed, composed of members all living in the same thoroughfare, so that a man had but to stir a few houses from his own door to enjoy his club and the society of his neighbours. "There was also," observes Mr. Timbs, " another inducement, for the streets of London were then so unsafe that the nearer to his home a man's club lay, the better for his clothes and his purse. Even riders in coaches were not safe from mounted footpads and from the danger of upsets in the huge ruts and pits which intersected the streets. But the passenger who could not afford a coach had to pick his way after dark along dimly-lighted, ill-paved thoroughfares, seamed by filthy open kennels, besprinkled from projecting spouts, bordered by gaping cellars, guarded by feeble old watchmen, and beset with daring street robbers and lawless 'rake-hells,' of the Mohock tribe, who banded into companies, and spread terror and dismay through the streets." The "street club," therefore, arose out of the instinct of mutual protection. It may be added that Stafford Street occupies as nearly as possible the site of Clarendon House, already mentioned by us under Piccadilly.

At the northern end of Albemarle Street, connecting Dover Street and Old Bond Street, is Grafton Street, which consists of spacious and old-fashioned mansions. At the house of Sir Ralph Payne (afterwards better known as the eccentric Lord Lavington) the leaders of the Opposition in Pitt's days frequently met. Erskine, having one day dined there, found himself so indisposed as to be obliged to retire after dinner to another apartment. Lady Payne, who was incessant in her attentions to him, inquired, when he returned to the company, how he found himself. Erskine took out a piece of paper, and wrote on it—

"'Tis true I am ill, but I cannot complain,
　For he never knew *Pleasure* who never knew *Payne*."

"Sir Ralph, with whom I was well acquainted," writes Sir Nathaniel William Wraxall, "always appeared to be a good-natured, pleasing, well-bred man ; but he was reported not always to treat his wife with kindness. Sheridan, calling on her one morning, found her in tears, which she placed, however, to the account of her monkey, who had expired only an hour or two before, and for whose loss she expressed deep regret. 'Pray write me an epitaph for him,' added she ; 'his name was *Ned*.' Sheridan instantly penned these lines :—

　　'Alas ! poor Ned !
　　My monkey's dead !
　　I had rather by half
　　It had been Sir Ralph !'"

At No. 4 in this street Henry, first Lord Brougham, resided during the last nineteen or twenty years of his life. He was born at Edinburgh in 1778, and coming to London to push his fortunes at the Bar, first made himself known to the political world by his advocacy of Queen Caroline, and afterwards by his zeal in the cause of Reform and Education. He was suddenly raised to the woolsack by the Whig party on their attaining to place and power under Lord Grey in 1830 ; but, for reasons never yet fully explained, he was not re-appointed after the Conservative interregnum five years later. He died somewhat suddenly at his residence at Cannes, in the south

of France, in 1868. He was a mathematician, a man of science, a linguist, and an orator, as well as a lawyer and statesman ; indeed, his general knowledge was so extensive that it was said of him in satire, that " if he had only known a little law he would have known a little of everything." His house was afterwards the Turf Club.

Here, at No. 19, lived for the last half century of his life Sir Alleyne Fitzherbert, a distinguished diplomatist, afterwards known as Lord St. Helen's, who, after having tried in early life nearly all the capitals of Europe, used to maintain that there was no other place but London that was worth living in. He was true to his principles, and he seldom if ever quitted the West-end, either winter or summer. He died in 1838.

Sir William Scott, afterwards Lord Stowell, who, in his sixty-eighth year, married the Dowager Marchioness of Sligo, lived for some time in this street. In our description of Doctors' Commons* will be found a detailed account of Sir William's marriage with this lady, as well as an anecdote referring more particularly to his residence in Grafton Street.

No. 10 was for many years the residence of Mr. William Holmes, M.P. for Berwick, and the "whipper-in" of the Tories in the House of Commons. He was an especial favourite of the Great Duke and of Sir Robert Peel, who used often to " drop in" upon him here.

Grafton Street, on account of its retired situation and the absence of a direct thoroughfare, has for several years been, as it were, an offshoot of "Club-land." At the present time there are the Grafton and the Junior Oxford and Cambridge, the latter occupying what was formerly the home of the Marlborough. The Turf Club, mentioned above, removed in 1875-6 to their new quarters in Piccadilly. In the south-east corner of this street Benjamin Tabart, the publisher, for some time had his shop ; his picture-books for children are well known.

Bond Street, which we now enter, dates from the year 1686, when it was built by Sir Thomas Bond. "In 1700," says Pennant, "Bond Street was built no further than the west end of Clifford Street. New Bond Street was at that time an open field, called the Conduit Mead, from one of the conduits which supplied this part of the town with water. Hatton, writing in 1708, describes it as "a fine new street, mostly inhabited by nobility and gentry."

The *Weekly Journal* of June 1st, 1717, observes,

"The new buildings between Bond Street and Mary-le-bone go on with all possible diligence, and the houses even let and sell before they are built. They are already in great forwardness." It is obvious to remark that as Old and New Bond Streets are one street, it is the latter to which allusion is evidently made in the above extract. Even a century and a half ago Bond Street was a region of fashion; or, to use the words of Pennant, in spite of the loose expression, "it abounded with shopkeepers of both sexes of superior taste." The same writer remarks, however, in 1805, that if its builder had been able to foresee the extreme fashion in reserve for the street, he would have made it wider. "But this," he philosophises, "is a fortunate circumstance for the Bond Street loungers, who thus get a nearer glimpse of the fashionable and generally titled ladies that pass and repass from two to five o'clock." Indeed, even down to the days of the Regency and the opening of Regent Street, the chief fashionable lounge in the West-end was along Old and New Bond Street; and as lately as the year 1823, the morning was the correct time for putting in an appearance there during "the London season."

The reader will be amused, we think, with the following extract from "A New Critical Review of the Public Buildings of London," in the year 1736:—"There is nothing in the whole prodigious length of the two Bond Streets or in any of the adjacent places, though almost all erected within our memories, that has anything worth our attention; several little wretched attempts there are at foppery in building, but they are too inconsiderable even for censure." How little could the writer of these lines imagine that in the course of a few years Bond Street, Old and New, would become one of the most fashionable streets of the district, and that its shops would be the chief emporium of articles of beauty and taste, only, at a later period, outdone by those of Regent Street.

"In February, 1768," writes Sir Walter Scott, "Lawrence Sterne expired at his lodgings in Bond Street, London, his frame exhausted by a long debilitating illness. There was something in the manner of his death singularly resembling the particulars detailed by Mrs. Quickly, as attending that of Falstaff, the compeer of 'Yorick,' for infinite jest, however unlike in other particulars." In vain did the female attendant, a lodging-house servant, chafe his cold feet, in order to restore his circulation. He complained that the cold came up higher, and he died without a groan. "His death took place much in the manner in which he himself had wished, and the last kind offices were rendered him not in his own house, or by the hand of kindred affection, but in a hired lodging and by strangers." Dr. Ferrier, however, adds, "I have been told his attendants robbed him even of his gold sleeve-buttons while he was expiring." Mr. P. Cunningham, in his "Handbook of London," identifies the house in which he died as No. 41 on the west side, "the silk-bag shop, now (1849) a cheese-monger's shop." His death, the date of which most writers fix as March 18th, 1786, was some-what sudden, for he had only just "come back to his lodgings in Bond Street" (writes Thackeray) "with his 'Sentimental Journey' to launch upon the town, eager as ever for praise and pleasure, as vain, as wicked, as witty, and as false as he had ever been, when death seized the feeble wretch."

In "Anecdotes of Distinguished Men," we read that "Sterne was no strict priest, but, as a clergy-man, not likely to hear with indifference his whole fraternity treated contemptuously. Being one day in a coffee-house, he observed a spruce powdered young fellow by the fireside, who was speaking of the clergy, in a mass, as a body of disciplined impostors and systematic hypocrites. Sterne got up while the young man was haranguing, and approached towards the fire, patting and coaxing all the way a favourite little dog. Coming at length towards the gentleman, he took up the dog, still continuing to pat him, and addressed the young fellow. 'Sir, this would be the prettiest little animal in the world had he not one disorder!' 'What disorder is that?' replied the young fellow. 'Why, sir,' said Sterne, 'one that always makes him bark when he sees a gentleman in black.' 'That is a singular disorder,' rejoined the young fellow; 'pray how long has he had it?' 'Sir,' replied Sterne, looking at him with affected gentleness, 'ever since he was a puppy!'"

Sterne was among the frequenters of Drury Lane Theatre in the days of Garrick. Mr. Cradock one day meeting him there, asked him why he did not try his hand on a comedy, especially as he was so intimate with the great actor. With tears in his eyes, Sterne replied, that there were two reasons which prevented him: firstly, that he had not the gifts of the comic muse; and secondly, that he was wholly unacquainted with the business of the stage. Possibly he was right; but we cannot help regretting that the author of "Tristram Shandy" never made an effort in that direction.

Poor Sterne was interred in the burial-ground belonging to St. George's, Hanover Square, where, curiously enough, a wrong date was cut upon his tombstone. He died poor, if not actually in debt. A letter addressed by him (probably from his lodgings) to Garrick, asking for a loan of ten pounds, just before leaving town on his "Sentimental Journey," is printed in *fac-simile* in Smith's "Historical and Literary Curiosities."

In this street, in 1769, lodged Pascal Paoli, the patriot of Corsica, and here he was constantly visited by Boswell, who, if the truth must be told, made himself somewhat foolishly conspicuous by dancing attendance upon him—so much so, indeed,

was paid for the painting of an English artist during his life-time.

Among the other eminent inhabitants of this street were Sir Thomas Lawrence, the distinguished President of the Royal Academy, and the Countess of Macclesfield, mother of the poet, Richard Savage. "She died here," says Mr. Peter Cunningham, "Oct. 11th, 1753, surviving both Savage and the publication of his 'Life' by Johnson."

GLOUCESTER HOUSE, PICCADILLY. (*See page* 286.)

as to be nicknamed "Corsica Boswell." Here, too, Boswell introduced Dr. Johnson to the General, thereby realising a proud feeling of hope which he thus expressed in his "Journey to Corsica:"— "What an idea may we not form of an interview between such a scholar and philosopher as Johnson, and such a legislator and general as Paoli?"

Here, too, Boswell had lodgings, where he would often entertain Dr. Johnson, Reynolds, and the rest of the literary circle of his time. It was stated in the *Times* of April 26th, 1875, that a picture of the interior of these lodgings, with portraits of the guests, a fancy scene, painted by Mr. W. P. Frith, was sold at Messrs. Christie and Manson's rooms, a few days before the above date, for upwards of £4,000—a larger sum than ever

At No. 24 Old Bond Street are the offices of the Artists' General Benevolent Institution, Artists' Orphan Fund, and the Arundel Society for Promoting the Knowledge of Art. The first-named of these institutions was founded in 1814, and incorporated in 1842; it affords relief to artists, whether members or not, as well as to their widows and children. The Arundel Society, which has for its object the promotion of the knowledge of art, by copying, reproducing, and publishing the most important works of the ancient masters, was founded in 1848, and is called after Thomas Howard, the celebrated Earl of Arundel in the reigns of James I. and Charles I., who has deservedly been called "the Father of *virtu* in England, and the Macenas of all politer arts," and whom we have already introduced to our readers in our account of Arundel House in the Strand.* Its members are divided into three classes—associates, life and annual subscribers, and honorary members—and its funds are applied to the publication of essays on art subjects, chromo-lithographs, engravings, photographs, &c., of the highest order of mediæval art; and it may safely be asserted that no society has done more than the Arundel in reviving a general appreciation of mediæval art. A minute account of the results achieved by the society may be found in two works issued by its secretary, Mr. F. W. Maynard, and entitled respectively

we may add, on the authority of Mr J. Larwood, in his " History of Sign-boards," that the sign of the " Coventry Cross " was borne by a mercer in New Bond Street at the end of the eighteenth century, this particular sign evidently being chosen on account of the silk ribbons manufactured in that town.

Of the librarians at different times inhabiting this street was Ebers, who lived at No. 27, and who, as Mr. John Timbs tells us, " in seven years lost £44,080 by the Italian Opera House, Haymarket." Of Hookham's Library, one of the fashionable lounges towards the close of the last

THE LONDON UNIVERSITY, BURLINGTON GARDENS. (*See page* 304.)

" Twenty Years " and " Five Years of the Arundel Society."

In this neighbourhood a club of gentlemen, mostly members of one or other of the Houses of Parliament, calling themselves " The Bohemians," still hold their musical Sunday gatherings, though their exact *locale* is kept a secret from the outer world. Bond Street, in fact, has long ranked high in the musical world for its devotion to the divine art.

The keepers of music-shops, it is well known, have usually adhered to the primitive practice of taking for signs some one or other of the instruments in which they deal, as, for instance, the " Hautboy," " The Violin," " The German Flute ; " and Messrs. Novello, the great musical publishers in Cheapside, have so far adhered to the custom as to carry on their trade under the sign of the " Golden Crotchet." While on the subject of signs

century, mention is thus made in George Colman's " Broad Grins : "—

" For novels should their critick hints succeed,
    The Muses might fare better when they took 'em ;
But it would fare extremely ill indeed
    With gentle Mr. Lane and Messieurs Hookham."

In New Bond Street, although, perhaps, not so ostentatious as those in the more general thoroughfares, such as Oxford Street or Regent Street, many of the shops are, nevertheless, extremely elegant, and the articles exhibited for sale are of the most *recherché* description. At the corner of Bruton Street is the shop of Mr. C. Hancocks, the great manufacturing jeweller. At 156 are the show-rooms of Messrs. Hunt and Roskell, formerly Storr and Mortimer, who succeeded to a large part of the connection of Mr. Hamlet. At No. 160 are the extensive show-rooms of Messrs. Copeland and Co. (formerly Messrs. Copeland and Spode), the eminent porcelain manufacturers, of Stoke-upon-Trent, almost the only rivals of Messrs. Wedgwood,

* See Vol. III., p. 71.

whom we have already mentioned in our account of the neighbourhood of Lincoln's Inn Fields.* Mr. Alderman Copeland, formerly Lord Mayor of London, was head of this firm.

At No. 116 in this street, Miss Clark, the great-granddaughter of Theodore, King of Corsica (who was buried at St. Anne's Church, Soho, and of whom we have already given some account in a former chapter †), was established as a miniature-painter early in the present century. Her card of address, with her modest prices and hours of attendance, is given *in extenso* in John Timbs' "Romance of London."

Dealers in pictures and other branches of the fine arts are numerous in this street; besides which the picture-galleries offer opportunities for a pleasing promenade for such as care to avail themselves of them. Foremost among these is the Doré Gallery, situated at No. 35. This exhibition, which includes some of the choicest productions of the distinguished French artist, M. Gustave Doré, is open daily all the year round. Among the pictures exhibited here are the "Massacre of the Innocents," the "Dream of Pilate's Wife," the "Night of the Crucifixion," and "Christ leaving the Prætorium." Of the last-named work the *Examiner* thus observes :—"We must go back to the Italian painters of the sixteenth century to find a picture worthy of being classed with this most stupendous achievement of the young French master. In gravity and magnitude of purpose, no less than in the scope and power of his imagination, he towers like a Colossus among his contemporaries."

At No. 47 is the Hanover Gallery, frequently used for the exhibition of pictures. No. 136 is the Grosvenor Gallery, which has become one of the popular exhibitions of the "London season," the pictures shown here being principally those of the "æsthetic" school. Scores of exhibitions of pictures and other curiosities, too numerous to particularise, have at various times existed in New Bond Street and its neighbourhood. The following curious notice of one such exhibition, quoted from the *Morning Chronicle*, of March 18, 1799, may be of interest to our readers in connection with this street :—"The real embalmed head of the powerful and renowned usurper, Oliver Cromwell, with the original dies for the medals struck in honour of his victory at Dunbar, are now exhibited at No. 5, in Mead Court, Old Bond Street (where the rattlesnake was shown last year); a genuine narrative relating to the acquisition, con-

cealment, and preservation of these articles to be had at the place of exhibition."

Cromwell's head, it appears, was exhibited here by an individual named Cox, who kept a museum of curiosities, and who had purchased it from one of the Russell family, in whose hands it had been for a century. When Cox parted with his museum, he sold the head to three individuals who all in their turn met with sudden deaths, and the head became the property of the daughters or nieces of the last survivor. These ladies, as we have mentioned in a previous chapter, being nervous at the idea of keeping in their house a relic so fatal, sold it to a medical man named Wilkinson.

At No. 21, in New Bond Street, was exhibited, in 1831, Haydon's picture of "Napoleon at St. Helena," painted for Sir Robert Peel, and upon which Wordsworth wrote one of his most beautiful sonnets.

Among the distinguished residents of this street Mr. Cunningham enumerates General Sir Thomas Picton, who fell at Waterloo, and Lord Nelson, who, as Southey tells us in his charming biography, was lodging here in 1797, after the battle of St. Vincent, and at the time when the news reached London of Lord Duncan's victory off Camperdown. By some accident or other the house was not illuminated; but when the mob was told that Admiral Nelson lay there in bed, badly wounded, it went off without breaking the windows.

At Long's Hotel, as we learn from his "Life" by Tommy Moore, Byron dined in company with Sir Walter Scott; and another hotel in this same street, "Stevens's," is mentioned by the same authority as one of Byron's "old haunts."

At No. 148, over a grocer's shop, the eccentric Lord Camelford had lodgings, preferring them to his magnificent mansion of Camelford House. It is recorded of him that in 1801, when all London was lit up with a general illumination on account of "the peace," no persuasion of friends, or of his landlord, could induce him to suffer a candle to be put in his windows. The mob, of course, attacked the house, and saluted his windows with a shower of stones. Lord Camelford rushed out with a pistol in his hand, and it seemed as if the day of public rejoicing was about to be stained with bloodshed. At last a friend and companion induced him to exchange his pistol for a good stout cudgel, which he laid about him right and left, till at length, overpowered by numbers, he was rolled over and over in the gutter, and glad to beat a retreat indoors, for once in his life crest-fallen. A year or two later we find his lordship still living here, when he fought with Captain Best that

---

memorable duel in which he fell mortally wounded "in the fields behind Holland House." The interior of Lord Camelford's lodgings is thus described in a note to the "Rejected Addresses:" —"Over the fire-place in the drawing-room . . . . were ornaments strongly expressive of the pugnacity of the peer. A long, thick bludgeon lay horizontally supported by two brass hooks. Above this was placed parallel one of lesser dimensions, until a pyramid of weapons gradually arose tapering to a horsewhip." No doubt its walls were decorated with portraits of the first "bruisers" of the day, and of the heroes of the "cock-pits," which then were still in vogue.

In this street, too, were the lodgings of "Squire Alworthy," a personage familiar to every reader of Fielding's "Tom Jones;" and many of the most touching scenes in that novel are laid in this thoroughfare.

Between Old Bond Street and Albemarle Street, on the site of a part of the gardens of Clarendon House (already described by us in our walk along Piccadilly), stood, till 1870, the Clarendon Hotel, one of the largest establishments of the kind in London. It had a frontage to either street, and contained large suites of apartments where royal and noble personages used to put up during their stay in London. Official banquets, too, were often held here in the first decade of Her Majesty's reign. Here were held the meetings of the Association of Baronets, instituted by the late amiable visionary, Sir Richard Broun, for the purpose of asserting the right of members of that order to the use of heraldic supporters, a coronet, the prefix of "honourable," and other more tangible and substantial advantages; but the association quietly died a natural death.

Among the records of the house was the *menu* of a dinner given by the late Lord Chesterfield in the year 1835, on resigning his office as Master of the Buckhounds. It is a curiosity in its way—the way of costly luxury; it is printed *in extenso* in the second volume of the "Club Life of London."

The mansion, before its conversion into an hotel, was occupied for two or three seasons by the Earl of Chatham as his town residence.

Stevens's Hotel, in Bond Street, was fashionable in the days of the Regency as the head-quarters for officers in the army, and "men about town." Captain Gronow tells us in his "Reminiscences" that if a stranger wanted to dine there, he would be "stared at by the servants and very solemnly assured that there was no table vacant." He adds that it was no uncommon thing to see thirty or even forty saddle-horses or tilburies waiting outside the

doors of this hotel; and that two of his old Welsh friends who resided here in 1815 qualified themselves for residence within its walls—in the eyes of "mine host," at all events—by "disposing of five bottles of wine daily." It is to be hoped that the gallant captain meant to add "between them;" but his phrase is a little ambiguous.

In this street, on its eastern side, about the year 1820, was a bazaar, called the Western Exchange, consisting of only one large room, well furnished with a variety of stalls. It had an entrance in the rear into the Burlington Arcade. The bazaar, however, proved a failure, and soon closed. Another bazaar was built in this street in 1879.

Clifford Street, which connects the north end of Savile Row with Bond Street, cutting Old Burlington Street at right angles, was built about the year 1740, and perpetuates the name of the Cliffords, Earls of Cumberland, the daughter and heiress of the last holder of that title having been the mother of the first Lord Burlington.

The house No. 7 was inhabited by Dr. Anthony Addington, a physician in good practice, and the father of Henry Addington, the first Lord Sidmouth, who was born in 1757, and who succeeded Pitt as Premier in 1801. It will be remembered that the latter, in some of the squibs of the day, was dubbed "The Doctor," partly, perhaps, owing to his parentage, partly to the story that it was by his advice that a pillow of hops was provided to cure the sleeplessness of George III. At No. 5 in this street Robert Liston, the celebrated surgeon, was living in the year 1841.

In this street, towards the end of the last century, was a debating society which lasted some few years. It was styled the Clifford Street Club, and met at the "Clifford Street Coffee House." Among its members were Lord Charles Townshend, and George Canning in his early prime. Political questions were here discussed, generally from a Liberal point of view, while foaming jugs of porter crowned the tables; and it was here that Canning first practised his tongue in political debate, on such subjects as the French Revolution. During the "sittings" of this club, porter was the only beverage indulged in by its members; and on one occasion, as John Timbs tells us, Canning compared a pot of this liquor to the eloquence of Mirabeau "as empty and vapid as his patriotism—'foam and froth at the top, heavy and muddy within.'"

On the north side is the shop of Messrs. Stulz, the fashionable tailors of the days of the Regency, who are said to have had half the members of the clubs of St. James's on their books.

At right angles with Bond Street, and forming,

together with Vigo Street, a direct communication into Regent Street, is the thoroughfare known as Burlington Gardens. Built about the year 1729, it consisted at first of small houses, scattered irregularly up and down. At the south-west corner, where the Gardens join Bond Street, and extending back to the Arcade, is the large warehouse of Messrs. Atkinson, the perfumers, established here in 1799. The opposite corner is occupied by the fashionable haircutters, Messrs. Truefitt, who have held it since 1810.

On the south side of Burlington Gardens, between the Arcade and the Albany, are the new buildings of the London University. The building, which is from the designs of Mr. Pennethorne, and was opened by Her Majesty in person early in the year 1870, occupies a site of about 250 feet long by 150 feet in depth, on which formerly grew two lines of tall poplars, which threw a graceful and grateful shadow over Burlington Gardens. The elevation is in the ornate Italian style, such as would have gladdened the heart of so great an admirer of classical architecture as the old Earl of Burlington, if he could wake up to life again.

As regards its ground-plan, it consists of two oblong blocks, the smaller of which stands behind and to the south of the principal one. The front presents a central portion of 120 feet long, flanked by two square towers, and extended further east and west by wings two storeys in height. These towers carry a clock and a sun-dial, and between them is a projecting portico, with five entrances. The portico, the centre, and the wings are all surmounted by ornate balustrades, on the pedestals of which are placed statues of eminent men, selected as fitting representatives of the various forms of academic culture. The statues over the portico are seated, those on the roof are standing, and there are also other standing figures in niches on the ground floor of each wing. The principal figures are those on the balustrade of the portico. These are by Mr. Joseph Durham—viz., Newton, Bentham, Milton, and Harvey, as representatives of the four Faculties of Science, Law, Arts, and Medicine. The figures on the central roof represent ancient culture in the persons of Galen, Cicero, Aristotle, Plato, Archimedes, and Justinian, the first three by Westmacott, and the last three by Woodington. The eastern wing is devoted to illustrious foreigners. On the roof-line are Galileo, Goëthe, and Laplace, by Wyon; in the niches are Leibnitz, Cuvier, and Linnæus, by MacDowell. The balustrade of the west wing is adorned with English worthies—Hunter, Hume, and Davy, by Noble; the niches being occupied by Adam Smith,

John Locke, and Bacon, by Theed. The individuals chosen to be represented, and also the sculptors, were selected by the joint action of the Senate of the University and the Metropolitan Board of Works. It was at first proposed to put Shakespeare in the place occupied by Milton, but the idea was overruled on the ground that the genius of the great dramatist was quite independent of academic instruction or rules. A statue of Shakespeare, however, has since been placed in the interior of the building.

Opposite to the centre of the portico is the principal entrance, with rooms to the right and left; beyond these is a fine and spacious corridor, running east and west. At the extreme west is the great library, used also as an examination hall, occupying the whole of that wing. To the east is the great theatre, or lecture hall, used for the purpose of conferring degrees, and capable of seating eight hundred persons, the benches rising behind one another after the fashion of an amphitheatre. It is well planned as to its acoustic properties. It is used occasionally, however, for other besides strictly academic purposes, such as for the meetings of the Royal Geographical Society. At each end of the corridor above mentioned are passages leading to the smaller examination halls and private rooms for the use of the examiners. The great staircase occupies a lofty hall, and leads to the first floor, where there is a library and common room for the use of the graduates. The staircase has marble balusters and hand-rails, and the floor of the main landing also is of polished marble. On this floor are also the senate-room and the offices of the registrar of the University.

The building is, perhaps, the finest modern example in England of the most refined and enriched style of Italian or "Palladian" architecture. The decorations are elaborate, abundant, and massive, and remarkable for a general character of flatness which is without a parallel in our time, and helps to subordinate mere ornamentation to the main outlines of form.

It is important to note here that the University of London is an examining, not strictly a teaching body. Its essential function is the bestowal of academical degrees on qualified candidates from all classes and denominations of Her Majesty's subjects, without distinction of caste or creed; and it was long without a home. For many years, in fact, since its commencement in 1838, when it grew out of the University, now University College, in Gower Street, it lived, so to speak, in furnished apartments, and, as a matter of course, had to shift its quarters from time to time. In consequence, it did not hold the position which it deserved in the republic of art, science, and the *belles lettres*. It is now, however, fairly at the head of all the higher education of the kingdom which is not given at Oxford and Cambridge; not, however, conferring it, but testing it from time to time. The number of candidates seeking to pass its examinations has now risen from twenty-three in the first year of Her Majesty's reign to about fifteen hundred annually; and it is honourably distinguished by the firmness with which it has insisted on a high standard being maintained by all who seek to become graduates of it. The Council comprises, or has comprised, many of the most eminent scholars and statesmen of the age, such as Grote, Thirlwall, Brougham, and Macaulay. Its board of examiners consists of men of high standing in the several branches of learning, who hold their appointments from year to year, when they are usually re-elected.

It is not a little singular to record the fact that in the first instance, when the Liberal party were in power, Mr. Pennethorne prepared a classical design for the university, being commissioned by Mr. Cowper-Temple, then Chief Commissioner of Public Buildings, but that when the Conservatives came into office in 1866, Lord John Manners insisted on an ecclesiastical structure being substituted, and that this was carried up some six or eight feet above the ground, when another change of Ministry revived the former commission, and the Palladian style conquered and prevailed.

Opposite, and extending northward to Clifford Street, is Old Burlington Street. If there is to be found in the West-end a dull, heavy, and unattractive street, it is this; and yet, in 1736, the author of "A New Critical Review of the Public Buildings" speaks of it as containing houses "in the finest taste of any common buildings that we can see anywhere; without the least affectation of ornament or seeming design at any remarkable elegance." He adds, "They need no ornament to make them remarkable." It is evident that the standard of architectural merit and beauty has considerably altered since the reign of George II. Mr. Planché tells us, in his agreeable "Recollections," that he remembers seeing blood running in kennels in Burlington Street, into which men, and women too, were dipping sticks and handkerchiefs, in front of the residence of Mr. F. Robinson ("Prosperity Robinson," afterwards Lord Goderich and Earl of Ripon), during the corn-law riots in 1815.

At the north end of this street, facing Boyle Street, a small and unimportant thoroughfare which connects the north end of Savile Row with that of Old Burlington Street, stood a large, heavy, and gloomy building, apparently almost without windows or doors. It was a school founded by Lady Burlington "for the maintenance, clothing, and education of eighty female children." It covered part of what was originally called the "Ten-Acres-Field." A new scheme for the remodelling of this institution was propounded in 1875–6; its endowment has since been made available for the education of boys as well as girls, and the school rebuilt. The name of Boyle Street serves to perpetuate yet another title of the house of Burlington

Adjoining this building on the east is the office of Messrs. Rushworth and Jarvis, the house agents and auctioneers. It is said to occupy the site of a summer-house which stood at the north-east corner of the gardens of Lord Burlington's mansion. At No. 8 lived Mr. Samuel Pepys Cockerell, F.S.A., father of the late Professor Cockerell, R.A.

At the corner of this street is the Burlington Hotel. Here Miss Florence Nightingale used to stay when in London, before and after the Crimean war, when her name first became known on account of her exertions in the cause of the sanitary condition of the British army.

On the north side of Burlington Gardens, occupying the space between Savile Row and Old Burlington Street, stands a handsome building used as the western branch of the Bank of England, and known as Uxbridge House. It was built by Vardy, assisted by Joseph Bonomi, for the first Earl of Uxbridge, the father of Field-Marshal, the first Marquis of Anglesey, who lost his leg at Waterloo. It was sold by his son and successor about the year 1855. It stands upon the site of a still earlier mansion, known as Queensberry House, which was built by Leoni for the celebrated Duke of Queensberry, the father of the "Piccadilly Duke" already mentioned. The poet Gay lived for many years as an inmate of its hospitable halls, enjoying the patronage and friendship of the duke, and of his eccentric wife, so well known to our readers as the friend of Pope, and celebrated in song as

"Kitty ever bright and young."

If we may believe Pope, who knew him well, Gay was quite a child of nature, wholly without art or design; one who spoke just what he thought and as he thought it. He dangled for twenty years about the Court, and at last obtained the offer of being made usher to the young princess. Secretary Craggs made Gay a present of stock in the South Sea year; and he was once worth £20,000, but lost it all again. He got about £500 by the first *Beggar's Opera*, and £1,100 or £1,200 by the second. Like most literary men, he was negligent of ways and means, and a bad manager. Latterly, however, the Duke of Queensberry took his money into his own hands, letting him have only what was necessary out of it, and as he lived at the duke's table, he could not have occasion for any large outlay; consequently he died worth upwards of £3,000.

Thackeray accuses the Duke and Duchess of Queensberry of having over-fed the poetical Gay,

Court. Lord Hervey, in his "Memoirs of the Reign of George II.," has thus characteristically described this *fracas*:—"Among the remarkable occurrences of this winter [1729], I cannot help relating that of the Duchess of Queensberry being forbid the Court, and the occasion of it. One Gay, a poet, had written a ballad opera, which was thought to reflect a little upon the Court, and a good deal upon the minister. It was called *The*

UXBRIDGE HOUSE. (*See page* 305.)

who, he says, "was lapped in cotton, and had his plate of chicken, and his saucer of cream, and frisked, and barked, and wheezed, and grew fat, and so ended." Congreve testifies that Gay was a great eater. "As the French philosopher used to prove his existence by *cogito, ergo sum*, the greatest proof of Gay's existence is *edit, ergo est*." It is not often now-a-days that literature finds itself so liberally rewarded in the persons of its followers.

The high-spirited Duchess of Queensberry, to whose kind intervention with Lord Bute even Thurlow was indebted for his silk gown, was Catherine Hyde, grand-daughter of the great Lord Clarendon. In order to promote the services of Gay, induced by her extraordinary friendship for him, the duchess sacrificed even the favour of the

Beggar's Opera, and had a prodigious run, and was so extremely pretty in its kind, that even those who were most glanced at in the satire had prudence enough to disguise their resentment by chiming in with the universal applause with which it was performed. Gay, who had attached himself to Mrs. Howard (then one of the ladies of the bed-chamber to Queen Caroline), and been disappointed of preferment at Court, finding this couched satire upon those to whom he imputed his disappointment succeed so well, wrote a second part to this opera, less pretty, but more abusive, and so little disguised that Sir Robert Walpole resolved, rather than suffer himself to be produced for thirty nights together upon the stage in the person of a highwayman, to make use of his friend, the Duke of Grafton's authority, as Lord Chamberlain, to put a stop to the representation of it. Accordingly this theatrical craftsman was prohibited at every playhouse. Gay, irritated at this bar thrown in the way both of his interest and revenge, zested this work with some supplemental invectives, and resolved to print it by subscription. The Duchess of Queensberry set herself at the head

King, when he came into the drawing-room, seeing her Grace very busy in a corner with three or four men, asked her what she had been doing. She answered, 'What must be agreeable, she was sure, to anybody so humane as his Majesty, for it was an act of charity, and a charity to which she did not despair of bringing his Majesty to contribute.' Enough was said for each to understand the other,

RICHARD BRINSLEY SHERIDAN. (*See page* 311.)

of this undertaking, and solicited every mortal that came in her way, or in whose way she could put herself, to subscribe. To a woman of her quality, proverbially beautiful, and at the top of the polite and fashionable world, people were ashamed to refuse a guinea, though they were afraid to give it. Her solicitations were so universal and so pressing that she came even into the Queen's apartment, went round the drawing-room, and made even the King's servants contribute to the printing of a thing which the King had forbid being acted. The

and though the King did not then (as the Duchess of Queensberry reported) appear at all angry, yet the proceeding of her Grace's, when talked over in private between his Majesty and the Queen, was so resented, that Mr. Stanhope, then Vice-Chamberlain to the King, was sent in form to the Duchess of Queensberry, to desire her to forbear coming to Court. His message was verbal. Her answer, for fear of mistakes, she desired to send in writing; she wrote it on the spot, and this is the literal copy :—

"'Feb. 27th, 1728-9.

"'The Duchess of Queensberry is surprised and well pleased that the King hath given her so agreeable a command as to stay from Court, where she never came for diversion, but to bestow a great civility on the King and Queen: she hopes by such an unprecedented order as this is, that the King will see as few as he wishes at his Court, particularly such as dare to think or speak the truth. I dare not do otherwise, and ought not, nor could have imagined that it would not have been the very highest compliment that I could possibly pay the King, to endeavour to support truth and innocence in his house, particularly when the King and Queen both told me that they had not read Mr. Gay's play. I have certainly done right, then, to stand by my own words rather than his Grace of Grafton's, who hath neither made use of truth, judgment, nor honour, through this whole affair, either for himself or his friends.

C. QUEENSBERRY.'

"When her Grace had finished this paper, drawn with more spirit than accuracy, she gave it to Mr. Stanhope, who desired her to think again, asked pardon for being so impertinent as to offer her any advice, but begged she would give him leave to carry an answer less rough than that she had put into his hands. Upon this she wrote another, but so much more disrespectful, that he desired the first again, and delivered it. Most people blamed the Court upon this occasion. What the Duchess of Queensberry did was certainly impertinent; but the manner of resenting it was thought impolitic. The Duke of Queensberry laid down his employment of Admiral of Scotland upon it, though very much and very kindly pressed by the King to remain in his service."

It was exactly eighteen years after penning the above protocol, that the Duchess of Queensberry found her way back to Court.

The author of the "New Critical Review of the Public Buildings of London," in the year 1736, speaks of Queensberry House as having no other faults but its bad situation, "over against a dead wall in a lane that is unworthy of so grand a building," and the fact that no wings can ever be added to it. The criticism, however, no longer holds good. "This fabric," adds the writer, "is evidently in the style of Inigo Jones, and not at all unworthy the school of that great master."

The large house fronting Burlington Gardens, extending from Old Burlington Street to Cork Street, long occupied by a younger branch of the Cavendish family, has lately been converted into an hotel.

Vigo Street (formerly called Vigo Lane), which, as we have said, connects Burlington Gardens with Regent Street, was named after a town in the north-west of Spain attacked and captured by the English forces under Drake, by Ormond, Rooke, and Stanhope, and also by Lord Cobham at various dates in the seventeenth and eighteenth centuries. It was probably built about the year 1720.

At right angles with this street, and opening out into Piccadilly nearly opposite St. James's Church, is Sackville Street, which was built about 1679-80, and was probably named after Sackville, the witty Earl of Dorset, by those who were anxious to perpetuate his memory. At all events, no proof can be found of any direct connection of its builders or of the former owners of the land on which it stands with the family which gave birth to a Buckhurst and a Dorset. Mr. Peter Cunningham tells us that it is "the longest street in London of any note without a turning on either side." It is now extensively occupied by wholesale warehouses of cloths and woollen fabrics.

The "Prince," an inn in this street, was one of the temporary dining-houses of the Literary Club of Dr. Johnson and his friends after they left the "Turk's Head," in Soho, and before repairing to the "Thatched House Tavern;" and here the Dilettanti Society met for some time in 1783.

In this street the Board of Agriculture, established in 1793 by the efforts of Sir John Sinclair and of Mr. Arthur Young, used to hold its meetings in the beginning of the reign of George IV. This board was subsidised by a grant of £3,000 annually from Parliament, to be dispensed in improving the practical agriculture of the kingdom.

No. 32 in this street is a perfect "rabbit-warren" of charitable and other institutions, the bare enumeration of which, as they stand mentioned in the "Post Office Directory," will be sufficient here :— The British Hairdressers' Benevolent Society, the British Archæological Association, General Domestic Servants' Benevolent Institution, Governesses' Benevolent Institution, The Irish Society, London Aged Christian Society, the Metropolitan Convalescent Institution, Milliners' and Dressmakers' Provident and Benevolent Institution, Naval and Military Bible Society, Royal Naval Female School Society, Society for the Relief of Distressed Widows, and the Pall Mall, Albany, and Albert Building Societies. Several of these institutions rely to a great extent for their support upon the voluntary contributions of the public; whilst others are self-supporting. It may not be out of place to remark here, that when M. Guizot was in this country he observed that nothing struck him more forcibly than the number of charitable institutions on the front of which were inscribed the words, "Supported by Voluntary Contributions;" and that they impressed him with a most favourable estimate of the English character. Besides the institutions named above, this house is also the head-quarters of the Albert Freehold Land and Building Society, the Irish Society, and the British Archæological Society. This last-named association is an offshoot of the Archæological Institute, and holds its own rival meetings and publishes its own "Transactions."

Of the distinguished residents in this street, in times past, have been Sir Everard Home (at No. 30), and Sir Gilbert Blane (at No. 8), both members of the medical profession.

Between Piccadilly and Regent Street, at a little distance eastward of Sackville Street, and near St. James's Hall, is Air (or Ayr) Street. It is stated on the authority of the rate-books of St. Martin's-in-the-Fields, that this street was built, at all events, as early as 1659, at which time it must have been quite at the western end of the town. But nothing is known as to the origin of its name, and it is quite innocent of literary or historic associations.

Parallel with Old Burlington Street on its west side, extending from Burlington Gardens to Clifford Street, is Cork Street, which perpetuates the name of one of four distinguished brothers of the House of Boyle, who all held peerages at the same time—a fact paralleled only by the Duke of Wellington and his three brothers. They were (besides Lord Burlington) Lord Cork, Lord Orrery, and Lord Broghill. A fifth brother was no less distinguished—the Honourable Robert Boyle, the philosopher. This street has only four houses on the eastern side. One of these belonged to the celebrated Field-Marshal Wade, for whom Lord Burlington built it in a fit of gratitude. It is described by the author of the "New Critical Review," as small, but chaste and simple in design, though rather overladen with ornament. Yet, he adds, "it is the only fabric in miniature I ever saw where decorations are perfectly proportioned to the space they are to fill, and do not by their multiplicity, or some other mistake, incumber the whole." The house was sold by auction in 1748. Horace Walpole tells us that it was regarded by Lord Chesterfield as such a toy that "he intended to take the house over against it to look at it;" and it was also commonly said of it that "it was too small to live in, and yet too big for a watch." Among the other eminent persons who lived in Cork Street were the haughty and imperious Mrs. (afterwards Lady) Masham, the celebrated bed-chamberwoman of Queen Anne's Court, and Dr. Arbuthnot, the physician, wit, and man of letters of the reign of Queen Anne. They both died here, the latter in February, 1735.

In this street is a public-house known as the "Blue Posts," for several generations a favourite dining-house for bachelors. Instead of a sign-board, and in the absence of a poetical and inventive taste, some innkeepers chose to denote their hostelry by the colour of some external feature of the fabric. Thus we read that there were "Black Posts" as well as "Blue Posts." Indeed, there was an inn rejoicing in that sign close by in Bond Street, immortalised by Etheredge in his comedy, *She would if she could.*

Savile Row, which extends northward from Burlington Gardens to Boyle Street and New Burlington Street, appears to have been for generations the favoured *locale* for the leading members of the medical profession.

No. 1 is the home of the Royal Geographical Society, which was founded in 1830 for the purposes of cultivating and extending geographical knowledge. It had its head-quarters in 1851 at No. 3, Waterloo Place; it was subsequently for a time settled in Whitehall Place, whence it removed to Savile Row in 1870.

It was this society which took a leading part in sending out Dr. Livingstone on those travels which have opened up a large portion of Central Africa to commerce and civilisation; and it was here that the embalmed body of David Livingstone (who had died in Africa several months previously), on being brought to London, was deposited prior to its being consigned to its last resting-place in Westminster Abbey, in April, 1874. The society has a large and well-selected library of works treating on those subjects which fall within its scope; and it gives an annual gold medal in recognition of services rendered to geographical science.

The adjoining house, No. 2, has been, since the year 1860, the head-quarters of the Roman Catholic body in London, in the shape of a club. It was founded in 1852, as the Stafford Club, so called from its original locality, occupying, as it did, the side of Crawley's Hotel, which faces Stafford Street. This club, however, was dissolved towards the close of the year 1875, after having been in existence for a little more than twenty years. In its place a new club has been established here, called the "St. George's;" the Duke of Norfolk was the chief mover of the establishment of the new club, and its success is largely due to the duke's exertions. It started with its full compliment of 350 members.

In 1826 Lord Maryborough (brother of the "great" Duke of Wellington) was living at No. 3; Sir Charles Mansfield Clarke at No. 10; and the Right Hon. George Tierney, M.P., at No. 11. No. 4 is the home of the Science (originally the Scientific) Club, established in 1874.

At No. 12 resided for many years Mr. George Grote, the distinguished historian of Greece. The eldest son of the late Mr. George Grote, of Badgmoor, Oxon., and a banker in London, he was born at Beckenham, Kent, in 1794. As a youth he entered his father's establishment as a clerk, and his leisure time was for many years afterwards spent in unremitting study. In 1832 he was returned to Parliament as one of the representatives of the City of London, and he held his seat for nine years as the champion of the ballot. His first publication was a pamphlet in reply to Sir James Mackintosh's "Essay on Parliamentary Reform" in the *Edinburgh Review;* it was printed anonymously in 1821. He afterwards wrote a small work on the "Essentials of Parliamentary Reform," "Plato and other Companions of Socrates," besides numerous essays, &c. His chief work, "The History of Greece," was published between 1846 and 1856. Mr. Grote was a trustee of the British Museum, a member of the Institute of France, Vice-Chancellor of the London University, and a Fellow of the Royal Society. He died here in 1871, and his remains were interred in Westminster Abbey. His widow, a lady of an old Kentish family, known as the authoress of "The Life of Ary Scheffer," died in 1878.

At No. 14 lived for many years Sir Benjamin Brodie, the eminent surgeon, and president at one time of the Royal Society. Sir Benjamin, who was of Scottish extraction, though the son of a Wiltshire clergyman, was one of the staff of the Medical School in Great Windmill Street, and a pupil of Sir Everard Home, at St. George's Hospital. He was Surgeon in Ordinary to George IV., and Serjeant-surgeon to William IV., and also to Her Majesty Queen Victoria. He was created a baronet in 1834, and he was the author of several works of the highest repute in the medical profession, especially on the generation of animal heat, the action of poisons, the nervous affections, &c. He was chosen to fill the presidential chair of the Royal Society in 1858. He died in 1862.

The adjoining house (No. 15) has been for some time the home of the Savile Club. At No. 17, formerly the residence of George Basevi, the architect, is the Burlington Fine Arts Club, which till about 1870 had its head-quarters at No. 177, Piccadilly. This club was established in 1866, "for the purpose of bringing together amateurs, collectors, and others interested in art; to afford ready means for consultation between persons of special knowledge and experience in matters relating to the fine arts; and to provide accommodation for showing and comparing rare works in the possession of the members and their friends." In the reading-room all periodicals, books, and catalogues, foreign as well as English, having reference to the world of art, are provided, so that the opportunity is afforded of obtaining knowledge of all sales of works of art, and of acquiring information on points relating to the history and condition of the fine arts both at home and abroad. In the gallery and rooms of the club arrangements are made for the exhibition of pictures, rare books, enamels, ceramic wares, coins, &c., and occasionally special exhibitions are held, having for their object the elucidation of some school, master, or specific art. When works of more than usual interest are on view, *conversazioni* are held. Two interesting gatherings of this kind took place in 1875. At one of them were exhibited the water-colour paintings of Turner's youthful friend, the artist Girtin (who was cut off at less than thirty years of age), and also the sketch models of the late eminent sculptor, Mr. J. H. Foley, comprising the designs for many of his most important works in London and elsewhere. On another occasion an almost perfect collection of Hollar's etchings were exhibited. In addition to its galleries of artistic objects, the house affords to members the ordinary accommodation and advantages of a London club.

At No. 20 lived and died Mr. Robert Vernon-Smith, many years one of the most laborious underlings in Lord Melbourne's and Lord John Russell's ministries, and afterwards Lord Lyveden. The house formerly belonged to his father, Mr. Robert Smith, brother of the witty Canon of St. Paul's, Sydney Smith, and known to society, from old Eton days, as "Bobus Smith." He was himself a wit, and deserves mention here as the founder of "The King of Clubs," which used to meet at the "Crown and Anchor," in the Strand, and which numbered among its members J. P. Curran, James Scarlett (afterwards Lord Abinger), Sam Rogers, the banker-poet, Lord Erskine, and Charles Butler, the Roman Catholic controversialist. Its talk was entirely of books, authors, and literature, politics being rigidly excluded. "Bobus Smith's" wife was one of the charming Miss Vernons, known as Horace Walpole's "Three Graces," the others being Lady Lansdowne and Lady Holland. Their mother was a daughter of the Countess of Ossory.

In this street lived and died Richard Brinsley Sheridan, the dramatist, wit, and politician. The history of the chequered career of this celebrity and bold companion of the Prince Regent has been often told. It has been said that when, by the assistance of his friends, he was installed in his residence in Savile Row, he boasted to one of his relations how carefully and regularly he was living—so much so that everything went on like clock-work. "Oh! that I can easily imagine," was the reply; "it goes on—tick! tick! tick!"

"His last scene," observes Sir N. W. Wraxall, "holds up to us an affecting and painful subject of contemplation. A privy councillor, the ornament of his age and nation, caressed by princes and dreaded by ministers, a man whose orations and dramatic works alike rank him among the most distinguished men of his own or of any period, he expired—though not in a state of destitution, like Spencer, like Otway, or like Chatterton, yet under humiliating circumstances of pecuniary embarrassments. His house in Savile Row was besieged by bailiffs, one of whom pressing to obtain entrance, and availing himself of the moment when the front door was opened by a servant, in order to admit the visit of Dr. Baillie, who attended Sheridan during his last illness, that eminent physician, assisted by the footman, repulsed him, and shut the door in his face. Dr. Baillie . . . . refused to accept any fee for his advice; and Earl Grey, who had so long acted in political union with Sheridan as a member of the Opposition, supplied him with every article for his comfort from his own kitchen. Nor, I have heard, did the Prince Regent forsake him in his last moments. If my information is correct, his Royal Highness sent him two hundred pounds, but Sheridan declined its acceptance, and returned the money." Sheridan died on the 7th of July, 1816, neglected by all but a few friends, among whom were the poets Rogers and Moore. Three or four days afterwards his body was carried to its last resting-place in Westminster Abbey, the pall being borne by dukes and other high personages, who had stood aloof from him in his difficulties and even in his last illness. Such is the way of the world!

No. 24, at the north-west corner, now a shop below and a private hotel above, is ambitiously styled Byron House, on account of a tradition—which, however, lacks verification—that the poet lived here about the time of his ill-starred marriage with Miss Milbanke.

At No. 34 in this street is an old-established charitable institution, the objects of which are clearly expressed in its title—the "Blind Man's Friend." It was founded by the late Mr. Charles Day, of the well-known firm of Day and Martin, of Holborn, who died towards the end of 1836, leaving £100,000 for the benefit of distressed persons suffering under the deprivation of sight. Between 200 and 300 blind persons are in the receipt of pensions of from £12 to £20 each. The entire income is about £4,000, and the election of the pensioners rests with the trustees.

At the back of Savile Row eastward, and running parallel between it and Regent Street, is Heddon Street, the entrance to which is on the west side of Regent Street. It is narrow and tortuous, and can scarcely be dignified with the name of a thoroughfare. The origin of its name is unknown, and its annals are a blank.

New Burlington Street, which we now enter, is a short thoroughfare, extending from the north end of Savile Row to the west side of Regent Street.

No. 6, on the north side, now the shop of Messrs. R. Cocks and Co., the eminent music publishers, was formerly the town residence of the Earl of Cork. Here, in the days of the Regency and later, the old eccentric Lady Cork held her "receptions," which were largely attended by the "upper ten thousand" and the rest of the world of fashion, in spite of her ladyship's well-known vice of "kleptomania"—a weakness in which she indulged so extensively and habitually, that her friends used to place pewter spoons and forks in their halls for her to carry off; in fact, all kinds of "dodges" were resorted to for the purpose of humouring her. "It was supposed," says Captain Gronow, "that she had a peculiar ignorance of the laws of *meum* and *tuum*; for her monomania was such that she would try to get possession of whatever she could place her hands upon; so that it was dangerous to leave in the ante-room anything of value. On application being made, however, the articles were usually returned the following day, the fear of the law acting strongly upon her ladyship's bewildered brain." And yet she reigned for many years a "queen of society" at the West-end, and, in fact, was the notorious "lion-hunter" of her age. At one time she would bring together such people as Sir Walter Scott; Betty, the "infant Roscius;" Belzoni, the Egyptian explorer; old Joseph Lankester, the schoolmaster; and other persons of note. Here, in 1840, the old countess died at the age of upwards of ninety. She was the last of the "Blue Stocking Club," of which we shall have more to say when we reach Portman Square, and was known in her youth as the lively and fascinating Miss Monckton. She "used to have the finest bit of blue at the house of her mother, Lady Galway," which was one of the haunts where that *coterie* assembled.

At Messrs. Colburn's, in this street, was published from its commencement, the *New Monthly Magazine*. It was started as a high Tory rival against the *Monthly Magazine* of Sir Richard Phillips. In 1820 Thomas Campbell became its nominal editor,

Physician." Redding accepted them, and ordered them to be set up in type, and to appear in the magazine. "It will scarcely be credited, but it is a fact," writes Mr. Redding, "that the packet was opened, Mr. Warren's paper canvassed among Colburn's *employés*, represented to him as not worth a sixpence, and returned by him to Mr.

SIR BENJAMIN BRODIE. (*See page* 310.)

the lion's share of the work, however, falling to Mr. C. Redding, on account of the poet's careless and indolent habits. About the same time it began to number among its writers Serjeant Talfourd. In connection with Mr. Colburn and the *New Monthly Magazine*, Cyrus Redding tells a good story with reference to a writer who subsequently became famous. Mr. Samuel Warren, then unknown to fame, sent for publication in the *New Monthly*, to Tom Campbell, or to his colleague, Cyrus Redding, the first few sheets of his "Diary of a Late

Warren without my knowledge. . . . The intercepted paper came out afterwards in *Blackwood*, and was followed by others equally good. Colburn then apologised, but not till the mischief was done. His regret was the greater because it appeared in his rival's pages." But what is the good of a responsible editor if his judgments are thus liable to revision by every ignorant shopman of a publisher? Other contributors afterwards joined the staff—viz., J. P. Curran, Joanna Baillie, Horace and James Smith, Bryan W. Procter (" Barry Corn-

HANOVER SQUARE, IN 1750.

wall "), Sir John Bowring, Henry Roscoe, W. M. Praed, Blanco White, "Morocco" Jackson, Miss Mary R. Mitford, Mrs. Hemans, and R. L. Shiel.

No. 8 is the publishing house of Messrs. Richard Bentley and Son. From this shop were issued the famous "Ingoldsby Legends," by the Rev. R. H. Barham (better known by his literary name of Thomas Ingoldsby); they were first sent as contributions to *Bentley's Miscellany*, and afterwards published separately. Mr. R. H. Barham, the witty author of these "Legends," was a minor Canon of St. Paul's and the vicar of a parish in Kent. He died in 1845. Charles Dickens and other authors frequently met at Mr. Bentley's table, and it was he who was the first editor of the *Miscellany*. At Messrs. Churchill's, the medical publishers (No. 11), are the offices of the British Medical Benevolent Fund, founded in 1836, for the relief of medical men, their widows and orphans, in temporary difficulty or distress, granting annuities to those who are incapable of providing for themselves. About 200 cases, it is stated, are relieved during the year.

In this street lived Mr. Joseph Planta, who for many years held the office of Under-Secretary of State for Foreign Affairs; and here he used to entertain George Canning, Baron Bulow, Lord Strangford, and other celebrities of that time, as his constant guests.

Here, too, lived Admiral Sir Joseph Sydney Yorke, K.C.B., some time M.P. for Sandwich, who was accidentally drowned in 1831. He was the third son of the Hon. Charles Yorke, who was appointed Lord High Chancellor in 1770, and who died suddenly, whilst his patent of creation as Lord Morden was in process of completion.

At No. 16 was, till 1882, the Royal Archæological Institute of Great Britain and Ireland. This body, for many years settled in the Haymarket, was established in 1843 under the title of the British Archæological Association. Its objects are "to investigate, preserve, and illustrate all ancient monuments of history, customs, art, &c., relating to the United Kingdom." The society possesses a good library, and a small but valuable collection of antiquities and drawings. The meetings of the members are held monthly during the London season, and the annual general Archæological Congress takes place in one of the cathedral cities or great towns of the kingdom.

CHAPTER XXV.

HANOVER SQUARE AND ITS NEIGHBOURHOOD.

"O could I as Harlequin frisk,
   And thou be my Columbine fair,
My wand should, with one magic whisk,
   Transport us to Hanover Square:
St. George's should lend us its aid."—"*Rejected Addresses.*"

Statue of William Pitt—Description of the Square in the Last Century—Harewood House—"Beau" Lascelles—Lord Rodney, and his Daughter's Clandestine Marriage—Lord Palmerston's Residence—Sir William Fairfax and Mrs. Somerville, and other Distinguished Residents—Zoological Society—Royal Agricultural Society—Royal College of Chemistry—The Oriental Club—The Arts Club—Hanover Square Rooms, now the Hanover Club—The building of New Streets in the Neighbourhood—Tenterden Street—Royal Academy of Music—Brook Street—George Street—St. George's Church—Fashionable Weddings—Dr. Dodd's Desire to become Rector—The Parish Burial-grounds—Distinguished Residents in George Street—Junior Travellers' Club—Maddox Street—Architectural Museum—The "Golden Star" Inn—Mill Street—Conduit Street—The Locality Three Hundred Years ago—Limmer's Hotel—The "Coach and Horses"—The "Prince of Wales" Coffee-house—A Batch of Architectural Societies—Trinity Chapel.

THIS square—perhaps in one way among the most popular in London, so closely connected as it is with the fashionable marriages solemnised in St. George's Church—was entirely unbuilt in 1716; but its name, which is mentioned in the plans of London of the year 1720, bears testimony to the loyalty of the Londoners who worshipped the "rising sun" in the person of George I. Both in the square itself, and in George Street adjoining, there are several specimens of the German style of building. The square covers about four acres of ground, and the centre is enclosed with a neat iron railing, within which, on the north side, is a colossal bronze statue of William Pitt, by Sir Francis Chantrey. This statue was not set up until 1831, when the statesman had been dead for more than a quarter of a century; it cost £7,000; and Mr. Peter Cunningham, who was present on the occasion, records the fact, that on the very day of its erection some advanced reformers endeavoured, though in vain, to pull it down with ropes. The figure is upright, in the act of speaking, and is one of the finest statues in London.

The *Weekly Medley*, in 1717, contains the following observations, which are interesting at the present time:—"Round about the new square, which is building near Oxford Road [now Oxford Street], there are so many other edifices that a whole magnificent city seems to be risen out of the ground, and one would wonder how it should find a new set of inhabitants. It is said it will be called by the name of Hanover Square. The chief persons that we hear of who are to inhabit that place when it is finished, having bought houses, are these following:—The Lord Cadogan, a general; also General Carpenter, General Wills, General Evans, General Pepper, the two General Stuarts, and several others whose names we have not been able to learn." It would appear, therefore, that its first tenants were mostly of the military order.

Strype tells us that the houses which in his time were in the process of creation were rapidly taken up; one of them he specifies by name, the mansion of " My Lord Cowper, late Lord High Chancellor of England;" and he adds that it was in contemplation to change the common place of execution from Tyburn to somewhere near Kingsland, in order to spare that square and the houses thereabouts—it must be supposed that he really means their inmates—the inconvenience and annoyance which might be caused by the execution of malefactors, which at that time went on rather by wholesale. But the square, though so aristocratic in its earlier inhabitants, does not appear to have been well looked after. At all events, we find plenty of complaints as to its condition half a century later. "As to Hanover Square," writes the author of " Critical Observations on the Buildings and Improvements of London," published in 1771, " I do not know what to make of it. It is neither open nor enclosed. Every convenience is railed out, and every nuisance railed in. Carriages have a narrow, ill-paved street to turn round in, and the middle has the air of a cow-yard, where blackguards assemble in the winter to play at hustle-cap, up to the ankles in dirt. This is the more to be regretted, as the square in question is susceptible of improvement at a small expense."

We gather from Dr. Hogg's work on "London as it is," published in 1837, that several at all events of the streets near Hanover Square, on the Grosvenor property, were not originally public thoroughfares. But the only gate now existing which bars the passage of carriages in this neighbourhood is that in Harewood Place, between the north side of this square and Oxford Street.

On the north side of the square, with its stables facing Oxford Street, is Harewood House, the residence of the Earl of Harewood. Of the interior of this mansion, Mr. T. Raikes gives us the following peep in his amusing " Journal: "—" The finest collection of old china in England will be found in the house of Lord Harewood, in Hanover Square, a nobleman whose agricultural pursuits and simple habits would give little reason to suppose that he was possessed of such an expensive article of luxury and taste. Fagg, the Chinaman, since the renewed rage in England for *old valuables*, has in vain offered Lord Harewood immense sums for this collection; but it was originally made by his elder brother, well known then as Beau Lascelles, who died unmarried, in 1814, and is always preserved in the family as a *souvenir* of him. The brothers were much attached to each other; but never was a greater contrast seen than in the refinement of the one and the simplicity of the other. Beau Lascelles was the essence of fashion of that day. He was a handsome man, rather inclined to be fat, which gave him a considerable resemblance to George Prince of Wales, whom he evidently imitated in his dress and manner. He was very high bred and amicable in society, and his taste in all that surrounded him was undeniable; his house, his carriages, horses, and servants, without any attempt at gaudy trappings, were the admiration of all the town, from the uniform neatness and beauty of their *tenue*. The *ensemble* of his equipage when he went to Court on a birthday might really be compared to a highly-finished toy. His house, though not large, was a museum of curiosities, selected with great taste and judgment, at a time when he had few competitors; and, had they all been preserved, they would now be of incalculable value. His life was luxurious but short, as he died at the age of fifty."

The gallant admiral, Lord Rodney, was living in this square in 1792. It is well known that his favourite daughter eloped to Gretna Green with Captain Chambers, a son of the eminent architect, Sir William Chambers. At first he was inclined to be angry, but he soon relented, and merely said, " Well, well! what is done can't be undone; but it's odd that my own family is the only crew that I never could manage, and I only hope that Jessy will never mutiny under her new commander ! "

The large house in the south-western corner, towards the close of the last century, was the town residence of Lord and Lady Palmerston, the father and mother of the late Premier. The house, which was one of the great centres of political and social reunions, is noted by Lambert, in his " History of London," as "the best piece of brick-work in the metropolis."

In 1816 Mrs. Somerville was residing in this square along with her parents, Sir William and

Lady Fairfax, and gratifying her new-born taste for astronomical and other science by attending the lectures at the Royal Institution. Here the Fairfaxes used to have little evening parties, and it was here that the late Sir Charles Lyell (as recorded in Mrs. Somerville's "Life") first met his future wife, the beautiful Miss Horner.

Among the other distinguished residents in the square have been Field-Marshal Lord Cobham, the owner of Stowe, and the friend of Pope; Sir James Clark, Physician to Her Majesty the Queen in 1841; and Ambrose Philips, the poet satirised by Pope, and author of the "Distressed Mother," who died in 1749. The mansion at the corner of Brook Street, now rebuilt and turned into the London and County Bank, was formerly called Downshire House. In 1826 it was inhabited by the Marquis of Salisbury. In 1835 it was held by another tenant, Prince Talleyrand, the ex-Minister of State in France, who used to gather round him the wits, *literati*, and diplomatists of the time. We shall meet him again at Kensington.

Of the houses which form the north-east side, one is occupied by the Zoological Society, whose offices have been located here since about 1846. The society was instituted in the year 1826, under the auspices of Sir Humphry Davy, Sir Stamford Raffles, and other eminent individuals, "for the advancement of zoology, and the introduction and exhibition of subjects of the animal kingdom, alive or in a state of preservation." In 1829 the society had a museum in Bruton Street, and subsequently in Leicester Square. This society took the place of the Zoological Club of the Linnæan Society, which had been broken up by internal differences. We shall have more to say about this society presently on reaching its gardens in the Regent's Park.

The Royal Agricultural Society of England has its offices at No. 12 (next door to the above). This society was established in 1838, for improving the general system of agriculture in this country, and engaging talented men in the investigation of such subjects as are of deep practical importance to the British farmer. Agricultural meetings are held annually in London and the country; the latter including a cattle-show, an exhibition of agricultural implements and inventions, and the awarding of prizes in either department. Its presidents, chosen annually, are almost always noblemen of high standing as practical farmers and breeders of stock.

At No. 15, on the north side of the square, and extending back into Oxford Street, is the Royal College of Chemistry. It was founded in 1845 "for the purpose of affording adequate opportunities for instruction in practical chemistry at a moderate expense, and for promoting the advancement of chemical science by means of a well-appointed laboratory and other appliances." The first stone of the laboratory, which has a handsome elevation on the south side of Oxford Street, was laid by the late Prince Consort in January, 1846. The fees for the students are in proportion to the number of days in each week that they attend.

At the north-west angle of the square, facing Tenterden Street, is the Oriental Club, founded about the year 1825, mainly through the influence and exertions of that accomplished writer and traveller, the late Sir John Malcolm. It was at first intended for gentlemen who have belonged to the civil or military services in India, or have been connected with the government of any of our Eastern dependencies. The building is constructed after the manner of club-houses in general, having only one tier of windows above the ground-floor. The interior received some fresh embellishment about the year 1850, some of the rooms and ceilings having been decorated in a superior style by Collman, and it contains some fine portraits of Indian and other celebrities, such as Lord Clive, Nott, Pottinger, Sir Eyre Coote, &c. This club is jocosely called by one of the critics of "Michael Angelo Titmarsh," the "horizontal jungle" off Hanover Square.

At No. 17 was established, about the year 1865, the Arts Club. It was instituted "for the purpose of facilitating the social intercourse of those who are connected, either professionally or as amateurs, with art, literature, or science." Charles Dickens belonged to this club, which numbers among its members very many of the Royal Academicians and others of the most rising artists of the day, with a goodly sprinkling of literary celebrities.

On the east side of the square, at the south-eastern corner of Hanover Street, the large building now known as the Hanover Square Club, or Cercle des Étrangers, had for many years, down to the beginning of 1875, borne the name of the Queen's Concert Rooms, more popularly known as the Hanover Square Rooms. The site of the building was anciently called the Mill Field (from a mill which adjoined it, and which Mill Street, hard by, still commemorates), or Kirkham Close. It was originally in the parish of St. Martin's-in-the-Fields, though in 1778 it was joined on to that of St. George's, Hanover Square. It appears to have formed part of the premises in the occupation of Matthew, Lord Dillon, the ground landlord being the Earl of Plymouth, who sold it to Lord Dunmore, who re-sold it to Sir John Gallini, by whom the house and the original concert-room were erected, in the first half of the reign of George III. Gallini, an Italian by extraction, but a Swiss by birth, who, coming to England, was engaged to teach dancing to the then youthful royal family, realised a fortune at the West-end, received the honour of knighthood, and married Lady Betty Bertie, daughter of Lord Abingdon. In 1774 Gallini, joining with John Christian Bach and Charles F. Abel, converted the premises into an " Assembly Room," no doubt, in order to act as a counter attraction to the fashionable gatherings in Soho Square, under the auspices of Mrs. Cornelys, and other places where music went hand-in-glove with masked balls and other frivolous dissipations. Two years later we find Gallini buying up the shares of his partners and carrying on the rooms upon his own account. Supported by the musical talent of Bach, Abel, and Lord Abingdon, and also, in emergencies, by the purse of the last, Gallini carried on here, from 1785 to 1793, a series of concerts, for which he contrived to gain the patronage of the Court. George III. himself was accustomed frequently to attend these concerts, together with Queen Charlotte ; and it is said that his Majesty showed such an active interest in the performances that he had a room added to the side, called the Queen's Tea Room : in this apartment, over the mantelpiece, was fixed a large gilt looking-glass, which he presented to the rooms for ever. In 1776 a committee of noblemen and gentlemen, consisting of Lord Sandwich, Lord Dudley and Ward, the Bishop of Durham, Sir Watkin Williams Wynn, Sir R. Jebb, and the Hon. Mr. Pelham, established the well-known " Concerts of Ancient Music," to the directorship of which soon afterwards were added Lord Fitzwilliam and Lord Paget, subsequently the Earl of Uxbridge. These memorable performances, which commenced their first season at the Tottenham Street Rooms, near Tottenham Court Road (subsequently converted into a theatre), and which from 1794 to 1804 had their head-quarters at the King's Theatre in the Haymarket, were removed hither in the latter year, and continued to flourish under the patronage of royalty and the leaders of the aristocracy—including the late Prince Consort, the Duke of Wellington, Lord Westmoreland, and others—down to June, 1848, when they were discontinued. King George III. took the warmest interest in these concerts, and not only occupied the royal box with his Queen and family night after night, but would constantly write out the programmes of the performances with his own hand. It is said the directors of these concerts paid Sir

John Gallini a rental of £1,000 a year for the use of the rooms. Mr. Greatorex was the conductor of these concerts from the commencement of the century down to his death in 1831, when he was succeeded by Mr. W. Knyvett. "The Concert of Ancient Music, at present more generally known by the appellation of the King's Concert," writes Sir Richard Phillips, in 1804, " is a branch that seceded from the Academy of Ancient Music. . . . It generally commences in February, and continues weekly on Wednesdays till the end of May. Six directors, chosen from among the nobility, select in turn the pieces for the night, and regulate all its principal concerns. The leading feature of its rules is the utter exclusion of all modern music. So rigid are its laws on this head, that no composition less than twenty-five years old can be performed here, without the forfeiture of a considerable sum from the director of the night." He adds, that two difficulties arise out of this stringent rule, a want of variety in the performances, and the "discouragement of living genius."

These rooms were also long used for the Philharmonic Concerts, established by Messrs. Cramer and Co., in 1813, under the auspices of the then Prince Regent. They were first held in the Argyll Rooms, at the corner of Argyll Place, and on those premises being burnt down in 1831, they were given at the concert-room of the Opera House ; but they were transferred to Hanover Square in 1833. It may not, perhaps, be out of place to mention here that the annual performance of the *Messiah* for the benefit of the Royal Society of Musicians was given here from 1785 to 1848.

In Jesse's " Life of Beau Brummell," the incident which is said to have given rise to the estrangement between the Prince Regent and the " Beau " is stated to have occurred at these rooms, although other writers have fixed upon St. James's Street as the scene, as we have mentioned in our account of that street ; nevertheless, the story told by Jesse will bear repeating :—" Lord Alvanley, Brummell, Henry Pierrepoint, and Sir Harry Mildmay, gave at the Hanover Square Rooms a *fête*, which was called the Dandies' Ball. Alvanley was a friend of the Duke of York ; Harry Mildmay, young, and had never been introduced to the Prince Regent ; Pierrepoint knew him slightly ; and Brummell was at daggers-drawn with his Royal Highness. No invitation, however, was sent to the Prince ; but the ball excited much interest and expectation, and to the surprise of the amphitryons, a communication was received from his Royal Highness, intimating his wish to be present. Nothing, therefore, was left but to send him an invitation, which was done in due form, and in the name of the four spirited givers of the ball. The next question was, how were they to receive their guest? which, after some discussion, was arranged thus:— When the approach of the Prince was announced, each of the four gentlemen took, in due form, a candle in his hand. Pierrepoint, as knowing the Prince, stood nearest the door with his wax-light,

were in front, and saw the Prince's face, say that he was cut to the quick by the aptness of the satire."

The entertainments provided in these rooms were not strictly confined to balls and concerts, for lectures, "readings," and public meetings innumerable have been held here; and in 1798 Miss Linwood here exhibited her "needlework pictures," prior to their final removal to Leicester

HAREWOOD HOUSE. (*See page* 315.)

and Mildmay, as being young and void of offence, opposite. Alvanley, with Brummell opposite, stood immediately behind the other two. The Prince at length arrived, and, as was expected, spoke civilly and with recognition to Pierrepoint, and then turned and spoke a few words to Mildmay; advancing, he addressed several sentences to Lord Alvanley, and then turning towards Brummell, looked at him, but as if he did not know who he was or why he was there, and without bestowing on him the slightest symptom of recognition. It was then, at the very instant he passed on, that Brummell, seizing with infinite fun and readiness the notion that they were unknown to each other, said aloud, for the purpose of being heard, 'Alvanley, who's your fat friend?' Those who

Square. In 1838-9, Dr. Chalmers, the celebrated Scotch divine, here delivered a series of lectures on the Church of England.

In 1845, at the death of the Misses Gallini, Sir John's nieces (the founders of the Roman Catholic Church in Grove Road, St. John's Wood), their freehold interest in Hanover Square Rooms was bought by Mr. Robert Cocks, the eminent musical publisher, who subsequently let them on a lease of twenty-one years to the committee of the club above mentioned. It is not, however, only with the two ancient institutions named above that the history of these rooms was interwoven, but with that of Mr. Henry Leslie's choir, and with the concerts of the Royal Academy of Music in Tenterden Street close by, which renewed its performances here in 1862. The large room, in its original state, was dull and heavy, owing to the architectural style of the date at which it was built; at one end was the ponderous royal box, and almost the only tasteful decoration consisted also gilt. The panels over the looking-glasses were filled with medallions, painted in *bas relief*, of the most celebrated composers—Handel, Beethoven, Bach, Rossini, Purcell, Weber, Haydn—accompanied by their names and dates; and the plinth

GEORGE STREET, HANOVER SQUARE, IN 1800.

of some paintings by the hand of Cipriani. In the winter of 1861-62, however, the rooms underwent a complete restoration and re-decoration, and they became the most comfortable concert-rooms in London, to say nothing of their great superiority to most large buildings in respect of acoustic properties. The large room had a slightly arched roof, richly gilt and ornamented with pictures; the walls on either side of the room were adorned with Corinthian columns with ornamental capitals, round the room was decorated in imitation of marbles of various patterns and colours.

On Saturday evening, December 19, 1874, took place the very last entertainment ever given in these time-honoured rooms. Mr. Cocks having placed them at the disposal of the Royal Academy of Music, a full orchestral and choral concert was given under the direction of Mr. Walter Macfarren. The work of altering the building to suit the requirements of a club was commenced immediately afterwards. The large room has been preserved unaltered, as far as possible; but in other respects the building has undergone a thorough transformation, and has been raised a couple of storeys in height; the additional floors being devoted to chambers for such members as may wish to make the club their home, either permanently or temporarily. On the ground-floor is the newspaper-room, which occupies the position of the old supper-room, to the left of the entrance in Hanover Street; the secretary's office, and also a writing-room. The principal lavatories, &c., are in the basement. The grand staircase, entirely of stone, is ornamented with statues holding jets of gas, and at the top is a large skylight, with an inner light of coloured glass. The first floor contains a smoking-room, card-room, wine-bar, and also the dining-hall. The last-named apartment has been formed out of the old concert-room, which has been somewhat curtailed in length; the east end, where the royal box formerly stood, is new; the pictures in the ceiling, mentioned above, where practicable, have been restored, and new ones inserted where necessary. On the second floor is a billiard-room, and also the drawing-room, which overlooks Hanover Square. The Hanover Square Club, as now established—whose object is much the same as that of the Travellers', embracing the introduction of foreigners—is not the first of that name which has existed; and it is probable that some house in the neighbourhood, in the time of the first two Georges, formed the head-quarters of a political association of persons zealous for the Hanoverian succession, which bore the same name; but the exact house which it occupied is not known.

In 1736 the *General Evening Post* of September 23rd contains the following paragraph, which shows pretty clearly the condition of the immediate neighbourhood of Hanover Square at that time, so far as the building of streets is concerned:—"Two rows of fine houses are building from the end of Great Marlborough Street through the waste ground and his Grace the Duke of Argyll's gardens into Oxford Road, from the middle of which new building a fine street is to be made through his Grace's house, King Street, and Swallow Street [now covered by Regent Street], to the end of Hanover Square, Brook Street, and the north part of Grosvenor Square, the middle of his Grace's house being pulled down for that purpose; and the two wings lately added to his house are to be the corners of the street which is now building." The street here spoken of is now called Princes Street, which opens into the north-east corner of the square.

This and Hanover Street, which connects the square with Regent Street at its south-east corner, were built about the same time, and bear testimony to the strong hold which the succession of the House of Brunswick had already taken on the feelings of the nation. Both streets are deficient in literary or personal associations; but it may be noted, that in the former Miss Emily Faithfull first started her "Victoria Press," through which she inaugurated her efforts to obtain remunerative employment for women.

In Tenterden Street, which connects the square at its north-west angle by a circuitous route with Oxford Street and the northern end of New Bond Street, is the Royal Academy of Music. It has been devoted to its present use almost since the formation of the Academy. The Academy itself was established in the year 1822, and a few years afterwards a charter was obtained from George IV. Here the Academy used to give its concerts until 1862, when the latter were transferred, as already stated, to the Hanover Square Rooms. The object of the Academy is the instruction of youth of either sex in every branch of musical education; and they are taught in classes by the first professors at a trifling charge. Since its foundation, it has supplied a large number of instrumental performers of no mean eminence to the various orchestras of London; and many of its pupils have become leaders and conductors of concerts, and also eminent musicians, whilst several have distinguished themselves as composers. Among the students here was Mr. Charles Dickens's sister Fanny, to fetch whom the future "Boz" would call at its doors every Sunday morning, and bring her back at night after spending the day in their wretched home in Upper Gower Street. The house, No. 4, on the north side, opposite the Oriental Club, was at one time the town residence of the Herberts, Earls of Carnarvon, who here used to entertain King George III. and his family with syllabub and tea in the terraced garden behind, which commanded a view of the Uxbridge or Tyburn Road. On the gardens of Lord Carnarvon's House, at the back, stands the carriage-factory of Messrs. Laurie and Marner, of which we shall have more to say when dealing with Oxford Street.

Brook Street, which connects the south-west angle of the square with New Bond Street and Grosvenor Square, will be more properly treated in a future chapter. Only a few of its houses stand to the east of Bond Street, and to these no literary interest attaches, unless it is worth while to mention the fact that one of them was the last abode of

Messrs. Saunders and Otley, librarians and publishers to the Queen, before the break-up of that firm, about the year 1865.

George Street, which dates its erection from the building of the square itself, and which, as we have observed above, is similar to it in the character of its architecture, passes from the centre of the south side of the square into Conduit Street. Of this street the author of "A New Critical Review of the Public Buildings of London" remarks that there is an inconsistency and a departure from the true rule of taste in making it wider at the upper than at the lower end, as quite reversing the perspective; and yet he says that the view down George Street from the top of the square, with St. George's Church in the front, is fine, and indeed "the most entertaining in the whole city," though it ought properly to end in something more attractive to the eye than the shops which now stand on the site of Trinity Chapel, in Conduit Street.

In a somewhat similar strain, but more rhapsodical style, Ralph remarks: "The sides of the square, the area in the middle, the breaks of building that form the entrance to the vista [of George Street], but above all the beautiful projection of the portico of St. George's Church, are all circumstances that unite in beauty and make the scene perfect." For ourselves, we prefer decidedly the view looking *up* the street towards the square, which throws the portico into bold relief against the sky. An *ascending* view of a church, too, is almost always preferable to what may be called a descending view.

The parish of St. George's was "carved" out of that of St. Martin's-in-the-Fields, and Mr. John Timbs says that the site of the church was given by a General Stewart. The fabric has been much admired by those who think that style of architecture appropriate for religious edifices. It was built in 1722-4; the designer and architect was named James. This was, to use Pennant's quaint expression, "one of the fifty [new churches] voted by Parliament, to give this part of the town the air of the capital of a Christian country." The writer of "A New Critical Review of the Public Buildings of the Metropolis," in 1736, mentions it as "one of the most elegant in London; the portico is stately and august, the steeple handsome and well-proportioned, and the north and east prospects very well worth a sincere approbation;" he complains, however, that its position is such as not to allow its beauties to be seen, for, "though situated in the very centre of the vista that leads to Grosvenor Square," it is so blocked up by houses as "only to be seen in profile." No doubt the beautiful pro-portions of its lofty Corinthian portico would form a fine object if there had been a broad street leading from Grosvenor Square to its western front; nevertheless, as it is, it is seen to great advantage from the junction of George Street and Conduit Street. The interior has been decorated in an ecclesiastical style, so far as possible, of late years. Over the altar is a fine painting of the Last Supper, ascribed to Sir James Thornhill; it is surmounted by a painted window, said to be of the sixteenth century; but the two ornaments do not harmonise. The window itself is said to have formerly belonged to a convent at Malines. The subject is "The Genealogy of Our Lord, according to His human nature, as derived from Jesse through the twelve kings of Judah, previous to the Babylonian captivity. In the centre of the lower part is the figure of Jesse seated; the roots of a vine are on his head; on his right are Aaron and Esaias; on his left, Moses and Elias."

Till within the last few years—or between the close of the last century and the year 1850, when Grosvenor Square was the centre of rank and fashion—St. George's enjoyed a monopoly of "fashionable" weddings, which has passed into a proverb. Here Sir William Hamilton was married on the 6th of September, 1791, to Emma Harte, afterwards so well known as "Emma Lady Hamilton," the friend of Nelson. Horace Walpole, in announcing the marriage to the Miss Berrys, tells them that "Sir William has just married his gallery of statues," alluding to the fact that his wife used to sit as a model to artists. Here, too, was married in the year 1839, the Marquis of Douro (now Duke of Wellington). The attesting witnesses, whose signatures may be seen in the marriage register, are his noble father, the great duke, and his three brothers—all peers of the realm—the Marquis Wellesley, Lord Maryborough, and Lord Cowley.

Mr. F. Locker, in one of his charming volumes of "Vers de Société," "takes off" to perfection a fashionable wedding at St. George's, and epigrammatically expresses all the good wishes which usually attend the brides who are "led to the altar" there :—

"She pass'd up the aisle on the arm of her sire,
　A delicate lady in bridal attire,
　　　　Fair emblem of virgin simplicity.
　Half London was there, and, my word! there were few
　Who stood by the altar or hid in a pew,
　　　　But envied Lord Nigel's felicity.

" O beautiful bride ! still so meek in thy splendour,
　So frank in thy love and its trusting surrender,
　　　　Going hence you will leave us the town dim !
　May happiness wing to thy bosom unbought,
　And Nigel, esteeming his bliss as he ought,
　　　　Prove worthy thy worship, confound him!"

But "fashionable" as the marriages mostly were that were performed in this church, they had their rude accompaniments : for instance, there were fees to be paid to "his Majesty's Royal Peal of Marrowbones and Cleavers : instituted 1719." "The book of their receipts," says a writer in 1829, "it seems, they carefully preserve. By the proceedings against the St. George's 'Marrow-bone and Cleaver Club' at Marlborough Street Office, by the Dowager Lady Harland, in their attempting to extort from her newly-married daughter, to whom they presented their silver plate, ornamented with blue ribbon and a chaplet of flowers, it appears the constable presented before the magistrate the book belonging to them, containing the names of a great many persons of the first consequence, who had been married at St. George's, Hanover Square ; all of whom had put down their names for a sovereign. In the course of a year, the sum gathered by these greasy fellows, as marriage-offerings, was £416 !"

The rectors of St. George's, in spite of the fashionable situation of the church, have not been on the whole distinguished, nor have many of them attained high dignities in the Church. To obtain this rectory the notorious Dr. Dodd offered to Lady Apsley, wife of the then Lord Chancellor, a *douceur* of three thousand pounds.

There are two burying-grounds belonging to this parish—one in the rear of Mount Street, Grosvenor Square, and the other on the north side of the Bayswater Road, Uxbridge Road. In the latter burial-ground for nearly fifty years reposed the remains of the gallant general, Sir Thomas Picton, who fell at Waterloo ; but in 1859 they were removed and deposited, with all due military honours, in St. Paul's Cathedral. There, too, lies poor Lawrence Sterne : we shall speak of him again when we reach Bayswater.

No. 25, about half way down on the eastern side, was the residence, for nearly a century, first of John Copley, the Royal Academician, and afterwards of his son, John Singleton Copley, Lord Lyndhurst, both of whom died here ; the former in 1815, and the latter in 1863. The future Chancellor was born in America in 1772, and at an early age was brought over to England by his parents, who were staunch royalists. The father was presented at Court, obtained the favour of George III. and Queen Charlotte, and enjoyed a prosperous career. The son obtained the highest honours at Cambridge, was called to the bar in due course, entered Parliament in middle life, and soon rose to be Solicitor and Attorney-General, and Master of the Rolls, and in 1827 succeeded Eldon as Lord Chancellor. He enjoyed the confidence of the Duke of Wellington and Sir Robert Peel, and at one time was sent for by the King to form an administration. The Whig party for many years feared nothing so much as the withering sarcasm of his annual reviews of the Parliamentary session, delivered by him in his place in the House of Lords. He again held the Great Seal under Sir Robert Peel in 1834–5 and in 1841–6. The walls of his house in George Street were hung with his father's historical paintings, including the "Death of Wolfe," the "Death of Lord Chatham," &c. It is remarkable that the united ages of the painter, the ex-Chancellor, and a sister amounted to nearly 270 years. After Lord Lyndhurst's death his house and the adjoining one were pulled down, and on their site was built the magnificent mansion of Mr. Gore-Langton.

The house, No. 15, formerly the town residence of the late Sir George Wombwell, one of the leaders of fashion in his day, and a friend of Count D'Orsay and the Fitzclarences, is now the Junior Travellers' Club.

Maddox Street, which runs from Regent Street to the east end of St. George's Church, dates from about 1720, and is probably named after the enterprising person who built it. In this street is the Museum of Building Appliances, which is in direct communication with, and indeed forms a part of, the Architectural Societies' House in Conduit Street. This museum, which was established in 1866, and enlarged in 1873, is "devoted to the reception of drawings, prospectuses, models, and specimen manufactures of every kind pertaining to the building trades." It was founded chiefly as a means of affording to patentees and inventors an "opportunity for the introduction of their improvements to those most interested in their adoption." The museum is open free daily throughout the year.

In this street is an inn now called the "Golden Star," but formerly the "Coach and Horses." It is remarkable that the "Golden Star" does not figure in Mr. Larwood's "History of Sign-boards." Less than half a century ago there were more than fifty inns in London rejoicing in the sign of the "Coach and Horses ;" but their number is much reduced now, having been superseded by railways and steam.

Close by Maddox Street, and also at the back of St. George's Church, is Mill Street, which perpetuates the fact of the mill standing hard by the site of Hanover Square, as mentioned above.

Conduit Street, which extends from Regent Street to Bond Street, across the south end of George Street, still preserves the memory of the conduit which stood in the centre of Conduit Mead—a large field—as lately as the year 1700, on which New Bond Street and its neighbouring streets have since been erected, but whereon Carew Mildmay told Pennant, in 1780, that he remembered shooting woodcocks when a boy. The same thing is said also of his contemporary, General Oglethorpe, who died in 1785, having lived to be upwards of ninety, and who, as Macaulay tells us, had "shot birds in this neighbourhood in Queen Anne's reign."

The Conduit Field in old days was a great "meet" for the Nimrods of the City. "On the 18th of September, 1562," writes Stow, "the Lord Mayor Harper, the aldermen, and divers other worshipful persons, rid to the Conduit-head before dinner. They hunted the hare, and killed her, and thence to dine at the Conduit-head. The Chamberlain gave them good cheer; and after dinner they hunted the fox. There was a great cry for a mile, then the hounds killed him at St. Giles's; great hallooing at his death and blowing of horns; and thence the Lord Mayor and all his company rode through London to his place in Lombard Street." It is amusing, after an interval of more than three hundred years, to read of a Lord Mayor going out from Cheapside and finding the hare and the fox in Marylebone, or possibly even nearer to the City, and thence making his return journey to his home in Lombard Street to the yelping of dogs and the lusty cheer of the huntsman's horn.

At the corner of Conduit Street and George Street is Limmer's Hotel, once an evening resort for the sporting world; in fact, it was a midnight "Tattersall's," where nothing was heard but the language of the turf, and where men with not very clean hands used to make up their books. "Limmer's," says a popular writer, "was the most dirty hotel in London; but in the gloomy, comfortless coffee-room might be seen many members of the rich squirearchy, who visited London during the sporting season. This hotel was frequently so crowded that a bed could not be had for any amount of money; but you could always get a good plain English dinner, an excellent bottle of port, and some famous gin-punch."

At the corner of this and Mill Street is the sign of the "Coach and Horses," serving as a sort of tap to "Limmer's," still bearing testimony to the sporting associations of the neighbourhood. Whilst the gentlemen Jehus put up at "Limmer's," their coachmen and grooms met here, and discussed all sorts of questions connected with horseflesh at a sociable "free and easy."

In this street was the "Prince of Wales" coffee-house, in which the mad Lord Camelford picked up, most gratuitously, his last quarrel with his friend Mr. Best, about a lady named Simmons—a quarrel which led to the duel fought by them in the grounds of Holland House, and his lordship's tragic death.

At No. 9, on the north side, between George Street and Regent Street, is a house formerly the town residence of the Earl of Macclesfield, but now entirely devoted to the architectural and building interests, for it contains within its walls the offices and rooms of the Architectural Association, the Architectural Publication Society, the Architectural Union Company, the District Surveyors' Association, the Photographic Society, the Provident Institution of Builders' Foremen and Clerks of Works, the Royal Institute of British Architects, the Society of Biblical Archæology, the Society for the Encouragement of the Fine Arts, and also an entrance to the Museum of Building Appliances, mentioned above. The rooms and gallery of the Architectural Association are used constantly during the "season" for exhibitions of architectural designs and paintings. The Royal Institute of British Architects was established in 1835 for the purpose of "facilitating the acquirement of architectural knowledge, for the promotion of the different sciences connected with it, and for establishing a uniformity and respectability of practice in the profession." The society has here founded a library of works, manuscripts, and drawings, illustrative, practically and theoretically, of the art; the publication of curious and interesting communications; the collection of a museum of antiquities, models, casts, &c.; with provision for performing experiments on the nature and properties of building materials. Its president is Mr. Horace Jones.

On the south side of the street, nearly facing George Street, is Trinity Chapel, a curious and interesting relic of London in the days of the Stuarts. Although they did not form part of the original edifice, yet the walls of the chapel which now present themselves to our view stand on the site of a movable tabernacle, or chapel on wheels, which was built by order of James II., to accompany him in his royal progresses and on his visits to the camp at Hounslow, in order that mass might be celebrated in his presence by his chaplain. The camp was at Hounslow when in the autumn of 1688 the king withdrew and abdicated; and as soon as his abdication was known to be a fact, the chapel was brought up by road to London, and placed upon the site now occupied by its successor. Dr. Tenison—afterwards Archbishop of Canterbury,

BERKELEY SQUARE. (See page 327.)

but at that time rector of St. Martin's-in-the-Fields—begged the new king and queen, William and Mary, to make over to him the structure, in order to turn it into a temporary church, or rather chapel of ease, for the use of the outlying portion of the inhabitants of his then wide and scattered parish. It was actually opened for service according to the rites of the Established Church in July, 1691, and among those who were present to hear the first Protestant of ease," without a district assigned to it; for the commissioners for church building in those days refused to allow a proposal which he made to that effect, on the ground that the site was not freehold. The latter, it appears, had been bestowed on the vicar and churchwardens of St. Martin's for the benefit of the poor of the parish, by whom it was turned into money, being purchased at the close of the last or very early in the present century for

LANSDOWNE HOUSE, IN 1800. (*See page* 327.)

sermon preached within its walls was John Evelyn, who thus writes in his diary :—" This church, being formerly built of timber on Hounslow Heath by King James for the mass priests, being begged by Dr. Tenison, was set up by that public-minded, charitable, and pious man." Pennant tells us that, " after having made as many journeys as the holy house of Loretto," it was altered into " a good building of brick, and has ever since rested on the same site." The houses on either side of the chapel were erected at the same time, forming part of the same insipid design, but such was the prevailing taste that they were then " considered by the public in general as highly ornamental to the street." It appears not to have been Dr. Tenison's fault that Trinity Chapel remained a mere " chapel

a " proprietary " chapel. The speculation would seem to have been successful, for a writer in the *Gentleman's Magazine* mentions it as one of the most fashionable places of worship at the West-end, " no pulpit being more frequently honoured by voluntary discourses from the most eminent dignitaries." Towards the commencement of the present century, the Rev. Dr. Beamish made it by his fervid and eloquent discourses, if not so fashionable, at all events so crowded, that it was impossible to accommodate the congregations which he drew together, without the erection of galleries. The chapel was plain and ugly enough before, but by this addition it was made fairly the most ugly of the then existing proprietary chapels. In the early part of the year 1875, it was decreed by the ground landlord that the site was required for secular building, and that the services in this chapel should be discontinued, and the fabric itself demolished.

George Canning lived for several years at No. 37, next door to the chapel, afterwards the residence of the excellent and benevolent Dr. Elliotson, to whom we are mainly indebted for the science of mesmerism, a study to which he devoted many years of his life, "and whose name," as Mr. John Forster observes, "was for nearly thirty years a synonym with all for unwearied, self-sacrificing, and beneficent service to every one in need." On the same side of the street was formerly, for very many years, before they removed into Brook Street, the shop of Messrs. Saunders and Otley, booksellers to the Queen, and for some time the publishers of "Lodge's Peerage." In this street died

quite suddenly, in 1832, Mr. E. Delmé Radcliffe, Gentleman of the Horse to George IV., whose racing studs he superintended. In his youth he was the best gentleman jockey in England, and lived much in the sporting circles of Carlton House. Mr. Raikes says, in his "Diary," that "from the time that he left Eton he never changed the style of his dress, wearing a single-breasted coat, long breeches, and short white-topped boots." Michael William Balfe, the composer, also resided in this street.

The eminent surgeon, Sir Astley Cooper, whom we have already mentioned in our account of Spring Gardens, lived in this street towards the end of his most successful professional career, after the futile attempt he made to retire from practice, making the large income of £15,000 a year; and here he died "in harness" in 1841.

CHAPTER XXVI.

BERKELEY SQUARE, AND ITS NEIGHBOURHOOD.

"Fountains and trees our wearied pride do please,
　　E'en in the midst of gilded palaces;
　　And in our town the prospect gives delight,
　　Which opens round the country to our sight."—*Sprat.*

Bruton Street—The "Great" Duke of Argyll—Anecdote of Sheridan—Museum of the Zoological Society—Berkeley Square—Lansdowne House and its Occupants—Horace Walpole—Lord Clive—Lady Jersey—Beau Brummell and his "Harbinger of Good Luck"—The Eccentric Sir John Barnard—Highwaymen and Footpads—Hay Hill—Bolton Row—"The Three Chairmen"—"The Running Footman"—Charles Street and its Noted Residents—Hill Street—The Blue-Stocking Club—Davies Street—Lord Byron and Joe Manton—Farm Street and the Roman Catholic Chapel—Mount Street—Martin Van Butchell, the Quack Doctor—The Coburg Hotel.

UNDOUBTEDLY there is a natural pleasure in a *rus in urbe*, which has no counterpart in any *urbs in rure*. It is this feeling to which must be ascribed the fact that in the most crowded parts of this great metropolis we leave open spaces, and plant them with trees, and rejoice to live in "squares" if our means will allow us. Still it was long before Nature asserted her sway. The majority of our squares, except those of Tyburnia and Belgravia, are the growth of the last century; and few of them existed before the accession of George III., their sites up to that time being mostly sheep-walks, paddocks, and kitchen-gardens.

Mr. Timbs tells us, what few of us remember or know, that it was at first attempted to call the squares by the strange and uncouth name of *quadrantes;* and Maitland, in his "History of London," retains the term, with only a slight alteration, when he mentions "the stately *quadrant* denominated King Square, vulgarly Soho Square." This name is probably known to few except very learned antiquaries, so wholly has it passed out of use.

We wish that we could endorse the words of Mr. John Timbs when he calls the garden spaces

or planted squares the most "recreative" feature of our metropolis. At all events, to the multitude the recreation is that of the eyes alone; for, except Leicester Square, not one of them is accessible to the weary working man, the public being allowed only to stare at them through the iron railings selfishly set round them.

But to proceed. Again bending our steps towards the west, we pass in a parallel line with Piccadilly, but in a somewhat "higher latitude." Leaving Conduit Street, which was our point of divergence at the conclusion of our last chapter, we step across Bond Street into Bruton Street, which leads direct into Berkeley Square. Bruton Street derived its name from Lord Berkeley of Stratton, whom we have already mentioned in connection with Piccadilly, and whose ancestors were known as the Berkeleys of Bruton. This street has had some distinguished residents in its time; among others, John, the second and "great" Duke of Argyll, who in the reign of William III. was Ambassador in Spain, and, after the Peace of Utrecht, Commander of the Forces in Scotland. He took part in the suppression of the rebellion of 1715. This duke is the same who is immortalised by Pope in the following lines :—

"Argyll, the state's whole thunder born to wield,
　And shake alike the senate and the field."

It may be remembered also that Sir Charles Hanbury Williams in his poems identifies the duke with this street :—

"Yes! on the great Argyll I often wait
　At charming Sudbrooke or in Bruton Street."

Sheridan also was living in this street in 1786. At this period his house was so beset with duns that, in spite of his seat in Parliament, even the provisions for his family had to be let down the area between the railings, as he was afraid to open the front door. Sir N. W. Wraxall tells a capital story *apropos* of this house and its occupant in that year :—"Sheridan," he writes, "entertained at dinner here a number of the (Whig) opposition leaders, though he laboured all the time under heavy pecuniary embarrassments. All his plate, as well as his books, were lodged in pawn. Having, nevertheless, procured from the pawnbroker an assurance of the liberation of his plate for the day, he applied to Beckett, the celebrated book-seller in Pall Mall, to fill his empty book-cases. Beckett not only agreed to the proposition, but promised to ornament the vacant shelves with some of the most expensive and splendid productions of the British press, provided that two men, expressly sent for the purpose by himself, should be present to superintend their immediate restoration. It was settled finally that these librarians of Beckett's appointment should put on liveries for the occasion, and wait at table. The company having arrived, were shewn into an apartment where, the book-cases being opened for the purpose, they had leisure, before dinner was served, to admire the elegance of Sheridan's literary taste, and the magnificence of his collection. But, as all machinery is liable to accidents, so in this instance a failure had nearly taken place, which must have proved fatal to the entertainment. When everything was ready for serving dinner, it happened that, either from the pawnbroker's distrust, or from some unforeseen delay on his part, the spoons and forks had not arrived. Repeated messages were dispatched to hasten them, and they at last made their appearance; but so critically, and so late, that there not being time left to clean them, they were thrown into hot water, wiped, and instantly laid on the table. The evening then passed in the most joyous and festive manner. Beckett himself related these circumstances to Sir John Macpherson."

In this street, for a time, resided Lord Brougham, when Lord Chancellor. No. 16 was the town house of the late and present Lord Granville, and at one time that of Lord Chancellor Cottenham. It passed afterwards into the hands of another well-known statesman, Lord Carnarvon. In 1841 No. 26 was the residence of Sir Matthew Tierney the favourite physician of George IV.

In Bruton Street was formerly the Museum of the Zoological Society, before or about the time of the establishment of its gardens in Regent's Park. The studio of Mr. Matthew Noble, the sculptor, was formerly in this street.

Berkeley Square, which we now enter on its eastern side, was built in 1698, and named after John, Lord Berkeley, of Stratton, whose mansion and grounds we have already described as situated on the north side of Piccadilly. From the rear of Devonshire House they extended back to Hay Hill, in the south-east corner of the square. In the centre of the square, which contains about five acres of ground, are some fine, tall, and shady plane-trees, which impart an air of cheerfulness and picturesqueness to the spot. Within the enclosure there was formerly an equestrian statue of George III., erected by the Princess Amelia. The statue, which was executed by Wilton, stood on a clumsy pedestal, and represented the king in the character of Marcus Aurelius. At one time this square was the most fashionable locality in London. The houses are rather heavy and monotonous in appearance; and a few link-extinguishers may still be seen flanking the doorways, reminding us of the days of sedan-chairs and cumbrous family coaches.

The magnificent mansion standing within its garden and gates, which occupies the southern side of the square, and has been for four generations the town-house of the Marquises of Lansdowne, was originally built by Robert Adam, the architect of the Adelphi, for John, Earl of Bute, the favourite Premier of George III. in his early days. It was scarcely finished when, in 1762, after an administration of about two years, during which he had brought the war with France and Spain to a close by the Treaty of Fontainebleau, Lord Bute suddenly threw up the reins of government, and retired into private life. The act was most unpopular. This magnificent residence, just completed and newly occupied, exposed his lordship to the most malignant comments; and his enemies asserted that he could not possibly have erected such a mansion by honest and fair means. They concluded, therefore, that he had either received large presents from the Court of France for signing the treaty, or had made large purchases in the public funds, previous to signing its preliminaries. The accusation was made publicly by others as well as by

"Junius," who in the plainest terms accused the earl of selling his country. It is not a little singular that, when some twenty years later the house passed by purchase into the hands of Lord Shelburne, afterwards Marquis of Lansdowne, the same accusation was revived, the public again raising an outcry to the effect that it could not have been bought except by moneys paid to his lordship for concluding the peace of 1783. Lord Shelburne, however, took no notice of the cry, for, according to Jeremy Bentham, he "was the only minister who did not fear the people."

Lord Bute was known to be, or at all events to have been, a poor man until called to the post of Premier; and his enemies were not slow to draw attention to the fact, that he could never have afforded to build such a house either from his patrimony or from his marriage with the daughter of Lady Mary Wortley Montagu. The "scandal" is recorded in the gossiping pages of Sir N. W. Wraxall, who adds, "As little could he be supposed to have amassed during his very short administration enough to suffice for such a building. The only solution of the difficulty, therefore, lay in imagining, however unjustly, that he had either received presents from France, or had made large purchases in the public funds previous to the signature of the preliminaries of peace " with that country. Whatever may have been the real solution of the mystery, there can be no doubt that the mansion brought nearly as much of public odium on Lord Bute as the building of Clarendon House, as we have already seen, had entailed a century before upon Lord Chancellor Hyde.

The story of Lord Bute's first introduction to royal circles is told at considerable length by Sir N. W. Wraxall. The substance of it is that in 1747, whilst living, from motives of economy, at a villa on the banks of the Thames, he was at Egham races, and that a shower coming on, and the Prince of Wales, accidentally finding him without a conveyance, offered to give him a seat in his own carriage, and took him to Cliefden, near Maidenhead, where he stayed the night. He rendered himself extremely acceptable to their royal highnesses, and thus laid the foundation, under the succeeding reign, of his elevation to the premiership—a promotion which may be said to have been a consequence of this turn in the chapter of accidents. When young he had a very handsome person; and long after he became a constant visitor and almost an inmate of Leicester House and of Cliefden, he would frequently play the part of " Lothario " in the private theatricals exhibited by the Duchess of Queensberry for the amusement

of those royal personages—a fact to which Wilkes alludes more than once with a sly *inuendo* in one of his publications. If this be really the true history of the rise of Lord Bute to place and power, it is but a modern instance of the Latin satirist's remark, " *Voluit Fortuna jocari.*"

In 1762 Dr. Johnson waited here on Lord Bute to thank him for the literary pension which, at his recommendation, the King had settled on him. Lord Bute on this occasion said to him expressly that this mark of royal favour was "given him not for anything he was to do, but for what he had already done." As Boswell remarks, Lord Bute on this occasion behaved in a very handsome manner. "A minister of a more narrow and selfish disposition would have availed himself of such an opportunity to fix an implied obligation on a man of Johnson's powerful talents to give him his support."

Lord Bute does not appear to have long resided here, for very soon after the mansion was completed it was sold to the Earl of Shelburne, afterwards first Marquis of Lansdowne. John Timbs tells us that "the price was £22,000, being some £3,000 less than it cost." He also mentions the *canard* which was current in the last century with respect to the house, namely, that " it was built by one Peace, that made by Lord Bute, in 1762, and paid for by another."

In the spring of 1780, on the failure of his publisher, Mr. H. Payne, of Pall Mall, George Crabbe, poor and unknown, came to this house, in order to ask for temporary aid; but he was refused by Lord Shelburne once and again. Crabbe's son tells us in his " Life " that " often in latter times he would express the feelings with which he contrasted his reception at this nobleman's door in 1780, with the courteous welcome which he received at a subsequent period in that same mansion, now Lansdowne House." " Dined at Lansdowne House," writes the poet, in his " Diary," in 1817. " My visit to Lord Lansdowne's father in this house, now thirty-seven years since ! " The only wonder that one feels in reading such an episode, even in a poet's life, is that he could condescend, when his name was known as the author of " The Village," to enter the doors of that Mæcenas from which he was so rudely repulsed when he needed temporary assistance.

With respect to the history of this house and its noble owners, we may be pardoned for drawing largely here upon one of the literary articles of the *Times :*—" In 1805 died the first Marquis of Lansdowne, having by that time passed very much out of popular notice ; and the principal cause of public regret for his demise was, that only a fortnight before his death he had declared his knowledge of the Junius secret, and yet among his papers was to be found no indication that could lead to its discovery. He was succeeded by his eldest son, the Earl of Wycombe, whose first act on coming into possession was to sell almost all the literary and artistic treasures which his father had accumulated with so much love and labour. The greater part of these were dispersed under the hammer of the auctioneer, many of the pictures going to enrich the National, the Grosvenor, and other galleries; only the Lansdowne MSS. were kept together, being purchased by the British Museum; while the Gallery of Antique Marbles was the sole portion of the collection for which the marquis showed any appreciation—his opinion being expressed in the fact that he purchased it from his father's executors for £6,000. If, however, this nobleman did not show much respect to his father's cultivated taste, he was not without a certain ancestral pride, for he tried to build a vessel on the principle of Sir William Petty's double-bottomed ship, that was to sail against wind and tide, a model of which was then, and is perhaps still, exhibited in the council-room of the Royal Society. Of nautical habits, he also erected, near the Southampton Water, a marine villa, in which, from dining-hall and private bower to kitchen and scullery, all was pure Gothic, while the gardens belonging to the castle were laid out at Romsey, some ten or twelve miles distant, on a site which formed the original estate of the Petty family. Here, if not in yachting voyages to Ireland or the Continent, he spent most of his time. In London he was a marked man—remarkable for his disregard of dress, and for the pride he took in appearing on the coldest days in winter without a great-coat and without gloves. He died in November, 1809, and was succeeded by his half-brother, the third Marquis, whose first care was to purchase the antique marbles from his sister-in-law; and there, at Lansdowne House, they may now be seen—some of them, as the youthful 'Hercules' and the 'Mercury,' justly considered the finest statues of the kind that have found their way to this country. As for the pictures, when the marquis succeeded to the title, in 1809, there was not one in this splendid mansion, with the exception of a few family portraits; but Lord Lansdowne set himself to the formation of a gallery, which now comprises nearly two hundred pictures of rare interest and value, but miscellaneous in their character, no school or master predominating, unless it be Sir Joshua Reynolds. Some of the portraits in this collection are of great interest. There is the celebrated portrait of Pope, by Jervas; Reynolds's wonderful portrait of Sterne; one of Franklin, by Gainsborough; a beautiful one of Peg Woffington, by Hogarth; Lady Hamilton appears twice—as a bacchante and a gipsy, from the pencil of Romney; Horner, the old college friend of Lord Lansdowne, is not forgotten; and, most interesting of all, there is the lovely portrait of Mrs. Sheridan, as St. Cecilia, painted by Reynolds."

It may recall with some vividness the fashion of those times if we record a little incident connected with this portrait. During the short-lived Ministry of " All the Talents " the Whig leaders celebrated their return to power by a continual round of festivities, in which Sheridan outvied all his colleagues. One Sunday (25th of May, 1806) he gave a grand dinner; on the Monday following a supper and ball, at which the dancing was prolonged to past eight o'clock next morning; on the Tuesday a christening, a masque, and another ball, the Prince being present on each occasion, and the Lord Chancellor Erskine, and the young Chancellor of the Exchequer, Henry Petty, being conspicuous among the dancers. On the occasion of this dinner, the portrait of Mrs. Sheridan was redeemed for one night only from the pawnbroker's, and exhibited in its place in the dining-room. When poor Sheridan died, it was still in possession of the pawnbroker; it then fell into the hands of Sheridan's solicitor, and from him it was purchased for £600 by Lord Lansdowne. In this little incident we get some glimpses of that conviviality for which the Whigs were distinguished. "Le Whig est la femme de votre Gouvernement," says Balzac; and the truth of the remark is especially illustrated in that social influence which the Whigs have always cultivated.

The name of Petty was assumed by the Hon. John Fitzmaurice, second son of Thomas, twenty-first Lord Kerry, and of Anne, only daughter of Sir William Petty, on inheriting the Petty estates on the death of his maternal uncle, Henry Petty, Esq., of Shelburne. He was created a peer of Ireland as Viscount Fitzmaurice, and soon after promoted to the Earldom of Shelburne. His son and successor, William the second earl, and the purchaser of Lansdowne House, was advanced to the Marquisate of Lansdowne in 1784. The above Sir William Petty, of whose talents and public services we have spoken in a previous chapter (page 256), is styled by Aubrey " a person of a great stupendous invention, and of as great prudence and humanity." Sir William was one of the members of the " Rota " or Coffee Club, to which John Milton and Pepys also belonged. The character of the club may be inferred from the lines in " Hudibras :"—

"————as full of tricks
　　As 'Rota-men' of politics."

Continuing our account of the mansion, we may simply state that it is large and of somewhat heavy proportions, and that the front is of white stone, ornamented with Ionic pillars and a pediment; but it is almost shut out from view by the rich foliage by which the mansion is surrounded; upon the gate-piers is a beehive, one of the crests of the house of Lansdowne. The pictures mentioned above are, for the most part, hung in a gallery of fine proportions (being 100 feet long by 30 wide); and besides these there is in the ante-room a copy of Canova's "Venus." The house also contains some fine specimens of antique busts and statues collected by Gavin Hamilton. The "classic" dining-room served for many years, with Holland House and Devonshire House, to bring together the principal leaders of thought and action belonging to the old Whig *coterie.* Here the Russells and Greys, and Sir James Mackintosh, would often meet around the hospitable table of Henry, the third marquis, so long the venerated "Nestor" of the Liberal party, who divided his time between this house and his seat of Bowood, in Wiltshire, till his death in 1863. Mr. Rush, the American Minister, was a frequent guest here in the days of the Regency, and he speaks of the hospitality of its "classic" dining-room in most glowing terms. We learn from Brougham's "Life" that cabinet councils were occasionally held here.

Among the most constant and most welcome guests here was "Tommy" Moore—"Anacreon Moore," as he was often called, in allusion to his light and sparkling verses.

Horace Walpole lived for the last fifteen years of his life at No. 11 on the east side of this square,

THE SIGN OF "THE RUNNING FOOTMAN." (*See page 334.*)

and here he died on the 2nd of March, 1797, a few years after succeeding to the Earldom of Orford, a title he scarcely ever cared to assume, preferring to be called plain "Horace Walpole" to the end. He thus writes to the Countess of Ossory, under date October, 1779, which fixes the date of his removal hither from Arlington Street, where we have already been introduced to him:—"I came to town this morning to take possession of [my house in] Berkeley Square, and am as well pleased with my new habitation as I can be with anything at present. Lady Shelburne's being queen of the palace over against me" (he is referring, of course, to Lansdowne House) "has improved the view since I bought the house, and I trust will make your ladyship not so shy as you were in Arlington Street."

Walpole was attacked at Strawberry Hill by the cold, about the close of November, 1796, and at the end of that month he removed to his house in Berkeley Square, which he never left again. On this cold supervened an attack of gout. He still amused himself with writing and dictating brief notes, instead of letters, and with the conversation of his friends; and, exhausted by weakness, sunk gradually and died painlessly, on the 2nd of the following March. On the death of Horace Walpole, the house passed to his niece, Lady Waldegrave, who was living here at the beginning of the present century.

It has been said of Horace Walpole, with some justice, by Mr. Charles Knight: "The chief value of his letters consists in his lively descriptions of those public events whose nicer details, without such a chronicler, would be altogether hid under the varnish of what we call history."

The house No. 13, two doors farther to the north, was at one time occupied by the late

Marquis of Hertford, who kept here the nucleus of the fine gallery of paintings now at Hertford House, Manchester Square.

No. 45, on the west side of the square, was the house of the great Lord Clive, the founder of our Indian Empire—"that second Kouli Khan," as

things being not sufficient to move his great mind." The house now belongs to his nearest representative, the Earl of Powis, who, though a Herbert by birth, bears the name of Clive.

An amusing story, showing how Lord Clive obtained his wife, is thus told by Sir Bernard

EXTINGUISHERS IN BERKELEY SQUARE.   (*See page* 327.)

Horace Walpole styles him. Sated with success and honours, his restless spirit seems to have enfeebled his nervous system, and there is too much reason to fear that he fell by his own hand, in November, 1774. Lord Clive in Dr. Johnson's opinion, was a man who, though loaded with wealth and what the world called honours, had yet "acquired his fortune by such crimes that his consciousness of this impelled him to cut his own throat, because he was weary of still life, little

Burke in his "Rise of Great Families:"—"Mr. Maskelyne (brother of Dr. Nevil Maskelyne, the Astronomer-Royal) went as a cadet to India, where he became acquainted with Mr. Clive (afterwards Lord Clive). The acquaintance ripened into intimate friendship, and led to constant association. There hung up in Mr. Maskelyne's room several portraits; among others a miniature, which attracted Clive's frequent attention. One day, after the English mail had arrived, Clive asked Maskelyne if he had received any English letters, adding, 'We have been very much misunderstood at home, and much censured in London circles.' Maskelyne replied that he had, and read to his friend a letter he then held in his hand. A day or two after, Clive came back to ask to have the letter read to him again. 'Who is the writer?' inquired Clive. 'My sister,' was the reply; 'my sister whose miniature hangs there.' 'Is it a faithful representation?' further asked Clive. 'It is,' rejoined Maskelyne, 'of her face and form; but it is unequal to represent the excellence of her mind and character.' 'Well, Maskelyne,' said Clive, taking him by the hand, 'you know me well, and can speak of me as I really am. Do you think that girl would be induced to come to India and marry me? In the present state of affairs, I dare not hope to be able to go to England.' Maskelyne wrote home, and so recommended Clive's suit, that the lady acquiesced, went to India, and, in 1753, was married at Madras to Clive, then rising to the highest distinction. Lord Clive returned to England in 1767, having done more to extend the English territory and consolidate the English power in India than any other commander. His name stands high on the roll of conquerors; but it is found in a better list—among those who have done and suffered much for mankind. He died at the age of forty-eight, in a fit of insanity, produced by the ingratitude and persecution of his country."

In another house in this square died, in 1762, Martha Blount, the friend and correspondent of Pope. At No. 48 resided Earl Grey for several years both before and after his premiership. In 1842 this square numbered among its residents Sydney Smirke, the architect, and Sir John Cam Hobhouse, afterwards Lord Broughton.

Another celebrated house in this square is No. 38, for half a century or more the residence of the Earl of Jersey. Here the celebrated Lady Jersey, the widow of the fifth earl—one of the female favourites of George IV., in the old days of Carlton House, and in after time one of the most omnipotent and imperious queens of "Almack's"—held her receptions. Half the fashionable world had the *entrée* to these, and the other half sought the privilege in vain, with watering lips. Lady Jersey was the daughter and heiress of Mr. Robert Child, the banker; and her large interest in the bank of Messrs. Child, at Temple Bar, and the income which she drew from it, threw a halo around her which blinded the upper ten thousand to the facts of her early married life.

A curious story which connects this square with a turn—though only a temporary turn—in the fortunes of "Beau" Brummell, of whom we have spoken in our chapter on Carlton House,* is told by Mr. Raikes in his "Journal:"—"At five o'clock on a fine summer's morning, in 1813, he was walking with me through Berkeley Square, and was bitterly lamenting his misfortunes at cards, when he suddenly stopped, seeing something glittering in the kennel. He stooped down and picked up a crooked sixpence, saying, 'Here is an harbinger of good luck.' He took it home, and before going to bed drilled a hole in it, and fastened it to his watch-chain. The spell was good: during more than two years he was a constant winner at play and on the turf, and, I believe, realised nearly £30,000."

The blind god, or goddess, of gain, however, appears speedily to have deserted him, for in 1816 he was obliged to fly the country on account of debt, and to retire to Calais, between which place and Caen, where he ultimately became English Consul, he spent his latter days.

Brummell outlived most of the Carlton House set: he died in 1840. Mr. Raikes describes him as tall, well-made, and of a good figure, and a general favourite in ladies' society. "Latterly," he writes, "he became bald, and continued to wear powder to the last of his stay in England, rather piquing himself on preserving this remnant of the *vieille cour* amidst the inroads of the Crops and Roundheads who dated from the French Revolution. He was always studiously, and even remarkably, well-dressed; never at all *outré;* and though considerable time and attention were devoted by him to his toilette, when once accomplished, it never seemed to occupy his attention. His manners were easy, polished, and gentleman-like, stamped with what St. Simon would call *l'usage du monde, et du plus grand, et du meilleur*, and regulated by that same good taste which he displayed in most things. No one was a more keen observer of vulgarism in others, or more piquant in his criticisms, or more despotic as an *arbiter elegantiarum;* indeed, he could decide the fate of a young man just launched into the world by a single word. His dress was the general model; and when he had struck out a new idea, he would smile at observing its gradual progress downwards from the highest to the lowest classes. . . . He was not only good-natured, but thoroughly good-tempered. I never remember to have seen him out of humour. His conversation, without having the wit and humour of Lord Alvanley, was highly amusing and agreeable, replete with anecdotes not only of the present day, but of

---

* See p. 96, *ante.*

society several years back, which his early introduction to Carlton House and to many of the Prince's older associates had given him the opportunities of knowing correctly." "Beau" Brummell, indeed, has never been equalled or paralleled since, not even by Count D'Orsay, whom he in some respects resembled.

In this square died, towards the close of the last century, the eccentric son of Sir John Barnard, sometime alderman of and M.P. for London, and one of those few members whose "price" even Sir Robert Walpole could not find out. This was the more remarkable in his case, as he was extremely penurious. Lord Chatham called him "the Great Commoner," probably in jest; but it is recorded that more than one high Minister of State constantly consulted him on all measures of finance, and that once, at least, he was offered the Chancellorship of the Exchequer. His son inherited his penurious tastes. The circumstances of his death were singular. One Monday morning he woke, having dreamed that he should die in the course of the week. He used to have a cup of chocolate for breakfast daily, and every Monday morning he gave his housekeeper the money for the weekly supply. He was so impressed with his dream, however, that he told her on this occasion to get only half the quantity. Before the fourth morning came he was found dead.

In the days of the Regency Berkeley Square probably vied with Grosvenor Square in being the most fashionable spot in the West-end, and the neighbourhood of both was constantly spoken of in the last century as the very type of London wealth, taste, hospitality, and luxury. Hence the sarcastic remark of Cawthorne—

"Alas! no dinners did he eat
In Berkeley Square or Grosvenor Street."

Nevertheless, in spite of its wealth and luxury, the locality seems to have had its drawbacks, for it enjoyed the unenviable distinction of being infested with highwaymen and footpads. According to Dr. Doran, the district around the square, Hay Hill, Hill Street, &c., continued to be a dangerous one down to the middle of the reign of George III. Lord Cathcart, in an unpublished letter to his son William, dated December, 1774, affords an instance of the peril which people ran on their way to the houses of Mrs. Montagu, Lady Clermont, Lady Brown, and other residents of that neighbourhood. Lord Cathcart tells his son that as his sisters and Mr. Graham (afterwards Lord Lynedoch) were going to Lady Brown's in a coach, they were attacked by footpads on Hay Hill. One opened the door and demanded the company's money.

The future Lord Lynedoch showed the stuff of which that gallant soldier was made. He upset the robber who addressed them, then jumped out and secured him. The confederate took to his heels. We may add, on the authority of Walker's "Original," that George IV. and the Duke of York, when very young men, were stopped one night by highwaymen on Hay Hill, whilst riding in a hackney coach, and robbed of what valuables they had about them.

Then, again, this neighbourhood has more than once been the scene of civil strife and bloodshed; and Mr. Planché tells us, in his agreeable "Recollections and Reflections," that he remembers seeing artillerymen standing with lighted matches by the side of their loaded field-pieces in Berkeley Square in the days of Lord Liverpool's ministry.

Hay Hill, which connects the south-east angle of the square with Grafton and Dover Streets, is a steep slope, and covers part of the site of the gardens belonging to Berkeley House. It is generally thought to derive its name, like Farm Street, on the other side of the square, from the rural manor of which it once formed a part. But Peter Cunningham considers it is a corruption of the "Eye" or "Aye," a brook which ran at its foot from Tyburn, which he supposes to be a corruption of "Eye-burn" or "Ay-burn."

Near this, in the reign of Queen Mary, as already mentioned, a skirmish took place between a party of insurgents, under Sir Thomas Wyatt, and a detachment of the royal army, in which the former were repulsed. After the subsequent defeat and capture of Sir Thomas Wyatt at Ludgate, he was executed, and, as Stow tells us, his head set up on a gallows at this very place.

According to the "Annual Register" for 1799, "Hay Hill was granted by Queen Anne to the then Speaker of the House of Commons; but much clamour being made about it as a bribe, . . . the Speaker sold it for £200, and gave the money to the poor. The Pomfret family afterwards purchased it, and it has lately been sold for £20,300."

At the foot of Hay Hill, in a lane leading towards Bruton Mews South, is a small public-house called the "Three Chairmen," pointing back to the days when sedan chairs were in fashion.

A narrow passage between the gardens of Lansdowne and Devonshire Houses leads to Bolton Row and Curzon Street. It is sunk below the level of the ground, and at one end is a flight of steps, with an upright iron bar in the centre. It is said that this bar was put up because a highwayman who had done some deed of violence in May Fair rode his horse through the defile, much to the danger of the foot-passengers. In Bolton Row, in the early part of the present century, resided Mr. Henry Angelo, the noted teacher of the noble art of fencing, who lived all his life in the world of fashion, and whose "Reminiscences" occupy two large volumes.

Charles Street and Hill Street, both on the western side of the square, are handsome thoroughfares; and the houses in both have always been tenanted by the highest and noblest families. In Hayes Mews, running northwards between these two streets, there is a public-house bearing the sign of the "Running Footman," much frequented by the servants of the neighbouring gentry. Upon the sign-board is represented a tall, agile man in gay attire, and with a stick having a metal ball at top; he is engaged in running, and underneath are the words, "I am the only running footman." We have given a copy of this curious sign on page 330. It is obvious that the very word "footman," still in constant use for a man-servant, implies the original purpose for which such a servant was kept—namely, to run alongside his master's carriage.

Chambers tells us in his "Book of Days," that the custom of keeping running footmen survived to such recent times that Sir Walter Scott remembered seeing the state-coach of John, Earl of Hopetoun, attended by one of the fraternity, "clothed in white, and bearing a staff." It is believed that the Duke of Queensberry—the "Old Q." already mentioned—who died in 1810, kept up the practice longer than any other of the London grandees; and Mr. Thoms tells an amusing anecdote of a man who came to be hired for the duty by that ancient but far from venerable peer. The duke was in the habit of trying the pace of candidates for his service by seeing how they could run up and down Piccadilly, watching and timing them from his balcony. They put on a livery before the trial. On one occasion, a candidate presented himself, dressed, and ran. At the conclusion of his performance he stood before the balcony. "You will do very well for me," said the duke. "And your livery will do very well for me," replied the man, and gave the duke a last proof of his ability as a runner by then running away with it.

In Charles Street, at No. 22, lived the Duke and Duchess of Clarence, prior to the accession of the former to the throne as King William IV. In this street, too, have resided at one time or another, the Earl of Ellenborough, some time Governor-General of India; Mr. James R. Hope-Scott, of Abbotsford, who came into possession of that property through his marriage with the grand-daughter and heiress of Sir Walter Scott; Mr. Thomas Baring, M.P., the distinguished master of finance, whose house was noted for its fine gallery of paintings; Admiral Sir Edward Codrington, the victor of Navarino, and subsequently M.P. for Devonport; Lady Grenville, sister of Lord Camelford, and widow of the Premier of 1806-7, the head of the "ministry of all the talents:" she lived till 1864, and died at the age of upwards of ninety.

Of John Street, which connects the western end of Charles Street with Hill Street, there is little or nothing to say, beyond the fact that it bears the Christian name of Lord Berkeley of Stratton, whom we have already mentioned. At the junction of these two streets stands Berkeley Chapel, one of the many proprietary chapels in the parish of St. George's, Hanover Square, to which a conventional district out of that parish has been attached. It dates from about 1750. Sydney Smith, at one time, was its officiating minister. Externally, it has as little to recommend it as most West-end proprietary chapels; but in 1874-5 its interior was decorated in good ecclesiastical taste.

Hill Street, so called from some trifling ascent on the farm of Lord Berkeley already mentioned, was erected in the early part of the last century. It comprises none but fine and handsome houses, and has always been inhabited chiefly by titled families, or, at all events, those of high aristocratic connections. Amongst its former residents Mr. P. Cunningham enumerates the "good" Lord Lyttelton; Mrs. Montagu, before she became a widow and removed to her more celebrated house in Portman Square; the first Lord Malmesbury; and Lord Chief-Justice Camden, who died here in 1794. In this street the late Lord De Tabley, better known by his former name of Sir John Leicester, made his fine collection of paintings of the English school. In 1826, it counted among its residents Mr. Henry Brougham, M.P. for Winchelsea; he lived at No. 5, the same house where, in 1835, resided Lord Albert Conyngham, afterwards Lord Londesborough. At No. 19 lived Mr. N. Ridley Colborne, afterwards Lord Colborne; both the latter were known for their galleries of pictures. At No. 9, in 1841, resided Admiral Sir Philip Durham, the last survivor, it is supposed, of those who escaped from the *Royal George*, when she went down at Spithead, with Admiral Kempenfelt and "twice four hundred men."

Sir N. W. Wraxall, in his "Historical Memoirs in his own Time," gives us a most interesting picture of the gatherings of literary celebrities and fashionable ladies under the roof of Mrs. Montagu, which were nicknamed the Blue Stocking Club, and into which, he tells us, he was introduced by Sir William Pepys. He describes minutely her dinners, and her evening parties, and the good looks and *esprit* of the hostess as she was seen in the season of 1776, when verging on sixty. Here frequently came the ponderous and sententious Dr. Johnson, as a satellite attendant on Mr. and Mrs. Thrale; Edmund Burke, grave and reserved, his society being more coveted than enjoyed; Lord Erskine, then just beginning to be known to fame as an orator; Dr. Shipley, the Bishop of St. Asaph, and his daughter, afterwards married to Sir William Jones, the Orientalist; Mrs. Chapone, who concealed the most varied and superior attainments under the plainest of outward forms; Sir Joshua Reynolds, with his ear-trumpet, prevented by deafness from joining in the general conversation; Horace Walpole, full of anecdote, gathered partly by contact with the world and partly by tradition from his father, the great Sir Robert; the learned and grave Mrs. Carter, the "Madame Dacier of England;" Dr. Burney, and his daughter, afterwards Madame D'Arblay, the author of "Evelina" and "Cecilia;" David Garrick, whose presence shed a gaiety over the whole room; the Duchess Dowager of Portland, grand-daughter of the Lord Treasurer Harley, Earl of Oxford; and Georgina, Duchess of Devonshire, then in the first bloom of youth.

Davies Street, which runs from the north-west corner of Berkeley Square, across Grosvenor and Brook Streets into Oxford Street, is named after Miss Mary Davies, the rich heiress of Ebury Manor, who carried the estate at Pimlico by marriage into the house of Grosvenor; or else, as Mr. Peter Cunningham suggests, after Sir Thomas Davies, some time Lord Mayor of London, who inherited a large part of the fortune of "the great Mr. Audley," whose name is connected with North and South Audley Streets. In this street lived "Joe Manton," the gun-maker, before his removal to Dover Street. When in London Byron used to go to Manton's shooting-gallery, to try his hand, as he said, at a wafer. Captain Gronow, in his agreeable anecdotes and reminiscences, tells us that Wedderburn Webster was present one day when the poet, intensely delighted with his own skill, boasted to Joe Manton that he considered himself the best shot in London. "No, my lord," replied Manton, "not the best, but your shooting to-day was very respectable;" upon which Byron waxed wroth, and left the shop in a violent passion.

The top of Davies Street runs into Oxford Street, not at right angles, as most of the other thoroughfares, but diagonally, and appears to follow the course of an old and narrow thoroughfare called Shug Lane, which, in the "New View of London," published in 1708, is mentioned as in a line with Marylebone Lane. The very name of Shug Lane, however, has long since passed away.

Farm Street, for such is the name by which the mews at the rear of the north side of Hill Street is dignified, contains the Jesuit Church of the Immaculate Conception, a handsome and lofty Gothic structure of the Decorated style, designed by Mr. J. J. Scoles, and built in 1848-9.

The fabric is the first possessed by the Jesuits in London since the expulsion of the order from Somerset House and St. James's under the Stuart sovereigns.* The front, which looks south instead of west, is a miniature reproduction of that of the Cathedral of Beauvais. The high altar, designed by the late Mr. A. W. Pugin, was the gift of Miss Tempest, and cost £1,000. The church has two other altars, and dwarf side-aisles. Having houses built up against it on either side, it is lit from a clerestory above.

Mount Street, which was built gradually at various dates, between the commencement and the middle of the last century, commemorates in its name a fort or bastion in the line of fortification so hastily drawn round the western suburbs in 1643, by order of the Parliament, when an attack from the royal forces was expected. There was a mount at the west end of this street, on the eastern border of Hyde Park. The eastern entrance to this street is in the corner of Berkeley Square, at the south end of Davies Street. Most of the street consists of shops, irregular in plan and size, and by no means of the first calibre.

Peter Cunningham tells us that in later times there was in this street a celebrated coffee-house, called "The Mount." It was probably one which was frequented by the charming Lawrence Sterne, towards the end of his life, whilst occupying the lodgings in Bond Street, where he died. From this coffee-house, at all events, many of his love letters to Mrs. Draper and other ladies are dated.

In Mount Street was living, at the commencement of the present century, a singular character, one Martin Van Butchell, a quack doctor and dentist of celebrity, who claimed to be able to cure the king's evil, teeth, ruptures, fistula, and every kind of evil to which flesh is heir, and who, consequently, obtained from his patients fees suited rather to the extent of their credulity than to that of his own merits. He applied, through the Lord Chamberlain of the Household, for the post of

* See Vol. III., p. 91.

GROSVENOR SQUARE. (*See page 339.*)

dentist to George III.; but when the consent of his Majesty was obtained, he said that he did not care for the custom of royalty. His wife having died, he had her body embalmed and kept in his parlour; and he outdid even this act of eccentricity by allowing his beard to grow, which at that time was reckoned sheer madness. He is said to have sold the hairs out of his beard at a guinea each to ladies who wanted to become the mothers

to make his wife and children dine by themselves, and to come when called by a whistle; he dressed his first wife in black, and his second in white, never allowing either a change of colour. He was also one of the earliest of teetotalers. He died in 1810.

No. 111, now occupied by a detachment of priests of the Order of Jesus, was at one time the manor house of an estate extending southwards to the

THE LOFT USED BY THE CATO STREET CONSPIRATORS, 1820. (*See page* 340.)

of fine children. He described himself in one of his printed circulars as "a British Christian man, with a comely beard full eight inches long." He used to ride about the West-end on a shaggy pony, always unclipped, of course, and painted with spots by the hand of its master. Its bridle was one of Van Butchell's contrivances, being really a blind, which could be let down over both the pony's eyes in case of the animal taking fright. He lived in the same house for nearly half a century, and never would go to visit a patient. "I go to none," he said and wrote, and he was true to his word, though as much as £500 was offered him to induce him to alter his resolution. And yet, when at home, he would sit and sell oranges, cakes, and gingerbread to the children at his doorstep. He used

borders of the property of the Berkeleys. In the garden behind it are some fine trees, which once stood, doubtless, in the open fields; and Farm Street in the rear still serves to keep up the tradition of its former rurality. A few doors west, on the southern side of the street, stands the Workhouse of St. George's, Hanover Square, a dingy and gloomy building externally. Nearly opposite to its gates, from the middle of Mount Street to Grosvenor Square, runs a short thoroughfare called Charles Street, of which there is little or nothing to say, beyond the fact that in it is the Coburg Hotel, kept by Francis Grillon, an offshoot of Grillon's Hotel, of Albemarle Street. In 1832, the Duchesse d'Angoulême, in her way from Edinburgh to France, held receptions at this hotel.

In this street, during the years 1767–68, when, as we have seen, he removed into the artistic neighbourhood of St. Martin's Lane, Josiah Wedgwood had his West-end show-rooms of pottery and porcelain, the royal arms over his door denoting— what at that time and in his case was no fiction —the patronage and custom of royalty which his firm enjoyed. Hither Queen Charlotte would drive from Buckingham House to see those art-treasures by the production of which Wedgwood was destined in a few short years to make the name of England famous in Continental courts. The fact is that the rooms here were small, and as the patronage of the wealthy classes poured in upon him in a stream, he soon found himself quite at a loss for room when large and handsome vases, as well as dishes and dinner-services, had to be displayed.

Charles Street was probably so called after one of the Stuart kings, from whose reign it dates. It may be interesting to record here that in the "Post Office Directory" for 1883 there are as many as forty Charles Streets mentioned as being within the limits of the metropolis, to say nothing of a Charles Square, three Charles Places, and a Charles Mews.

CHAPTER XXVII.

GROSVENOR SQUARE, AND ITS NEIGHBOURHOOD.

A Critical Reviewer's Opinion of the Square in the Last Century— Sir Richard Grosvenor—The Statue of George I.—Linkmen and Oil-Lamps— A House raffled for—Mr. Thomas Raikes—Anecdote of Charles Mathews—Beckford of Fonthill, and Lord Nelson—The Earl of Derby and Miss Farren, the Actress—The Earl of Harrowby and the Cato Street Conspiracy—Lord Stratford de Redcliffe—The Earl of Shaftesbury —Dr. Johnson—Lower Grosvenor Street—A Curious Exhibition—Brook Street and its Distinguished Residents—North and South Audley Streets.

THIS square was the last addition in point of date, and also the farthest addition westward, to the metropolis at the time when "The New Critical Review of the Public Buildings of London" was published, namely, in 1736. It was intended to be the finest of all the then existing squares ; but the writer of that work condemns it as hopelessly falling short of any such a design. In fact, he laughs at it as a miscarriage in its execution, utterly wanting in harmony of plan, and irregular in its details. He speaks of the east side as the best of the four ; but even this he censures severely, and he cannot find terms bad enough to describe the "triple house on the north side," which, he suggests, "could have been built only with the view of taking in some young heir to buy it at a great rate." He praises, however, the expensive taste with which the centre of the square was laid out, though he condemns the brick enclosure round it as clumsy, and a "blemish to the view which it was intended to preserve and adorn." The brick enclosure happily is no more, having long since given place to iron railings. As for the south and west sides, they are, in the author's opinion, "little better than a collection of whims and frolics in building, without anything like order or beauty, and therefore deserving no further consideration." The purer taste of our own day, however, will see merits, if not beauty, in the variety of styles introduced into the houses which form the square ;

and the owner of the freehold, the head of the Grosvenor family, will be able to laugh at the attempt to "write down" his ancestors' fine and important contribution to the grandeur of the West-end. The real fact is that many of the houses are built of red brick, but they have noble stone facings, and being each of a different pattern, though uniform in general appearance, they give to the square a pleasing variety in details, without detracting from its dignity.

That the square was built a long time before the year above mentioned is clear from the fact, that as early as 1716 Pope speaks of it in a letter to his friend and correspondent, Miss Martha Blount.

Previous to the completion of the houses between New Bond Street and Hyde Park, the erections here were called "Grosvenor Buildings ;" but in the year 1725, says the author of the "Beauties of England," Sir Richard Grosvenor, Bart. (who was in right of the manor of Wimondham, Herts, Grand Cup-bearer at the coronation of George II., and who died in 1732), assembled his tenants and the persons employed in the buildings to a splendid entertainment, when he named the various streets. At the same period he erected the gate in Hyde Park, now called by his name." Sir Richard, to whom this square owes its origin, was, says Malcolm, "as great a builder as the Duke of Bedford." The landscape garden, which occupies the centre of the square, was laid out by Kent, and the enclosure can boast a few trees, though not so handsome as the plane-trees of Berke ey Square.

There was formerly in the centre of the square a gilt statue of George I. on horseback, but the pedestal is now vacant. This statue was made by Van Nort, and was erected by Sir Richard Grosvenor in 1726, "near the redoubt called Oliver's Mount." Soon after it was put up, says Malcolm, "some villains dismembered it in the most shameful manner, and affixed a traitorous paper to the pedestal."

Before several of the houses in this square, and indeed in other streets at the West-end, may still be seen specimens of the iron link-extinguishers on the top of the railings. Numerous allusions to the link-boys and their calling are to be found in the plays and lighter poems of the last century, and links were commonly carried before carriages at the West-end until about the year 1807, when the introduction of gas gradually superseded their use. The link-men and link-boys would appear to have been a disorderly class, and the profession to have been followed as a cloak for thieving. Thus Gay writes in his "Trivia :"—

> "Though thou art tempted by the linkman's call,
> Yet trust him not along the lonely wall :
> In the midway he'll quench the flaming brand,
> And share the booty with the pilfering band."

It is worthy, perhaps, of a note, as showing the reluctance of our aristocracy to adopt new-fangled fashions, that Grosvenor Square was the last street or square which was lit with oil; the last oil-lamp there was not superseded by gas until 1842. The inhabitants for many years opposed the intrusion of so vulgar a commodity as gas, and preferred to go on as their fathers had gone on before them. What we have here said about the opposition to the introduction of gas in this locality may serve to remind the reader of Macaulay's words respecting the obstruction offered, less than two centuries ago, to Edward Fleming's first attempt to light the streets of London with oil. "The cause of darkness was not undefended. There were fools in that age who opposed the introduction of what was called 'the new light' as strenuously as fools in our own age have opposed the introduction of vaccination and railroads, and as strenuously as the fools of an age anterior to the dawn of history doubtless opposed the introduction of the plough and of alphabetical writing."

In 1739, says a writer in the *Gentleman's Magazine*, "the centre house on the east side of the square was raffled for, and won by two persons named Hunt and Braithwaite. The possessor valued it at £10,000, but the winners sold it two months afterwards for £7,000 to the Duke of Norfolk." The house was built on ground held by Sir Richard Grosvenor for eighty-four years from 1737, at a ground-rent of £42 per annum.

Malcolm, writing at the commencement of this century, humorously observes that his readers "must know that this square is the very *focus* of feudal grandeur, elegance, fashion, taste, and hospitality," and that "the novel-reader must be intimately acquainted with the description of residents within it, when the words 'Grosvenor Square' are to be found in almost every work of that species written in the compass of fifty years past."

Grosvenor Square, as may naturally be supposed, though only a century and a half old, has had plenty of distinguished inhabitants. In it, in 1832, was living Mr. Thomas Raikes, the accomplished author of the "Journal" from which we have so often quoted. Here Mr. Raikes used to entertain not only many of the leading politicians and statesmen of the day, but also Pope the actor, the elder Mathews, Tom Sheridan, Charles Calvert, and other genial acquaintances. One evening, when the above-named guests were present, a comical incident occurred, which Mr. Raikes records in his "Journal:"—"In the course of conversation, Pope alluded to an old gentleman in the country who was so madly attached to the society of Mathews, that whenever he came to town he went straight to his house, and if he did not find him there, would trace him and follow him wherever he might happen to be. This did not excite much attention, but about nine o'clock we all heard a tremendous rap at the door, and my servant came in saying that there was in the hall a gentleman who insisted on seeing Mr. Mathews. The latter appeared very disconcerted, made many apologies for the intrusion, and said that he would get rid of him instantly, as he doubtless must be the person who so frequently pestered him. As soon as he had retired, we heard a very noisy dialogue in the hall between Mathews and his friend, who insisted on coming in and joining the party, while the other as urgently insisted on his retreat. At length the door opened, and in walked a most extraordinary figure, who sat down in Mathews's place, filled himself a tumbler of claret, which he pronounced to be execrable, and began in the most impudent manner to claim acquaintance with all the party, and say the most ridiculous things to every one. We were all for the moment thrown off our guard ; but we soon detected our versatile companion, who really had not taken three minutes to tie up his nose with a string, put on a wig, and otherwise so to metamorphose himself that it was almost impossible to recognise him."

It had been foretold to Mr. Raikes at Paris some years previously that he would one day be arrested for debt; and the prophecy was thus fulfilled. Mr. Raikes shall tell his own story:—"The repairs of my house were being performed by contract; but the builder failed before his work was concluded, and the assignee claimed of me the whole amount of the sum agreed. This I would not pay further than it had been fairly earned. The difference was only £150; but the assignees sent a bailiff to my house and arrested me, while my carriage was waiting to convey me to dinner at the Duke of York's, where the story caused considerable merriment."

The town residence of Mr. Beckford, the famous owner of Fonthill Abbey, in Wiltshire, was in this square; and on one occasion Lord Nelson was on a visit here, at a time of general scarcity, when persons in every rank of life denied themselves the use of that necessary article of food, bread, at dinner, and were content, for the sake of example, with such vegetables as the season afforded. Lord Nelson, however, contrary to the established etiquette of the dinner-table, called for bread, and was respectfully told by one of the servants in waiting that, in consequence of the scarcity of wheat, bread was wholly dispensed with at the dinner-table of Mr. Beckford. Nelson looked angry; and desiring his own attendant to be called, he drew forth a shilling from his pocket, and commanded him to go out and purchase him a loaf; observing, that after having fought for his bread, he thought it hard that his countrymen should deny it to him.

Here, at No. 23, lived Edward, the twelfth Earl of Derby, after his marriage with Miss Farren, the celebrated actress, whose mother lived with his lordship and her daughter, and died here in 1803. Miss Farren's first patronesses and acquaintances in London were Lord and Lady Ailesbury and Mrs. Damer, to whom she had been introduced by the Duchess of Leinster, who knew something of her family in Ireland. The house was the town residence of the Earls of Derby until about the year 1852, when the then head of the house of Stanley removed to St. James's Square.

It was at No. 39 in this square, then, as now, the house of the Earl of Harrowby, that the Cabinet Ministers of George IV. had arranged to dine on the 23rd of February, 1820, when they were prevented by a preconcerted plan for their assassination, which is known to history as the Cato Street conspiracy, from the place between Marylebone and the Edgware Road where it was concocted, and which is now called Horace Street. The head of this conspiracy was a discharged soldier, named Arthur Thistlewood, who had been imprisoned for twelve months for annoying Lord Sidmouth. Along with a band of a dozen or more desperadoes, it had been arranged that some of them should watch the door of Lord Harrowby's house, where, whilst one of the gang delivered a pretended dispatch-box, the rest were to rush in and kill all the King's ministers, Lords Sidmouth and Castlereagh being especially marked out for vengeance. From Grosvenor Square they were to rush off to the barracks in Hyde Park, and thence to attack the Bank of England and the Tower of London, as they expected that they would have the people with them. Meantime, however, the Government had obtained scent of the intended massacre, through the agency of a spy, and whilst the assassins were assembled in a stable-loft in Cato Street, and arming themselves by the light of a candle for the execution of their plan, they were surprised by a body of Bow Street officers, who made their way up the ladder into the loft. The leader of the officers, on calling upon Thistlewood to surrender, was shot dead; the lights being put out, a fearful *mêlée* followed; in the midst of it Thistlewood managed to escape, but he was captured early next morning. Along with nine of his comrades, he was safely lodged in the Tower next day; and it may be remarked that they were the last prisoners confined in that fortress. In the following April the conspirators were brought to trial, when Thistlewood and three of his chief accomplices were sentenced to death, and the rest were transported for life. It is stated in Mr. John Timbs' "Romance of London," on the authority of the late Sir R. Thierry, a judge in the Australian colonies, that two at least of the persons transported for this crime rose in the course of time to independent positions at Bathurst and Sydney, and became respectable members of society.

The corner house of the square, between Upper Grosvenor and South Audley Streets, was for many years the residence of Lord Stratford de Redcliffe, better known by his former name of Sir Stratford Canning, "the greatest of diplomatists of his age, the highest authority on all subjects connected with Turkey and the East, and the only man in Western Europe of whom the Ottoman Porte was really afraid." Here he produced a drama, a volume of poems, and sundry essays on religious subjects at an age when most men are rather inclined to throw the pen aside than to take it in hand. He died in 1880.

Besides the members of the aristocracy named above, this square has numbered among its inhabitants, at one time or another, Bishop Warburton, author of the "Divine Legation;" Lord Chancellor Hardwicke; Lord North, when Premier; Henry Thrale, of Streatham; Sir Thomas Stamford Raffles; and John Withers and Sir George Beaumont, the great patron of art and artists. He had part of his gallery at the house already mentioned as belonging to Lord Stratford de Redcliffe. In 1841 Lord Canning and Lord Granville (then Lord Leveson) were living together at No. 10. Among its more recent inhabitants may be mentioned the late Mr. Joseph Neeld, M.P., whose fine gallery of paintings was at No. 6; and the Earl of Shaftesbury, who has lived at No. 24 for more than thirty years. The philanthropy of the last-named nobleman, although so well known, is fairly entitled to a word or two of recognition here, particularly in his efforts to ameliorate the condition of the lowest orders of society. The Ragged School movement, of which Mr. John Forster epitomises the history in his "Life of Dickens" by saying that it was begun by a shoemaker of Southampton and a chimney-sweep of Windsor, was carried out to its present length and its present success mainly under the auspices of Lord Shaftesbury; and the same writer tells us that in thirty years the schools had passed some thirty thousand children through them, and that it is computed that for a third of that number honest means of employment have been found by the same agency.

We have already had occasion, more than once, to speak of the conflicts that took place in this neighbourhood during the civil wars. It is said that the line of fortifications thrown up at that time, by order of Cromwell, ran diagonally across the space occupied by this square from the mound, or mount, at the western extremity of what is now, from that circumstance, called Mount Street, as we have already mentioned. Apart from this, there are few, if any, historical events connected with the square; indeed, it may be said that it is almost of too recent growth to have much of a history.

That Johnson was a frequenter of so fashionable a region as Grosvenor Square may be set down by Mr. Timbs, or by others, among "Things not Generally Known." But Mr. Smith, in his "Book for a Rainy Day," tells us that he once saw the burly doctor "follow a sturdy thief who had stolen his handkerchief in Grosvenor Square, seize him by the collar with both hands, and shake him violently; then, letting him loose, give him such a powerful smack on the face as sent him reeling off the pavement." Independent as he was in all his ideas, the learned doctor once fairly owned that if he was not plain Dr. Johnson, of Lichfield, Oxford, and Bolt Court, he would desire to be "Grosvenor of that ilk."

The Count de Melfort, in his "Impressions of England," remarks that Grosvenor and St. James's Squares clearly have the first rank to themselves. This may have been a just remark at the time when he wrote, in the reign of William IV., but it would scarcely be true now that Belgrave Square has come to be the centre of attraction and fashion. However, they all owe their precedence to the fact that they are mainly occupied by the highest of the aristocracy, and that there is not a plebeian "professional" man—not even a titled M.D.—living in them.

At the south-eastern corner of the square, and extending eastward towards Bond Street, is Lower Grosvenor Street. Writing at the commencement of the present century, the author of the "Beauties of England" states that it "consists of a great number of excellent houses, the majority of which are inhabited by titled persons and affluent families. Indeed, a bare list of the persons of distinction residing in this neighbourhood would comprehend a great portion of the present British peers."

Here, in 1784, was living Mr. John Crewe, M.P. for Cheshire, and subsequently Lord Crewe, already mentioned as the last survivor of Fox's friends at "Brooks's" Club. His wife, who was a most zealous Whig, gave at her house a splendid entertainment in commemoration of the return of Mr. Fox for Westminster, in May of the above year. "The intimate friend of Fox, and one of the most accomplished and charming women of her time," writes Sir N. W. Wraxall, "she had exerted herself in securing his election, if not as efficaciously, yet as enthusiastically as the Duchess of Devonshire herself. On this occasion the ladies, no less than the men, were all habited in blue and buff. The Prince of Wales, too, was present in that dress. After supper, a toast having been given by his Royal Highness, consisting of the words 'True blue and Mrs. Crewe,' which was received with rapture, the lady rose and proposed another health, expressive of her gratitude, and not less laconic, namely, 'True blue, and all of you.'"

Mr. Peter Cunningham enumerates among the other residents the Countess of Hertford (celebrated in Thomson's "Seasons," Spring), Miss Vane, the mistress of Frederick, Prince of Wales; Mrs. Oldfield, the actress; Admiral Jervis, afterwards Earl St. Vincent; Dr. Matthew Baillie (brother of Agnes and Joanna Baillie); and last, not least, Sir

Humphry Davy, when he became President of the Royal Society. Mr. Fox Maule, afterwards Lord Dalhousie, and the accomplished Mr. H. Gally Knight, M.P., author of "An Architectural Tour in Normandy," also lived here.

And yet this highly aristocratic street has been occasionally invaded by plebeian exhibitions. At No. 68, for instance, was, in 1818-20, Duburg's Exhibition. This consisted of models in cork of

On the north of the open fields, says Macaulay, the Oxford Road, in the reign of Charles II., ran between hedges. "Three or four hundred yards to the south were the garden walls of a few great houses, which were then considered as quite out of town. Here was a spring from which, long afterwards, Conduit Street was named." From this stream or brook—which came down from Tyburn, and found its way across Piccadilly, as we have

CURZON CHAPEL, MAY FAIR. (*See page* 352.)

ancient temples, theatres, &c., in Rome and other Italian cities, and in the south of France, all formed to a scale, and executed so as to convey a faithful representation of the ruins as they then stood. Mr. Rush, the ambassador from the United States of America, writes in his "Court of London," under date May, 1819: "Went to see the cork models in Lower Grosvenor Street. There was a representation of the amphitheatre at Verona, and of that at Rome; of Vergel's tomb; of the Cascade near Tivoli; of the Grotto of Egeria; of Vesuvius in a state of eruption; and of various other things of antiquity. I rank it among the most curious exhibitions that I have seen in London." No. 16 was for some time the home of the Royal Institute of British Architects.

already seen—the neighbourhood was called the Brook Field. The earliest instance of the name occurring is, perhaps, in the *London Gazette* of September, 1688:—"His Majesty has been graciously pleased to grant a market for live cattle to be held in Brookfield, near Hyde Park Corner, on Tuesday and Thursday in every week. The first market day will be held on the first Thursday in October next, and afterwards to continue weekly on Tuesdays and Thursdays—the Tuesday market in the morning for cattle, and the afternoon for horses." The land, however, being wanted for building purposes, and the market not proving very attractive, the latter was dropped, and the services of designers and architects were called in. Many of the original houses still remain; they mostly date from the middle of the last century. The principal street that sprung up in these fields—running from Hanover Square across Bond Street, Davies Street, and Grosvenor Square, towards Hyde Park—naturally took the name of Brook Street.

This street has for a century been the residence of successful surgeons and physicians. Hither Sir Charles Bell, in the height of his fame, removed about the year 1831, and here he lived till his final settlement in Edinburgh, in 1835. Sir Henry Holland, the fashionable Court physician, resided for upwards of fifty years at No. 25, formerly the residence of Edmund Burke. His house was a centre of literary and scientific society, and around his table often were gathered the Macaulays, the Wilberforces, and Sydney Smith (whose daughter he married), as well as Lord John Russell, Lord Melbourne, and other political leaders. He attended the deathbeds of no less than five Premiers, and of several members of our own and some other royal houses. He was the physician to the Princess Charlotte, and at a later date to Her Majesty and the late Prince Consort. He was created a baronet in 1853. He was the author of very many important medical works and books of travel, and he made it a rule of his life, and one which he observed until the very last year of his life, to travel abroad every summer. He died in October, 1873, at the age of eighty-five. Lady Holland's name is well known in the world of letters as the author of the "Life" of her accomplished and witty father, "the Canon of St. Paul's."

Sir William Gull, physician extraordinary to Her Majesty, is another distinguished resident in this street. He was created a baronet in 1872, on the recovery of the Prince of Wales, after a dangerous attack of fever, through which Sir William attended his Royal Highness as his chief medical adviser.

At No. 50 lived Sir Jeffrey Wyatville, the restorer of the architecture of Windsor Castle.

Handel likewise resided in this street. Mr. J. T. Smith, in his "Antiquarian Rambles," fixes the house exactly; it was "No. 57 on the south side, four doors from Bond Street, and two from the gateway." On the same side of the street, between Bond and Davies Streets, is Claridge's—formerly Mivart's—hotel, noted as the place where royal and distinguished personages from foreign countries usually "put up."

At No. 20 was held the first entertainment given by the Society of Painters in Water Colours.

In Woodstock Street, which lies between Oxford Street and Brook Street, Johnson was once living in lodgings, accompanied by his wife, on his second journey to London, in the autumn of 1737, before he took up his residence in Castle Street, and made the acquaintance of Edmund Cave. He does not, however, appear to have remained here long, finding it possibly too far from the scene of his literary labours at Clerkenwell in the days when there were no omnibuses or "underground" railways.

TIDDY DOL.
From a Contemporary Print.　(*See page* 346.)

Grosvenor Square is connected with Oxford Street, at its north-east corner, by a thoroughfare of inferior appearance, built about 1770, and called Duke Street, probably after the Duke of Cumberland. It requires no further notice here.

At the north-west corner of the square, which also it connects with Oxford Street, is North Audley Street—so called, not from the Lords Audley, as is often supposed, but after Mr. Hugh Audley, a barrister of the Inner Temple, who, seeing the tendency of London to increase in a westerly direction, bought up the ground hereabouts for building purposes, and having started with a very small capital, died in 1662, leaving property to the tune of nearly half a million. The land taken up by him is described in an old survey, to be seen among the maps of George III., in the British Museum, as "lying between Great Brook Field, and the Shoulder of Mutton Field." The history of this individual may be found in a curious pamphlet, entitled, " The Way to be Rich, according to the practice of the great Audley, who began life, with £200, in the year 1605, and died worth £400,000 this instant November, 1662."

Here lived and here died, in 1770, at the age of upwards of ninety, General Lord Ligonier, one of the last survivors of the Duke of Marlborough's campaigns, and the correspondent of nearly all the eminent statesmen of the reigns of George II. and George III.

In this street was the " Vernon's Head," the sign of Admiral Vernon, the hero of Portobello, set up in commemoration of the capture of that town in 1739. The house was converted into a private residence in 1882-3. Opposite is St. Mark's Church, originally a chapel of ease to St. George's, Hanover Square, though now it has a district assigned to it, and has become, to some extent, independent of the mother church. It is in the Ionic style of Grecian art. It was erected by Mr. John Deering, R.A., in 1828.

South Audley Street, which runs southward from the south-western corner of Grosvenor Square, was not built till many years after North Audley Street, namely, about 1728; it comprises far finer houses, and has been tenanted by the highest families; and many foreigners of distinction, diplomatists, and others, have lived in it temporarily. Charles X. of France, for instance, in his exile, occupied No. 72; Louis XVIII. also lived here at one time, but the house is not identified, even by Mr. P. Cunningham. General Paoli, of Corsican fame; Sir William Jones, the great Eastern scholar; and Sir Richard Westmacott, the sculptor, are also named as residents here. Mr. Cunningham also tells us that Sir Richard Westmacott executed all his principal works at the house No. 14, now the residence of the Hon. Edward Leveson-Gower, brother of Lord Granville.

In this street, too, lived Mr. Robert Berry, the father of the charming Misses Berry, the friends and correspondents of Horace Walpole, of whom we shall have more to say in our next chapter.

Horace Walpole complains, in a letter to one of these ladies, that he has "no Audley Street" to receive him of an evening—alluding, no doubt, to his cousins, the Conways, to whose house he also refers in another letter, complaining that "all Audley Street is off to Yorkshire," and that town is dull and lonely.

No. 74 in this street, lately the residence of the

Earl of Cawdor, was for the best part of a century the house of the Portuguese Ambassador. In this street, at No. 77, was living, in 1820, Alderman (afterwards Sir Matthew) Wood; and here, on the 6th of June in that year, Queen Caroline, the injured consort of George IV., arriving from the Continent, took up her residence. Here she received the formal addresses from the common councilmen and livery of London, and here she would appear on the balcony, and bow to the mob assembled in the street below. Here her Majesty continued to reside till the commencement of her trial in Westminster Hall, which lasted from the 19th of August down to the 10th of November. During these long and weary weeks, the Queen was accommodated with apartments more conveniently situated in St. James's Square, at the house of Sir Philip Francis, as we have already seen. The sad story of the Queen's last few days is thus told by Hughson :—" On the death of George III., the Princess of Wales, who had been several years residing on the Continent, became Queen-consort of England, and resolved on immediately proceeding thither. On the 6th of June, 1820, her Majesty arrived in London, and took up her temporary residence at the house of Alderman Wood, in South Audley Street. The alderman met her Majesty at Montbarde, in France, and accompanied her through the rest of her journey. On the 16th, the common council, and on the 3rd of the following month, the livery of London, presented addresses to her Majesty on her return. On the 19th of August, the proceedings on the Bill of Pains and Penalties commenced in the House of Lords, which lasted till the 10th of November, when her Majesty was acquitted. It is impossible, in the limits of this work, to describe the state of the metropolis during these unpopular proceedings ; on their close, the town was illuminated for three nights, and, on the 29th, the Queen went to St. Paul's Cathedral to return thanks." It is difficult to imagine what the special mercies were for which her Majesty gave "thanks" on this occasion. Her death happened in the following August.

Queen Caroline, however, was not the only royal personage who has lived in this street; for, in 1826, at Cambridge House (now Curzon House) resided the Duke of York, after he gave up his newly-built mansion in the stable-yard at St. James's. The house has been, at a later date, the residence of Earl Howe.

In the above year, too, Lord John Russell lived in this street; his house, however, has been converted to business purposes, and now serves as a hairdresser's shop. In 1841 the name of Lord Sydenham occurs among the list of residents here.

Among the inhabitants of this street, in 1763, was Lord Bute, as we learn from a notice in a contemporary journal, which tells us that, " in the July of that year, two women were sent by Lord Bute's order to Bridewell, for singing political ballads before his lordship's door in South Audley Street."

On the eastern side of this street is one of those proprietary chapels of ease, with which we have seen this fashionable district abounds. It is a dull, heavy structure, dating from the last century. In its vaults repose some distinguished characters: Lady Mary Wortley Montagu; Ambrose Philips, the poet; Philip, Earl of Chesterfield, who was carried hither from Chesterfield House, in 1773; and John Wilkes, who was buried here from Grosvenor Square, in 1797. A mural tablet in the chapel bears an inscription, said to be from his own pen :—" The remains of John Wilkes, a friend to Liberty."

In this street are the pottery-galleries of Messrs. Goode, where are displayed the celebrated productions of the Messrs. Minton. The chief stores of the Lambeth Art *Faience* have for many years past been kept at this establishment, which is said to be the most extensive of its kind in Europe.

At the corner of South Street stands a house of a very marked character, and by many attributed to Inigo Jones. The building is heavy and dull to a degree; massive cornices, small window-panes set in massive frames, and a bay-window over a portico, projecting partly over the pavement in South Street, are its chief architectural features. The house was formerly the residence of General Gascoyne, the colleague of Canning in the representation of Liverpool.

Audley Square—as it is the fashion to style a few dull, heavy, substantial houses which recede a little from the road on the eastern side of South Audley Street, just above Chesterfield House—scarcely deserves a separate notice, but may be regarded as a part of South Audley Street; and the only fact recorded in its annals is, that Mr. Spencer Perceval, the premier, whose assassination we have recorded,† was born in it in the year 1762.

Chesterfield House, at the bottom of this street, we shall describe in our next chapter.

CHAPTER XXVIII.

MAY FAIR.

"The morals of May Fair."

Derivation of the Name of May Fair—The Earliest Notice on Record of St. James's Fair—Description of the Fair in the Last Century—Puppet Shows—The Eccentric " Tiddy Dol "—Suppression of the Fair—The Rev. Dr. Keith's Chapel, and the Clandestine Marriages there—The Marriage of " Handsome Tracy "—Miss Elizabeth Gunning and the Duke of Hamilton—Extracts from the Marriage Registers of St. George's, Hanover Square—Curzon Street—The Misses Berry—Epigram by Horace Walpole—Distinguished Residents of Curzon Street— Hertford Street—Dr. Jenner—The " Dog and Duck "—Shepherd's Market—" Kitty Fisher "—Seamore Place—Chesterfield Street—The Hon. Mrs. Norton—Queen Street—Chesterfield House, and its Reminiscences.

THIS spot, which embraces in its somewhat vague and undefined area the present Curzon Street, Hertford Street, and Chesterfield House and gardens, took its name, in the days of Edward I., from an annual fair, which that king privileged the hospital of St. James's to keep " on the eve of St. James', the day, and the morrow, and four days following," as has already been stated in our account of St. James's Palace.* Pepys speaks of it as St. James's Fair, a name which expresses it geographically with sufficient accuracy, at a time when all to the north and west of St. James's Hospital was an open field.

The following amusing notice of " the Fair in St. James's " is quoted from Mackyn's Diary by Mr. Frost, in his " Old Showmen of London," as the earliest on record :—" The xxv. day of June [1560]. Saint James's fayer by Westminster was so great that a man could not have a pygg for money ; and the bear wiffes had nether meate nor drink before iiij. of cloke in the same day. And the chese went very well away for 1d. q. the pounde. Besides the great and mighti armie of beggares and bandes that were there."

Beyond the fact that it was postponed for a few weeks or months in 1603, on account of the plague, nothing more is recorded concerning this fair till 1664, in which year, Mr. Frost tells us, " it was suppressed, as considered to tend rather to the advantage of looseness and irregularity, than to the substantial promotion of any good, common and beneficial to the people."

It is to be hoped that the bad character of the fair, as given by the *Observator* somewhat later, in the reign of Queen Anne, is a little exaggerated. The editor writes:—"Oh! the piety of some people about the Queen, who can suffer things of this nature to go undiscovered to her Majesty, and consequently unpunished! Can any rational men imagine that her Majesty would permit so much lewdness as is committed at May Fair, for so many days together, so near to her royal palace, if she knew anything of the matter? I don't believe the patent for that fair allows the patentees the liberty of setting up the devil's shops and exposing his merchandise for sale." As to the precise nature, however, of this diabolic ware and "merchandise" he does not enlighten us in detail.

According to Mr. Frost, in his work quoted above, "May Fair" did not assume any importance till about the year 1701, when the multiplication of shows of all kinds caused it to enlarge its sphere of attractions. "It was held," he writes, "on the north side of Piccadilly, in Shepherd's Market, Shepherd's Court, White Horse Street, Sun Court, Market Court, and on the open space westwards, Chapel Street and Hertford Street, as far as Tyburn (now Park) Lane. The ground-floor of the Market House, usually occupied by butchers' stalls, was appropriated during the fair to the sale of toys and gingerbread, and the upper portion was converted into a theatre. The open space westwards was covered with the booths of jugglers, fencers, and boxers, the stands of mountebanks, swings, round-abouts, &c.; while the sides of the streets were occupied by sausage-stalls and gambling-tables. The first-floor windows were also, in some instances, made to serve as the proscenia of puppet-shows."

"I have been able to trace," he adds, "only two shows to this fair in 1702, namely, Barnes and Finley's, and Miller's, which stood opposite to the former, and presented 'an excellent droll called *Crispin and Crispianus*, or a shoe-maker a prince, with the best machines, singing, and dancing ever yet in the fair.'" The fair, on this occasion, drew together a large concourse of persons, and an attempt to exclude some young women of light character resulted in a riot. The young women, arrested for the purpose of being turned out, were rescued by some soldiers; a conflict ensued, other constables came up, and the "rough" element, of course, took part with the accused women. In the end one constable was killed and three others seriously injured. The man who actually dealt the fatal blow to the unfortunate constable managed to escape; but a butcher who had been active in the affray, was tried for his part in the affair, convicted, and hung at Tyburn. This tragical occurrence helped, no doubt, to bring the fair itself into dis-

credit, especially among the respectable inhabitants of the neighbourhood of Piccadilly."

Pennant, who remembered the last "May Fair," describes the locality as "covered with booths, temporary theatres, and every enticement to low pleasure." A more minute description of the scene, evidently drawn from the life, is given by an antiquary named Carter, in the *Gentleman's Magazine* for 1774.

"A mountebank's stage," this person tells us, "was erected opposite the 'Three Jolly Butchers' public-house, on the eastern side of the market area, now the 'King's Arms.' Here Woodward, the inimitable comedian and harlequin, made his first appearance as 'Merry Andrew;' from these humble boards he soon after made his way to those of Covent Garden Theatre. Then there was a 'beheading of puppets,' in a coal-shed attached to a grocer's shop (then Mr. Frith's, now Mr. Frampton's). One of these mock executions was exposed to the attending crowd. A shutter was fixed horizontally, on the edge of which, after many previous ceremonies, a puppet was made to lay its head, and another puppet instantly chopped it off with an axe. In a circular staircase-window, at the north end of Sun Court, a similar performance by another set of puppets took place. In these representations the late punishment of the Scottish chieftain, Lord Lovat, was again brought forward, in order to gratify the feelings of southern loyalty at the expense of that farther north."

"After the Scottish rebellion of 1745," writes Chambers, in his "Book of Days," "the beheading of puppets formed one of the most regular and attractive parts of the exhibitions at the 'May Fair,' and was continued for several years. The last great proprietor of such puppet-shows was a man named Flockton, whose puppets were in the height of their glory about 1790, and who retired soon after on a handsome competence." A puppet-show, we may add, under the name of the Marionettes, was revived at St. James's Hall about the year 1872.

At these annual gatherings in May Fair, too, was to be seen "Tiddy Dol," the eccentric vendor of gingerbread, whom we have mentioned in our account of the Haymarket, and who figures in Hogarth's well-known picture of the "Idle Apprentice" at Tyburn, where he, in his ornamental dress, is seen in the crowd holding up a gingerbread cake in his hand and addressing the mob. Here, too, was to be seen a Frenchman, whose name has passed away, who submitted to the curious his wife's powers of physical endurance. Fragile and delicate as she appeared, she would (so it was stated) raise from the floor a blacksmith's anvil by the hair of her head, which she twisted round it; and then, lying down, she would have the anvil placed on her bosom, while a horse-shoe was forged upon it with the same heavy blows which may be heard and seen in a blacksmith's shop.

In "Malcolm's Anecdotes" (vol. ii.) is preserved an advertisement of this fair from one of the London papers of the time :—"In Brookfield market-place, at the east corner of Hyde Park, is a fair to be kept for the space of sixteen days, beginning with the 1st of May; the first three days for live cattle and leather, with the same entertainments as at Bartholomew Fair, where there are shops to be let, ready built, for all manner of tradesmen that usually keep fairs, and so to continue yearly at the same place."

May Fair, which had long been falling into disrepute, ceased to be held in the reign of George I. It was "presented by the grand jury of Middlesex for four years successively as a public scandal; and the county magistrates then presented an address to the Crown, praying for its suppression by royal proclamation." Its abolition was brought about mainly through the influence of the Earl of Coventry, to whose house in Piccadilly it was an annual nuisance.

In 1721, as we learn from the *London Journal* of May 27th in that year, "the ground upon which the May Fair formerly was held is marked out for a large square, and several fine streets and houses are to be built upon it." The idea of a "square," however, was never realised.

In recording the downfall of May Fair and of its doings, the *Tatler* announces that "Mrs. Saraband, so famous for her ingenious puppet-show, has set up a shop in the Exchange, where she sells her little troop under the name of jointed babies."

The fashionable locality now known as May Fair, in the days of George I. and George II., however, enjoyed, on other grounds than that of the annual fair, a celebrity almost unique, and rivalled only by the Fleet Prison, of which we have already spoken.* Here was a chapel for the celebration of private and secret marriages, which stood within a few yards of the present chapel in Curzon Street. It was presided over by a clergyman, Dr. George Keith, who advertised his business in the daily newspapers, and, in the words of Horace Walpole, made "a very bishopric of revenue." This worthy parson having contrived for a long time to defy the Bishop of London and the authorities of Church and State, was at length

excommunicated for "contempt" of the Church of which he was a minister; but he was impudent enough to turn the tables upon his superior, and to hurl a sentence of excommunication at the head of his bishop, Dr. Gibson, and the judge of the Ecclesiastical Court. Keith was sent to prison, where he remained for several years. His "shop," however, as he called it, continued to flourish under his curates, who acted as "shopmen;" and the public was kept daily apprised of its situation and its tariff, as witness the following advertisement in the *Daily Post* of July 20th, 1744: "To prevent mistakes, the little new chapel in May Fair, near Hyde Park corner, is in the corner house, opposite to the city side of the great chapel, and within ten yards of it, and the minister and clerk live in the same corner house where the little chapel is; and the licence on a crown stamp, minister and clerk's fees, together with the certificate, amount to one guinea, as heretofore, at any hour till four in the afternoon. And that it may be the better known, there is a porch at the door like a country church porch."

But the rank and fashion of May Fair did not care whether the fees demanded were high or low, provided they could get the marriage ceremony performed secretly and expeditiously, yet legally. "Sometimes," writes Charles Knight, in "Once upon a Time," "a petticoat without a hoop was led by a bag-wig and sword to the May Fair altar, after other solicitations had been tried in vain." As an instance of the way in which this marriage, not *à la mode*, worked in West-end society, let us take the following sketch from Horace Walpole in his best style :—"Did you know a young fellow that was named 'Handsome Tracy?' He was walking in the Park with some of his acquaintance, and overtook three girls; one was very pretty. They followed them; but the girls ran away; and the company grew tired of pursuing them, all but Tracy. He followed them to Whitehall Gate, where he gave a porter a crown to dog them. The porter hunted them, and he the porter. The girls ran all round Westminster, and back to the Haymarket, where the porter came up with them. He told the pretty one that she must go with him, and kept her talking till Tracy arrived, quite out of breath, and exceedingly in love. He insisted on knowing where she lived, which she refused to tell him; and after much disputing, went to the house of one of her companions, and Tracy with them. He there made her discover her family, a butter-woman in Craven Street, and engaged her to meet him next morning in the Park; but before night he wrote her four love-letters, and in the last offered to give two hundred pounds a year and a hundred a year to Signora la Madre. Griselda made a confidence to a staymaker's wife, who told her that the swain was certainly in love enough to marry her, if she could determine to be virtuous, and to refuse his offers. 'Ay,' says she; 'but suppose I should, and should lose him by it?' However, the measures of the cabinet council were decided for virtue; and when she met Tracy next morning in the Park, she was

concocted and cemented, turned out a happy one afterwards.

But the butterman's daughter was far from being the only person who found her way through this little chapel into the matrimonial "ship of fools." Everybody has heard of the three Miss Gunnings, whose beauty and attractions set the West-end in a perfect flame in the reign of George II., the eldest of whom was married to the sixth Earl of Coventry.

CLARIDGE'S HOTEL. (*See page 343.*)

convoyed by her sister and brother-in-law, and stuck close to the letter of her reputation. She would do nothing; she would go nowhere. At last, as an instance of prodigious compliance, she told him that if he would accept such a dinner as a butterman's daughter could give him, he should be welcome. So away they walked to Craven Street; the mother borrowed some silver to buy a leg of mutton, and kept the eager lover drinking till twelve o'clock at night, when a chosen committee accompanied the faithful pair to the minister of May Fair. The doctor was in bed, and swore he would not get up to marry the king, but added that he had a brother over the way who perhaps would, and who did marry them." It is to be hoped that the union, thus hastily and thoughtlessly

One of these young ladies here went through the marriage ceremony, which gave her the coronet of a duchess. Horace Walpole thus records the fact in his gossiping letters, under date February 27th, 1752:—" The event that has made the most noise since my last is the extempore marriage of the youngest of the Miss Gunnings, who have made so vehement a noise of late. About a fortnight since, at an immense assembly at my Lord Chesterfield's, made to show the house, which is really most magnificent, the Duke of Hamilton made violent love at one end of the room while he was playing faro at the other; that is, he saw neither the bank, nor his own cards, which were of three hundred pounds each; he soon lost a thousand. . . . Two nights afterwards he found himself so impatient, he sent for a parson. The doctor refused to perform the ceremony without license or ring, so the duke swore he would send for the archbishop. At last they were married with a ring off the bed-curtain at half an hour after twelve at night, at the May Fair Chapel."

At last even the people of rank and "quality," the inhabitants of May Fair, grew frightened at their own practices; and, as a consequence, an

in the little chapel here. The entries in these volumes extend over nearly twenty years; and there is a duplicate set in the Bishop of London's registry covering, probably, a somewhat larger period.

Dr. Keith himself was a clergyman from the north of the Tweed, but he had been driven from Scotland on account of his attachment to Episcopacy. He had set up a marriage office in the Fleet Prison,

CHESTERFIELD HOUSE, 1760.   (*See page* 353.)

Act was passed forbidding clandestine marriages. On the day previous to its coming into operation no less than sixty-one marriages were registered here. The Act itself was passed in the previous year, though its operation was delayed till Lady-day, 1754. During this period of suspense, Walpole writes to Montague:—"The Duchess of Argyll harangues against the marriage bill not taking place (*i.e.*, effect) immediately, and is persuaded that all the girls will go off before next Lady-day."

Among the registers of St. George's, Hanover Square, are three dingy volumes, marked "A," "B," and "C," respectively, containing such records as exist of about 7,000 marriages which were performed by the Rev. Mr. Keith and other clergymen

but had been forced to abandon it. He found, however, a better opening here, and a richer class of customers. It is said that, in one morning during the Whitsun holidays, he tied up in the silken bonds of matrimony a greater number of loving couples than had been married at any ten churches within the "bills of mortality." But this surely must have been an exaggeration.

While in prison, Keith seems to have had a keen eye to business. During his incarceration his wife died, and he kept her corpse embalmed and unburied for many months, and by that means ingeniously contrived to turn the circumstance into an advertisement of his trade. At all events, here is a record of his proceedings taken from the *Daily Advertiser* of January 30, 1750:—"We are informed that Mrs. Keith's corpse was removed from her husband's house in May Fair the middle of October last, to an apothecary's in South Audley Street, where she lies in a room hung with mourning, and is to continue there till Mr. Keith can attend the funeral. The way to Mr. Keith's chapel is through Piccadilly, by the end of St. James's Street, and down Clarges Street, and turn on the left hand." Then follows the announcement that the marriages are still carried on as usual by "another regular clergyman," as quoted above.

In the *Connoisseur* for October, 1754, are the following witty and satirical remarks *apropos* of the then recent Act for preventing clandestine marriages, and its effects on Keith's chapel :—" I received a scheme from my good friend Mr. Keith, whose chapel the late Marriage Act has rendered useless on its original principles. The reverend gentleman, seeing that all husbands and wives are henceforth to be put up on sale, proposes shortly to open his chapel on a new and more fashionable plan. As the ingenious Messrs. Henson and Bever have lately opened, in different quarters of the town, repositories for all horses to be sold by auction, Mr. Keith intends setting up a repository for all young males and females to be disposed of in marriage. From these studs (as the Doctor himself expresses it) a lady of beauty may be coupled to a man of fortune, and an old gentleman who has a colt's tooth remaining may match himself with a tight young filly. The doctor makes no doubt but his chapel will turn out even more to his advantage on this new plan than on its first institution, provided he can secure his scheme to himself, and reap the benefits of it without interlopers from the *fleet* (*sic*). To prevent his design being pirated, he intends petitioning the Parliament that, as he has been so great a sufferer by the new Marriage Act, the sole right of opening a repository of this sort may be vested in him, and this, his place of residence in May Fair, may still continue the grant for marriages." Here follows a "Catalogue of Males and Females to be disposed of in Marriage to the best bidder, at Mr. Keith's Repository, in May Fair :"—

"A young lady of £100,000 fortune—to be bid for by none under the degree of peers, or a commoner of at least treble the income.

"A homely thing, who can read, write, cast accounts, and make an excellent pudding—this lot to be bid for by none but country parsons.

"A very pretty young woman, but a good deal in debt, would be glad to marry a member of Parliament, or a Jew.

"A blood of the first-rate, very wild, and has run loose all his life, but is now broke, and will prove very tractable.

"Five Templars—all Irish. No one to bid for these lots of less than £10,000 fortune."

The concluding announcement in the article is as follows :—

"Wanted, a dozen of young fellows, and one dozen of young women, willing to marry to advantage ; to go to Nova Scotia."

The following extracts, taken at random from the register-books at St. George's, above mentioned, will serve to show that the private marriages celebrated in Dr. Keith's little chapel were not confined to the lower or rougher element, but were often taken advantage of by the "upper ten thousand :"—

"1748, March 23.—Hon. George Carpenter and Frances Clifton."

"1749, September 14.—William, Earl of Kensington, and Rachel Hill, Hempstead."

"1751, May 25.—Henry Trelawney, Esq., and Mary Dormer, St. Margaret's."

"1751, July 21.—Edward Wortley Montagu and Elizabeth Ashe, St. Martin's Fields."

"1752, June 30.—Bysshe Shelley and Mary Catherine Michell, Horsham."

"1751, May 25.—Hon. Sewallis Shirley and Margaret, Countess of Oxford."

"1753, March 15.—James Stewart Stewart, Esq., and Catherine Holoway, of St. Matthew's, Friday Street."

"1752, February 14.—James, Duke of Hamilton, and Elizabeth Gunning."

Of the lady whose name is contained in the last-mentioned entry we have already spoken. We may add, however, that she was the second of three fair sisters, of Irish extraction, without fortune, but closely related to the first baronet of the same name. Miss Elizabeth Gunning was not content with a single dukedom, for, after the death of the Duke of Hamilton, she married John, Duke of Argyll, and was eventually created a peeress of Great Britain in her own right, as Baroness Sundridge and Hamilton. The last time she appeared at any public assembly was at a pic-nic ball at Marseilles, during a three months' sojourn of the family in France in 1785. With reference to that event, a writer of that period observes : "I had the honour of dining with them that day, and the duchess, as soon as possible, retired from the company to dress. She came down to coffee in all her splendour ; every one was struck with astonishment ; and I could not refrain from saying that I thought her Grace really looked as well as when I first saw her in the court-room in England as Duchess of Hamilton. The duke, with a smile, replied, 'Less aided then, perhaps, than now, sir.' Her Grace could not but be apprised of the wonder that was excited, and the Lieutenant of Police, rather too loudly, exclaimed, 'I have never seen any one so completely beautiful before.'" Her elder sister, Maria, was the wife of George William, sixth Earl of Coventry, and lived close by, in Piccadilly.

The marriages at May Fair Chapel, if not quite so loosely conducted as they were at the Fleet, were at least attended with the same evils, and afforded the same facilities for the accomplishment of forced and fraudulent unions. For instance, marriages could be antedated without limit, on payment of a fee, or not entered at all. Parties could be married without declaring their names. It was a common practice for women to hire temporary husbands at the Fleet, in order that they might be able to plead coverture to an action for debt, or to produce a certificate in case of their being *enceinte*. These hired husbands were provided by the parson for five shillings each; sometimes they were women. It appears that, for half-a-guinea, a marriage might be registered and certified that never took place. The marriage of the Hon. H. Fox, son of the first Lord Holland, to the daughter of the Duke of Richmond, at the Fleet, in 1744, and the increase of these irregular practices, led to the introduction of the Marriage Act. The interval between the passing of the bill and its coming into operation, as we have stated, afforded a rich harvest to the parsons of the Fleet and May Fair. In one register-book there are entered 217 marriages which took place at the Fleet on the 25th of March, 1754, the day previous to the Act coming into force. Clandestine marriages continued at the Savoy till 1756, when a minister and his curate being transported, an effectual stop was put to them.

To return once more to Dr. Keith, we may add that, in spite of being a person of loose morals, and frequently performing the marriage service in a state of intoxication, he published at least one religious treatise—"The Guide; or, the Christian Pathway to Everlasting Life." He lived to be nearly ninety, and died in 1758.

Curzon Street was so named from the ground landlord, George Augustus Curzon, third Viscount Howe, ancestor of the present Earl Howe. In this street, in November, 1852, died at No. 8, at the age of ninety, Miss Mary Berry, one of the two Misses Berry who enjoyed for so many years the friendship of Horace Walpole; and, indeed, the lady to whom, when late in life he succeeded to the earldom of Orford, he made an offer of his hand and his coronet. She and her younger sister, Agnes, were the daughters of a Yorkshire gentleman, Mr. Robert Berry, who lived in South Audley Street, as already stated in our last chapter. Walpole first met them when on a visit at Wentworth Castle, in Yorkshire, and the friendship there made proved a lasting one. "The young ladies," says Mr. Robert Chambers, in his "Book of Days," "afterwards took up their abode at Twickenham, in the immediate neighbourhood of Strawberry Hill, with whose master a constant interchange of visits and other friendly offices was maintained. Horace Walpole used playfully to call them his 'two wives,' corresponded with them frequently, told them many stories of his early life, and what he had seen and heard, and was induced by these friends, who used to take notes of his communications, to give to the world his 'Reminiscences of the Courts of George I. and II.' On Walpole's death, the Misses Berry were left his literary executors, with the charge of collecting and publishing his writings. This task was accomplished by Mr. Berry, under whose superintendence an edition of Walpole's works was published, in five quarto volumes. He died, a very old man, in 1817; and his daughters, for nearly forty years afterwards, continued to assemble around them all the literary and fashionable celebrities of London. Agnes, the younger sister, pre-deceased Miss Berry by about a year and a half. Miss Berry was an authoress, and published a collection of 'Miscellanies' in 1844. She also edited about sixty letters, addressed to herself and her sister by Horace Walpole, and came chivalrously forward to vindicate his character against the sarcasm and aspersions of Lord Macaulay in the *Edinburgh Review*."

The following epigram on the Misses Berry was written by Horace Walpole, on their paying a visit to his printing-press at Strawberry Hill, soon after their return from a visit to Italy and a stay at Rome :—

> "To Mary's lips has ancient Rome
>   Her purest language taught;
> And from the modern city home
>   Agnes its pencil brought.
>
> "Rome's ancient Horace sweetly shouts,
>   Such maids with lyric fire;
> Albion's old Horace sings nor paints—
>   He only can admire.
>
> "Still would his griefs their fame record,
>   So amiable the pair is;
> But ah! how vain to think his word
>   Can add a straw to Berry's."

Sir Henry Halford, the Court physician, during his long reign of successful practice, lived for many years in this street, as also did the Princess Sophia

Matilda of Gloucester. The name of Madame Vestris also appears as the occupier of No. 1, in the year 1826. Here, too, Tobias Smollett was living, in third-rate lodgings, when he heard the news of the victory of Culloden.

Mr. Peter Cunningham enumerates, as residents of this street, Pope's Lord Marchmont, and Richard Stonehewer, the friend and correspondent of the poet Gray, at No. 41. In 1808, Francis Chantrey was living in this street, before his marriage, while first beginning to make his name famous as a sculptor. Whilst here, he received his first great order, from Mr. Alexander, the architect. It was for four colossal busts of Howe, St. Vincent, Duncan, and Nelson, for the Trinity House, with duplicates for the Royal Naval Asylum at Greenwich. He had already occupied rooms in Chapel Street, close by, where we find him in 1804, when he sent his first work for exhibition to the Royal Academy, of which he afterwards became so leading a member.

In the large house on the north side of the street, enclosed in its own grounds, and embowered in a grove of plane-trees, nearly opposite Curzon Chapel, lived Lord Wharncliffe, the great-grandson of Lady Mary Wortley-Montagu, and editor of her works. The house is still the property of his descendants. Curzon Chapel—a chapel of ease—is a large, dull, brick building, on the south side ; and it stands within a few yards of the spot whereon Dr. Keith's unlicensed chapel formerly flourished.

Hertford Street—a somewhat dull and heavy thoroughfare, running parallel with Curzon Street on its south side, and crossing the top of Down Street, which it connects with Park Lane—has long been one of the most fashionable thoroughfares in this aristocratic neighbourhood, and is often mentioned as typical of the height of fashion in the days of William IV. and the early part of the reign of Queen Victoria.

In No. 14 lived Dr. Jenner, for a few years, from 1804, a man sadly in advance of his age, as may be inferred from the fact that, in spite of his wonderful discovery of vaccination, which arrested the ravages of the small-pox, he was unable to make a good professional connection at the West-end, and returned to Gloucestershire in disgust. His merits have been somewhat tardily acknowledged by the erection of a statue. The first Earl of Liverpool, father of the prime minister, died here in 1808. At No. 10 lived, in the last century, Lord Sandwich, famous for his musical parties : the house was afterwards inhabited by General John Burgoyne, the unsuccessful hero of the American War ;

and subsequently, for a short time, by Richard Brinsley Sheridan. At No. 30 was living, in 1841, Mr. H. B. Trelawny, Lord Byron's companion in his last expedition to Greece, and in whose arms the poet breathed his last. In this street resided the late Sir Charles Locock, Bart., the eminent physician-accoucheur to Her Majesty, who died in 1875 ; and that consummate lawyer and accomplished scholar, Sir Alexander Cockburn, Lord Chief Justice of England, who died in 1880.

But Hertford Street is rich also in its past memories of quite another kind. As nearly as possible on its site there stood, a couple of centuries ago, a public-house, with gardens attached, called "The Dog and Duck," from the diversion of duck-hunting by spaniels which was carried on there. The fun was to watch the duck dive in order to escape from the dog's jaws ; and it was quite a fashionable sport in the suburbs of London till the early part of the present century, when it was superseded by pigeon-shooting. Mr. Larwood, in his "History of Sign-boards," describes it as an old-fashioned wooden house, extensively patronised by the butchers, and other rough characters, during the "May Fair" time. The pond in which the sport took place was situated behind the house, and, for the benefit of the spectators, was boarded round to the height of the knee, in order to preserve the over-excited spectators from involuntary immersions. The pond, he adds, "was surrounded by a gravel walk, shaded by willow-trees."

In the immediate neighbourhood of Curzon and Hertford Streets are a number of small and dingy streets and lanes, the names of which help to perpetuate the market formerly held here, such as Market Street, Shepherd's Market, and Shepherd's Street. But this market, rural as the name may sound, is not so called from any pastoral associations, but from a certain Mr. Shepherd, or Sheppard, to whom once belonged the ground on which the "May Fair" was held. We fear, therefore, that all poetical thoughts of shepherds and shepherdesses going there a-Maying must be dismissed as baseless fictions. In Carrington Street, an insignificant thoroughfare between Down Street and Park Lane, there was a riding-school ; and in this street lived the noted "Kitty Fisher."

Seamore Place is the name of a row of handsome but somewhat old-fashioned mansions, which occupy a sort of *cul de sac* at the western end of Curzon Street. They are only nine in number, and their chief fronts look westward over Hyde Park. In one of them, Lady Blessington, with her daughter and her son-in-law, Count D'Orsay, resided during a part of her widowhood, from about

1836 to 1840, surrounded by all the fashionable butterflies of the world of *bon ton*, whose admiration she so much courted. Whilst living here, too, she followed her bent by penning and sending some of her best known contributions to the literature of the day. We shall have to speak of her career hereafter, when we come to Gore House, between Knightsbridge and Kensington. Here, too, at one time, resided Lord Normanton.

Chesterfield Street, which runs out of Curzon Street northwards to Charles Street, was so called out of compliment to the great, or rather the polite, Lord Chesterfield, whose grounds it bounded on the east. In this street lived " Beau" Brummell for some years, after his retirement from the army, and while he still basked in the sunshine of royal favour among the circle of the Prince of Wales at Carlton House. Here, consequently, the Prince would frequently come of a morning in order to see the " Beau" make his toilette, and to learn the art of tying his neckerchief *à la mode*. And here the Prince would continue to sit so late into the evening that he would send his horses home from the door, and insist on taking a quiet chop or steak with his host, but with no intention of returning home till he was half-seas over, and the streaks of early morning were appearing in the sky.

Here, too, was living, in 1847, the gallant admiral, the Earl of Dundonald, formerly known as Lord Cochrane, when his name was formally restored to his rank in the navy and to the roll of the Knights of the Order of the Bath, by an order of the Queen in Council; and from this street he dated his letter of thanks to Mr. Douglas Jerrold for having advertised that tardy act of justice in the public press.

At No. 1 in this street lived that amiable, talented, and eccentric personage, Mr. J. W. Ward, afterwards Mr. Canning's Secretary for Foreign Affairs, and eventually known as Lord Dudley; and No. 11 was for many years the residence of Sir Robert Adair, the distinguished diplomatist. He died here in 1855. In this street, too, at No. 3, has lived, for upwards of thirty years, the Hon. Mrs. Norton, the poetess. By birth a Miss Caroline Sheridan, one of three beautiful grand-daughters of Richard Brinsley Sheridan, in early life she married the Hon. George C. Norton, a brother of the late Lord Grantley. She contributed to the annuals from a date prior to her marriage, and is known to the world as the authoress of several poems, which have taken a high stand in English literature, among which should be mentioned "The Undying One," based on the legend of the Wan-

dering Jew, "The Child of the Islands," "The Dream," and the "Lady of La Garaye."

The next turning on the east of Charles Street is Queen Street, where the ever youthful widow of the last Viscount Saye and Sele died in 1789, at the age of ninety-four, a lady about as celebrated as Queen Elizabeth for her fondness for dancing, in which she indulged almost to the last week of her long life. She was supposed to be the original of the Viscountess delineated in Hogarth's print of the " Five Orders of Periwigs, Coronets, &c." * It may be added that here, too, Lord John Russell was living in 1835, whilst M.P. for South Devon and for Stroud.

Chesterfield House, to which we now turn, stands at the junction of South Audley and Curzon Streets, and was built on ground belonging to Curzon, Earl Howe, by Isaac Ware, the same who edited " Palladio" for Philip, fourth Earl of Chesterfield. From one of Lord Chesterfield's " Letters to his Son," dated " March 31, O.S., 1749, Hotel Chesterfield," and from a quotation in No. 152 of the *Quarterly Review*, we get a fair account of the house when newly built. In the former his lordship writes: " I have yet finished nothing but my *boudoir* and my library; the former is the gayest and most cheerful room in England; the latter the best. My garden is now turfed, planted, and sown, and will, in two months more, make a scene of verdure and flowers not common in London." The writer in the *Quarterly Review* says: " In the magnificent mansion which the earl erected in Audley Street you may still see his favourite apartments, furnished and decorated as he left them—among the rest, what he boasted of as 'the finest room in London,' and, perhaps, even now it remains unsurpassed, his spacious and beautiful library looking on the finest private garden in London. The walls are covered half-way up with rich and classical stores of literature; above the cases are in close series the portraits of eminent authors, French and English, with most of whom he had conversed; over these, and immediately under the massive cornice, extend all round, in foot-long capitals, the Horatian lines—

' NUNC. VETERUM . LIBRIS . NUNC. SOMNO . ET .
   INERTIBUS . HORIS :
  DUCERE . SOLICITÆ . JVCUNDA . OBLIVIA . VITÆ.'

On the mantelpieces and cabinets stand busts of old orators, interspersed with voluptuous vases and bronzes, antique or Italian, and airy statuettes, in marble or alabaster, of nude or semi-nude opera nymphs." The columns of the screen facing the court-yard, and also the spacious marble staircase, were brought from Canons, near Edgware, the mansion of the "princely" Duke of Chandos, which was pulled down in the year 1744, and the costly materials dispersed by auction. Among the historic relics which found a place here was a lantern of copper gilt, for eighteen candles, which

In 1869 this splendid mansion was—or, rather, so it was reported—doomed to be abolished; but it was purchased by a City merchant, Mr. Charles Magniac. Although it is no longer inhabited by the family of the noble earl whose name it bears, its walls still remain, and doubtless its interior is

THE GRAND STAIRCASE, CHESTERFIELD HOUSE.

was bought at the sale at Houghton, Sir Robert Walpole's seat. An amusing story is told with reference to the portraits of Lord Chesterfield's ancestors, which hung upon the walls of the library. As a piece of satire on the boast of ancestry so common at that time in great families, his lordship, it is said, placed among these portraits two old heads, which he inscribed "Adam de Stanhope" and "Eve de Stanhope." Surely no one could beat that.

but little altered in its general appearance from what it was in the above year, when the following description was written:—"The house itself has many fine points, and in others, it must be owned, it is slightly disappointing. Passing from the porter's lodge across a noble court paved with stones, and entering the hall, the visitor cannot fail to be struck by the grand marble staircase, up and down which the great Chandos must have walked when it stood beneath his own palatial roof at Canons.

And, apart from historical traditions, it is really a staircase for *ideas* to mount, especially when one is met on its first landing, not only by busts of Pitt and Fox, but by a lofty clock, apparently of antique French construction, and which looks as though it had, at some time or other, chimed out the hours at the two fiddles in bas-relief, gilt and crossed one over the other, are scarcely to be compared in appearance with harps, lyres, &c., the usual metaphorical tributes to the Muse of Melody, the Muse of Apollo, to Orpheus, and to Sappho; and that one is more reminded of the violinists who played

THE EARL OF CHESTERFIELD. (*See page* 356.)

Versailles, long ere gay courtiers there perceived the shadow of the scaffold cast by the coming event of the 'Great' Revolution.

"Entering the music-room by means of this same staircase, we confess to some sense of disappointment. Not, of course, that we had expected to be greeted by any harmony of sweet sounds, any music from the spheres, but that the symbolism of decoration on the walls, on the ceiling, and the mantelpiece, might, on the whole, have been more graceful and more appropriate than it is, considering that prominent parts at the Court of France in the reign of Louis XIV., and at the beginning of that of Louis XV., than of the divine origin of music itself, which such a room ought to suggest. More pleasingly reminded, however, of that same Court is the visitor on descending to the reception-rooms on the lower floor, and entering the drawing-room, which is especially called the French room. There not only do the panelling of the walls, and the construction of the various pieces of furniture transport one back to the glories of the *ancien régime* of the time when Chesterfield enjoyed its society, but the looking-glasses, one over the fire-place and another facing it, appear as though they had mirrored that society, and not only mirrored but *multiplied* it; for these looking-glasses, being severally formed of various panels, fit, mosaic-like, one into another, and the divisions of these panels being ornamented by wreaths of painted flowers, &c., the beholder is reproduced again and again, and, in many a fantastic multiform, may judge of himself under various, not to say versatile, aspects.

"In one of the apartments—another drawing-room, to which this French *salon* leads—hangs a large chandelier, formed of pendent crystal, which once belonged to Napoleon I. Historically, this chandelier is so luminous in interest that it re-quires a narrative to itself; but the effect of it is somewhat heavy, owing to the large size of the crystal drops.

"The mantel-shelf in this room is classically beautiful; and amongst the pictures on the walls is a fine copy of Titian's 'Venus,' the original of which—if we remember aright—hangs in the Uffizii Gallery at Florence. But, perhaps, the most interesting apartment in the whole house is the library. There, where Lord Chesterfield used to sit and write, still stand the books which it is only fair to suppose that he read—books of wide-world and enduring interest, and which stand in goodly array, one row above another, by hundreds. . . In another room, not far from the library, one seems to gain an idea of the noble letter-writer's daily life, for we can still see its ante-chamber, in which the aspirants for his lordship's favour were sometimes kept waiting*—aspirants to favour who afterwards, in various ways, achieved fame for transcending that of 'their then patron.' On the garden-front outside is a stone or marble terrace, overlooking the large lawn, stretching out in lawn and flower-beds behind the house. Upon this terrace Chesterfield, doubtless, often walked, snuff-box in hand, and in company with some choice friends—let us say from France —friends with whom he might gossip on matters connected with the courts, and camps, and cabinets of his day." The old earl, it would seem, was fond of the repose which his garden and court-yard afforded; for the late Earl of Essex, who died in 1839, the husband of Kitty Stephens, used to say that he remembered, as a boy, seeing the courtly old earl sitting on a rustic seat in front of his mansion, and basking in the sun.

Chesterfield House is one of the few private houses in London which M. Grossley, in his "Tour to London," allows to be equal to the hotels of the nobility in Paris. After it was sold to Mr. Magniac, as above stated, that gentleman consider-ably curtailed the grounds in the rear, and erected a row of handsome buildings overlooking Chester-field Street, to which has been given the name of Chesterfield Gardens.

Philip Dormer Stanhope, fourth Earl of Chester-field, was the son of Philip, third Earl, and of Lady Elizabeth Savile, daughter of the Marchioness of Halifax. His grandmother superintended his education till his eighteenth year, when he went to Cambridge. After his university career he spent a few years in foreign travel, mixing freely with the best society of the chief Continental towns, and at the Hague, adding to his many accomplishments the pernicious vice of gaming. While at Paris he received his final polish under the tuition of the beauties of that place, and, no doubt, gained much of the experience which forms the ground-work of the advice, which he afterwards transcribed in his "Letters" for the very questionable benefit of his son.

Before the death of his father, he sat in the House of Commons as representative of two Cornish boroughs, St. Germains and Lostwithiel, and became a distinguished speaker; and after his accession to the title, in 1726, and his con-sequent removal to the Upper House, he soon obtained some slight celebrity as an orator. His Court favour varied greatly. During the life of George I., he was appointed Gentleman of the Bedchamber to the Prince of Wales; but on that prince's accession as George II., he was greatly disappointed by the absence of that royal favour which he conceived he had a right to expect. He was, however, in the following year appointed Am-bassador to Holland, where he greatly distinguished himself by his diplomatic talent; and it was at the expiration of his two years of service there that, on his return to England, he was appointed Lord Steward of the Household; but having joined a strong opposition against Walpole, and incurring the decided enmity of the king, he was dismissed from this situation with marks of strong resentment. There are various stories as to the radical cause of the king's dislike to the brilliant statesman, but probably any one of them would have been suffi-cient to create, at the least, a decided coldness. Archdeacon Coxe's version of it is confirmed by Walpole, who was concerned in it, in his memoir of George II.; but there is a discrepancy as to dates, and a tone of improbability about some of the details, which throw more than a shadow of

---

* The room is immortalised in Mr. E. M. Ward's picture, "Dr. Johnson in the Ante-room of Lord Chesterfield." In this picture the Canons staircase is well shown in the back-ground.

doubt over the whole. Briefly, it runs to the following effect : that Chesterfield had ardently desired the post of Secretary of State, and an arrangement had been made in his favour ; upon which he had an audience of the Queen, to which he was introduced by Walpole, and immediately after paid a longer visit to Lady Suffolk, then reigning favourite, than was approved of by the Queen, who thereupon procured that his appointment should not take place. Here it may be remarked that Chesterfield had been intimately acquainted with Mrs. Howard long before she had attracted the notice of Queen Caroline or George II.; and further, that, having been created Countess of Suffolk in 1731, and thus set at her ease as to money matters, she was well disposed to leave the Court, but did not do so till 1735, three years after the dismissal of Chesterfield, to which Archdeacon Coxe represents her retirement as the ominous preliminary! Walpole relates a similar parallel indiscretion of Chesterfield's ; and it appears that it was not till two years before the earl's death that he was informed, by Horace Walpole himself, that the cause of his disgrace was his having offended the Queen by paying court to Lady Suffolk. Be this as it may, there was another and more probable cause for the royal dislike, which lay in his marriage with the daughter of George I. and the Duchess of Kendal, Melosina de Schulenburg, created, in her own right, Countess of Walsingham, and considered, as long as her father lived, one of the wealthiest heiresses in the kingdom. George I. opposed the inclinations of his tall, dark-haired, and graceful daughter, in consequence of Chesterfield's notorious addiction to gambling ; but, a very few months after Chesterfield's dismissal from court, Lady Walsingham became Lady Chesterfield. Her husband's house in Grosvenor Square was next door to the Duchess of Kendal's, whose society he much frequented ; and it was she who suggested legal measures respecting a will of the late king, which George II. was said to have suppressed and destroyed, and by which, as the duchess alleged, a splendid provision had been made for Lady Walsingham ; and at last, rather than submit to a judicial examination of the affair, George II. compromised the suit by a payment of £20,000 to the Earl and Countess of Chesterfield. These things were not likely to smooth the way for the ex-Lord Steward's return to St. James's ; nor was it facilitated by his inveterate habit of ridiculing and disparaging the Electorate and all its concerns, which he continued to his dying day.

His marriage took place in 1733 ; fourteen years after, in 1747, he commenced building the "rather fine house," as he described it, in May Fair. When the famous boudoir of blue damask and gold, of which much has been said, and more hinted, was finished, and to which Madame de Monconseil contributed the two magnificent *bras de porcelaine* to be placed on each side of the costly mantelpiece, the lordly owner took possession of the house, a year before the other rooms were finished, their slow progress greatly vexing him. In 1745 his lordship was admitted a member of the Cabinet, and in the next year appointed Lord-Lieutenant of Ireland. Three years later we find the earl retiring from the office of principal Secretary of State, to which the king had been constrained, by his undoubted talent, to appoint him ; and thus at the early age of fifty-four, he resigned finally the cares of official life. He was, nevertheless, still an active member of the Upper House, and among the measures with which his name is identified are some of historical importance. In spite of much opposition, within and without of the House, he carried the Bill for the Reform of the Calendar, and gave us the "new style," which set our calculation of the year in harmony with that of the rest of Western Europe.

Dr. King, in "Anecdotes of his Own Times" (1819), says that the earl resigned his employment of Secretary of State because "he would not submit to be a cipher in his office, and work under a man who had not a hundredth part of his knowledge and understanding, and resolved to meddle no more in public affairs. However," he adds, "he was lately so much disgusted with our bad measures, that he could not help animadverting on them, though in his usual calm and polite manner. His petition to the king is an excellent satire, and hath discovered to the whole nation how, at a time when we are oppressed with taxes, and the common people everywhere grown mutinous for want of bread, the public money is squandered away in pensions, generally bestowed upon the most worthless men."

It was during Lord Chesterfield's last brief tenure of the seals of office that Dr. Johnson's eagerly-sought introduction to him took place. The then unknown author, whose dictionary, now a great fact, was then merely an idea floating in the brain of an apparently ordinary mortal, waited in the ante-room of the Secretary of State, and when, having seen Colley Cibber preferred before him, he was admitted, he received, besides approval of his plan, a donation of ten guineas ! Not many months before he had received fifteen guineas for "The Vanity of Human Wishes." And many years after, he remarked to Boswell: "Sir, ten pounds were to me at that time a great sum."

"The world has been for many years," writes Boswell, in his "Life of Johnson," "amused with a story, confidently told, and as confidently repeated, with additional circumstances, that a sudden disgust was taken by Johnson upon occasion of his having been one day kept long in waiting in Lord Chesterfield's ante-chamber, for which the reason assigned was, that he had company with him; and that, at last, when the door opened, out walked Colley Cibber; and that Johnson was so violently provoked when he found for whom he had been so long excluded, that he went away in a passion, and never would return. I remember having mentioned this story to George, Lord Lyttleton, who told me he was very intimate with Lord Chesterfield; and holding it as a well-known truth, defended Lord Chesterfield by saying, that 'Cibber, who had been introduced familiarly by the backstairs, had probably not been there above ten minutes.' It may seem strange even to entertain a doubt concerning a story so long and so widely current, and thus implicitly adopted, if not sanctioned, by the authority which I have mentioned; but Johnson himself assured me that there was not the least foundation for it. He told me that there never was any particular incident which produced a quarrel between Lord Chesterfield and him; but that his lordship's continued neglect was the reason why he resolved to have no connection with him.

"When the dictionary was upon the eve of publication, Lord Chesterfield, who, it is said, had flattered himself with expectations that Johnson would dedicate the work to him, attempted, in a courtly manner, to soothe and insinuate himself with the sage, conscious, as it should seem, of the cold indifference with which he had treated its learned author; and further attempted to conciliate him, by writing two papers in *The World*, in recommendation of the work; and it must be confessed that they contain some studied compliments, so finely turned, that if there had been no previous offence, it is probable that Johnson would have been highly delighted. Praise, in general, was pleasing to him; but by praise from a man of rank and elegant accomplishments he was peculiarly gratified.

"This courtly device," continues Boswell, "failed of its effect. Johnson, who thought that 'all was false and hollow,' despised the honeyed words, and was even indignant that Lord Chesterfield should, for a moment, imagine that he could be the dupe of such an artifice." His expression to Boswell concerning Lord Chesterfield, upon this occasion, was: "Sir, after making great professions, he had for many years taken no notice of me; but when my dictionary was coming out, he fell a-scribbling in *The World* about it. Upon which I wrote him a letter, expressed in civil terms, but such as might show him that I did not mind what he said or wrote, and that I had done with him."

Dr. Johnson appeared to have had a remarkable delicacy with respect to the circulation of this letter; for Dr. Douglas, Bishop of Salisbury, informed Boswell that, having many years ago pressed him to be allowed to read it to the second Lord Hardwicke, who was very desirous to hear it (promising at the same time that no copy of it should be taken), Johnson seemed much pleased that it attracted the attention of a nobleman of such a respectable character; but, after pausing some time, declined to comply with the request, saying, with a smile, "No, sir, I have hurt the dog too much already," or words to this purpose.

Dr. Adams expostulated with Johnson, and suggested that his not being admitted when he called on him, to which Johnson had alluded in his letter, was probably not to be imputed to Lord Chesterfield; for his lordship had declared to Dodsley that "he would have turned off the best servant he ever had if he had known that he denied him to a man who would have been always more than welcome." And in confirmation of this, he insisted on Lord Chesterfield's general affability and easiness of access, especially to literary men. *Johnson:* "Sir, that is not Lord Chesterfield; he is the proudest man this day existing." *Adams:* "No, there is one person, at least, as proud; I think, by your own account, you are the prouder man of the two." *Johnson:* "But mine was *defensive* pride." This, as Dr. Adams well observed, was one of those happy turns for which Johnson was so remarkably ready.

Johnson having now explicitly avowed his opinion of Lord Chesterfield, did not refrain from expressing himself concerning that nobleman with pointed freedom. "This man," said he, "I thought had been a lord among wits, but I find he is only a wit among lords!"

Johnson's remark on Lord Chesterfield's "Letters to his Son"—a natural son, of course, for the title passed at his death to a cousin—is well known to most readers of modern literature: "Take out the immorality, and the book should be put into the hands of every young gentleman."

Of Lord Chesterfield we are told by the Hon. G. Agar-Ellis, afterwards Lord Dover, in the *Keepsake*, that "the love of literature, and, still more, any talent for it, was so rare an attribute in a 'man of quality,' that his lordship, in his day, stood almost alone as a noble author, and as the Mæcenas of all others." But the first of these assertions is surely an exaggeration; and as to the latter character, Lord Chesterfield's treatment of Dr. Johnson, in his own courtly mansion, was not very much like that of the courteous and kindly Mæcenas to the poet Horace.

A good story is told by Mr. Frost, in his "Old Showmen," respecting Lord Chesterfield. His lordship once made a wager with Heidigger, a Swiss by birth, and by office Master of the Revels, and who had the reputation of being "as ugly as sin," that he could find an uglier person in the course of a week. The seven days elapsed, and Lord Chesterfield lost his wager.

One of his lordship's most familiar acquaintances was the elder brother of the first Lord Rokeby, called "*Long* Sir Thomas Robinson" on account of his height, and to distinguish him from Sir Thomas Robinson, first Lord Grantham. Hawkins relates how that Lord Chesterfield "employed him as a mediator with Johnson, who, on his first visit, treated him very indignantly." It was on his request for an epigram that Lord Chesterfield made the distich :—

> " *Un*like my subject will I make my song:
> It shall be witty, and it shan't be *long;* "

and it was he to whom he said in his last illness,

" Ah, Sir Thomas, it will be sooner over with me than it would be with you, for I am *dying by inches*." Lord Chesterfield was very short. Sir Thomas did not long survive his witty friend, and died in 1777.

Lord Chesterfield had but one child—the illegitimate son, Philip Stanhope, to whom his famous "Letters" were addressed; and he, after disappointing Chesterfield's expectations, was carried off in the prime of life. The aged peer survived him some five years, and died in 1773, almost an octogenarian.

Lord Chesterfield's wit did not die with him, for even his will contained a grim satire on the Dean and Chapter of Westminster, some of whose lands, adjoining Chesterfield House, were taken by the earl, after a hard bargain, for the purpose of forming Stanhope Street. The substance of the clause in the will referred to is to the effect that, if his "godson," as he calls him, Philip Stanhope, should at any time indulge in horse-racing, or the keeping of race-horses or hounds ; or if he should reside for one night at Newmarket during the time of the races there, or should lose in any one day the sum of £500 by gambling, then he should forfeit and pay out of his estate the sum of £5,000, "to and for the use of the Dean and Chapter of Westminster." As his death took place before that of the earl, the Dean and Chapter could have no claim upon the estate of the "godson," as the contingent interest never accrued in their favour.

CHAPTER XXIX.

APSLEY HOUSE AND PARK LANE.

——— " Tecto quum vidit in illo
Magnum habitatorem."—*Juvenal.*

Situation of Apsley House—George II. and the Apple-stall Keeper—Henry, Lord Apsley, purchases the Site, and builds a Mansion—The First Earl Bathurst—Apsley House purchased by the Nation for the Duke of Wellington—Description of the Building—The Picture-Gallery—The Duke's Temporary Unpopularity, and Attack of the Mob on Apsley House—The Waterloo Banquets—The Waterloo Shield—Biographical Notice of the Duke of Wellington—Memorials of the Illustrious Duke—The " Curds and Whey House "—Hyde Park Corner—A Singular Panic—Park Lane—A Strange Abode—Park Lane Fountain—Holdernesse House—Great Stanhope Street—Tilney Street—Dean Street—Dorchester House—South Street—Chapel Street—Grosvenor House—The Grosvenor Family—Dudley House—Upper Brook Street—Park Street—Green Street—Norfolk Street—The Murder of Lord William Russell—Camelford House.

QUITTING May Fair, we now turn to the southwest, down Hamilton Place, in order to look in upon Apsley House, with which we were obliged to deal very briefly in our walk along the mansions of Piccadilly. This house, so many years the residence of the late, and still the residence of the present Duke of Wellington, forms a conspicuous object on entering London from the west, occupying as it does the corner of Hyde Park and Piccadilly. Its situation is one of the finest in the metropolis, standing upon the rising ground

overlooking the parks, and commanding views of the Kent and Surrey hills in the far distance. Its site is said to have been a present from George II. to a discharged soldier, named Allen, who had fought under that king at Dettingen. His wife here kept an apple-stall, which by the thrifty couple was turned by degrees into a small cottage. The story of this present has been often told, but it will bear telling yet once again :—When London did not exist so far as Knightsbridge, George II., as he was riding out one morning, met Allen, who

HYDE PARK CORNER IN 1750. (From Mr. Crace's Collection.)

doubtless showed by his garments that he had once belonged to the army; the king accosted him, and found that he made his living by selling apples in a small hut. "What can I do for you?" said the king. "Please your majesty to give me a grant of the bit of ground my hut stands on, and I shall be happy." "Be happy," said the king, and ordered him his request. Years rolled on; the apple-man died, and left a son, who from dint of industry became a respectable attorney. The then Chancellor gave a lease

house which he built upon it the name by which it is still known. The mansion was originally of red brick, and though solid and substantial, it had no great architectural pretensions.

The father of Lord Chancellor Apsley, the first Earl Bathurst, was one of the most genial and agreeable of the friends of Pope, who has referred to him in the often quoted lines in terms of respect and affection :—

THE DUKE OF WELLINGTON IN 1842. (*After a Sketch by "H. B."*)

of the ground to a nobleman, as the apple-stall had fallen to the ground. It being conceived the ground had fallen to the Crown, a stately mansion was soon raised, when the young attorney put in claims; a small sum was offered as a compromise, and refused; finally, the sum of £450 per annum, ground rent, was settled upon.

In 1784, Allen's son or other kin sold the ground to Henry, Lord Apsley, Lord Chancellor, afterwards second Lord Bathurst, who gave to the

"Oh! teach us, Bathurst, yet unspoiled by wealth,
   That secret rare, between th' extremes to move
   Of mad good-nature and of mean self-love."

His lordship appears to have been of a particularly lively and cheerful disposition, and to have preserved his natural vivacity to the very last. To within a month of his death, which happened on the 16th of September, 1775, at the age of ninety-one, he constantly rode out on horseback for two hours before dinner, and regularly drank his bottle of claret or madeira after dinner. Some amusing anecdotes have been told of this old Lord Bathurst, which will bear telling over again. He used to repeat often, with a smile, that Dr. Cheyne had assured him, fifty years before, that he would not live seven years longer, unless he abridged himself of his wine. About two years before his death, he invited several of his friends to spend a few cheerful days with him at his seat, near Cirencester; and being, one evening, very loth to part with them, his son (then Lord Chancellor) objected to their sitting up any longer, adding, that health and long life were best secured by regularity. The earl suffered his son to retire, but as soon as he left the room, exclaimed, "Come, my good friends, since the old gentleman is gone to bed, I think we may venture to crack another bottle!"

In 1820 the mansion was purchased by the nation, and settled as an heirloom on the illustrious dukedom of Wellington. It was then leasehold only. Mr. Peter Cunningham tells us that "the Crown's interest in Apsley House was sold to the duke by indenture, dated the 15th of June, 1830, for the sum of £9,530, the Crown reserving, however, a right to forbid the erection of any other house or houses on the same site." The principal front, next Piccadilly, consists of a centre with two wings, having a portico of the Corinthian order, raised upon a rusticated arcade of three apertures, leading to the entrance hall. The west front consists of two wings; the centre slightly recedes, and has four windows with a balcony. The front is enclosed by a rich bronzed palisade, corresponding with the gates to the grand entrance to the Park. In the saloon is a colossal statue of Napoleon, by Canova.

In 1828 the mansion was enlarged, and the original exterior of red brick was faced with a casing of Bath stone, designed by Mr. B. Wyatt. At this time the front portico and the west wing were added; but, says Mr. Peter Cunningham, "the old house still remains intact, so much so, indeed, that the hall door and knocker belonged to the original Apsley House." In the upper part of the west wing is the Waterloo Gallery, nearly a hundred feet in length. This noble apartment is splendidly decorated, and richly gilt. The ball-room extending the whole depth of the mansion, and the small picture gallery, which together form a suite, are both superb rooms. On the ground-floor, at the north-west angle, looking into the little garden which divides the house from Hyde Park, is the modest chamber used by the great Duke as a bedroom to the last year of his life. It is plainly furnished, with a small iron bedstead and a plain

writing table; a few books, which were the duke's favourite companions, still remain where their great master left them. This room was shown to the public, along with the rest of the house, for a few days in 1852, the year of the duke's death, and a striking proof it gave of his simplicity and studied avoidance of all that savoured of luxury. The house contains several fine pictures, amongst others a full-length portrait of George IV., in the Highland costume, by Sir David Wilkie. This picture was damaged by a stone during the Reform Bill riots, but the injury has been skilfully repaired. There are also portraits of the Emperor Alexander and the Kings of Prussia, France, and the Netherlands, and of several of the duke's companions-in-arms, and pictures of the battles which he fought. Among the latter is Sir William Allan's celebrated painting of the "Battle of Waterloo, with Napoleon in the Foreground," of which the duke is said to have remarked that it was "good, very good; not too much smoke." Then there are several portraits of his great rival, Napoleon; also Wilkie's "Chelsea Pensioners reading the Gazette of the Battle of Waterloo," which was painted for the duke. The gallery contains besides a collection of other subjects, sacred and profane, by the old masters and painters. Dr. Waagen, in his work on "Art and Artists in England," speaks with great enthusiasm of the specimens of Sir David Wilkie in this collection; as also of a "Christ on the Mount of Olives," by Corregio (captured in Spain from Joseph Bonaparte); besides others by Velasquez, Claude Lorraine, Jan Steen, and Teniers.

In the tumults which broke out in London in 1831 on account of the opposition of the duke and the Tory party to the first Reform Bill, the windows of Apsley House were broken by the mob. In consequence of this, the duke had all his windows cased with iron shutters, like those of shop-fronts in our leading thoroughfares, and made bullet-proof; and though often entreated to have them removed when his popularity returned, he steadily refused to allow the change to be made, as he had no confidence in the smiles of popular favour, and would often say that they were a standing proof of the vanity of the world's applause. With reference to the manner in which the fury of the multitude in the above-mentioned year vented itself on the duke, we glean a little intelligence in the following extract from Mr. Raikes' "Journal:"—
"I can remember well," he writes, "the time when the duke returned to England, after his brilliant campaigns, crowned with the battle of Waterloo; at that time he was cheered by the people wherever he went, and lauded to the skies. Afterwards, at

the period of the Reform Bill, the fickle people forgot all his services, and constantly hooted him in the streets. One morning, as he was coming from the Tower on horseback, the rascally mob attacked him with so much virulence and malice, that he was exposed to considerable personal danger in the street. I was in that year at a ball given by him at Apsley House to King William IV. and his Queen, when the mob were very unruly and indecent in their conduct at the gates; and on the following days they proceeded to such excesses, that they broke the windows of Apsley House, and did much injury to his property. It was then that he caused to be put up those iron blinds to his windows, which remain to this day as a record of the people's ingratitude. Some time afterwards, when he had regained all his popularity, and began to enjoy that great and high reputation which he now, it is to be hoped, will carry to the grave, he was riding up Constitution Hill, in the Park, followed by an immense mob, who were cheering him in every direction; he heard it all with the most stoical indifference, never putting his horse out of a walk, or seeming to regard them, till he leisurely arrived at Apsley House, when he stopped at the gate, turned round to the rabble, and then pointing with his finger to the iron blinds which still closed the windows, he made them a sarcastic bow, and entered the court without saying a word."

The shutters remained outside the windows of the house down to the death of the duke in 1852, after which they were removed by his son and successor.

On every 18th of June to the last, the duke celebrated his Waterloo dinner in the large gallery. Mr. Rush, in his "Court of London," mentions dining here in the summer of 1821, when the king (George IV.) was a guest, with most of the royal dukes, the foreign ambassadors, and the duke's old companions in arms. He thus describes the after-dinner scene:—"The king sat on the right hand of the duke. Just before the dessert courses, the duke rose and gave as a toast, 'His Majesty.' The guests all rose and drank it in silence, the king also rising and bowing to the company. A few minutes afterwards the king gave 'The Duke of Wellington,' introducing his toast with a few remarks. The purport of these was, that had it not been for the exertions of 'his friend upon his left' (it was so that he spoke of the duke), he, the king, might not have had the happiness of meeting those whom he now saw around him at that table; it was, therefore, with peculiar pleasure that he proposed his health. The king spoke with great emphasis and great apparent pleasure. The duke made no

reply, but took in respectful silence what was said. The king himself continued sitting whilst he spoke, as did the company in profound stillness under his words."

These banquets were continued from year to year down to the duke's death. As years rolled on, the familiar faces gradually fell off, and the number of chairs for his guests—his old comrades in arms—grew smaller and smaller.

AUTOGRAPH OF THE DUKE OF WELLINGTON.

On state occasions, the chief ornament of the duke's sideboard was the celebrated shield presented to him by the City of London. It is of pure gold, and was manufactured by Messrs. Rundle and Bridge, from the designs of Thomas Stothard, R.A. On it are represented, in bas-relief and in alto, the most important of the duke's victories; and it is said that its cost was nearly £15,000. In fact, a dinner at Apsley House has been almost described in anticipation by Virgil, in a passage of his "Æneid," thus translated by Dryden:—

> "On Tyrian carpets, richly wrought, they dine;
> With loads of massive plate the sideboards shine;
> And antique vases, all of gold embossed
> (The gold itself inferior to the cost
> Of curious work), where, on the sides, were seen
> The fights and figures of illustrious men,
> From their first founder to the present Queen."

Down to within a few weeks of his death, the duke used to ride out every afternoon, on his way to the Horse Guards or the Park. His appearance, as he passed from the gate of Apsley House into Piccadilly, at his accustomed hour, was one of the sights of London which "country cousins" were regularly taken to see; and, attired in a plain blue frock-coat, with white waistcoat and trousers, with a groom riding behind him, he was "the observed of all observers." "A stranger could recognise him amidst the peers by the marked respect they showed to him. The duke was the best-known and most popular man in London. There were people constantly waiting at the entry to the House of Lords, and not unusually in the vicinity of the Horse Guards, to get a peep at him; and he had been so long accustomed to acknowledge the homage paid to him by all classes, on his appearing in public, that the habit had become mechanical with him. Every well-bred person raised his hat to the duke; and the duke, sitting on horseback in his calm, impassive manner, and looking straight before him, lifted two fingers towards his hat to everybody. It was quite a scene when he chanced to walk along Regent Street, or some of the more frequented thoroughfares in the neighbourhood of the Horse Guards or the Houses of Parliament. A knot of followers instantly fell into his wake, augmenting as he proceeded. Shopkeepers rushed to their doors, or peered out of their windows, to catch a glance of him. 'The Duke!' passed from lip to lip. You could see in the countenance of all sorts of people as they approached and passed—and all sorts of people is a wide word in the streets of London—a pleased expression as they recognised the duke. It was less striking to observe the respectful greetings of the better-conditioned classes, than the cordial interest which the common people evinced in the great captain. The omnibus-driver would point him out to his outside passengers; the cad on the steps behind, to his 'insides.' The butcher's boy, as he dashed along on his pony, drew bridle to look at the duke. Cabmen, cadgers, costermongers, and *gamins*, gentle and simple, young and old, paused for a moment to gaze at the man whom they delighted to honour."

To write a complete biography of "the duke" would be altogether beyond our province, for to do that would be almost equivalent to writing a history of Europe during the time in which he lived. Suffice it then for us to say that he was the third son of Garrett, first Earl of Mornington, and brother of the Marquis Wellesley, and that he was born in 1769. Entering the army in 1787, he commenced his actual service in the field in 1794. Shortly afterwards, he was returned to the Irish Parliament for the borough of Trim, County Meath; and in 1806, he was chosen to represent Newport in the House of Commons. In the following year he was appointed Chief Secretary for Ireland. His Grace was for upwards of a quarter of a century Lord Warden of the Cinque Ports, and besides the honours and emoluments bestowed upon him for his brilliant services by the British Government, he received almost every foreign order of distinction, to the number of seventeen. As a parliamentary orator he spoke plain and to the point, and his correspondence was remarkable for its laconic brevity. To sum up, in the words of one of his biographers, it may be said that "throughout his long career, he appears the same honourable and upright man, devoted to the service of his sovereign and his country, and just and considerate to all who served under him. As a general, he was cautious, prudent, and careful of the lives of his

men; but when safety lay in daring, as at the battle of Assaye, he could be daring in the extreme. He enjoyed an iron constitution, and was not more remarkable for his personal intrepidity than for his moral courage. The union of these qualities obtained for him the appellation of the 'Iron Duke,' by which he was affectionately known in his later years. . . . His tastes were aristocratic, and his aides-de-camp and favourite generals were almost all men of family and high connections. Altogether, he was the very type and model of an Englishman; and in the general order issued by the Queen to the Army, he was characterised as 'the greatest commander whom England ever saw.'"

On the 14th of September, 1852, the "great Duke" died at Walmer Castle, his official residence as Lord Warden of the Cinque Ports. On that morning his valet called him as usual at six o'clock. Half an hour afterwards he entered the room and found his master ill. At four o'clock in the afternoon, after an epileptic fit, the great soldier breathed his last. Of all his crowd of illustrious friends, only two were near him—Lord and Lady Charles Wellesley, who were staying on a visit. So little did he anticipate death that he had appointed that day to meet the Countess of Westmoreland at Dover to see her off by packet to Ostend. The chamber in which he died had much the appearance of that at Apsley House described above; it was a little room with a single window, which served as his library and study, and an iron bedstead three feet wide.

Apsley House stood between two other memorials of the illustrious duke—a colossal figure mounted on horseback surmounting the arch at the top of Constitution Hill, and the statue of Achilles in Hyde Park. The first of these statues was modelled by Mr. Matthew C. Wyatt and his son, James Wyatt; it occupied three years, and is said to have taken more than one hundred tons of plaster. It represents the duke upon his horse "Copenhagen," at the field of Waterloo. The entire group weighs forty tons, and is nearly thirty feet high. The erection of this statue, in 1846, which cost about £30,000, originated from the close contest for the execution of the Wellington statue in the City. The archway on which this statue stood was erected by Mr. Decimus Burton, in 1828. It is Corinthian, and on each face are six fluted pilasters, with two fluted columns, flanking the single archway, raised upon a lofty stylobate or plinth, and supporting a richly-decorated entablature, in which are sculptured alternately "G. R. IV.," and the imperial crown within wreaths of laurel. The massive iron gates, bronzed, are enriched with the royal arms in a circular centre. In 1882–3, in order to relieve the block caused by the traffic at Hyde Park Corner, it was decided to set the archway 200 feet back, and to form a new roadway across the corner of the Green Park, connecting Hamilton Place with Halkin Street. At the present time (Jan., 1883), it is undecided where the statue of the duke will be re-erected.

The statue in its original position had always been an object of interest to visitors to the metropolis. "On fine afternoons," writes Mr. John Timbs, "the sun casts the shadow of the duke's equestrian statue full upon Apsley House, and the sombre image may be seen gliding, spirit-like, over the front." But this will now be seen no more.

Of the statue of Achilles, erected in the duke's honour by the ladies of England, we shall have more to say when we come to our chapter on Hyde Park. It has not, however, been by the aid of statuary alone that the memory of the duke has been kept alive; for it is said that within twenty-five years after he fought his last crowning battle, there were already in Europe seven bridges, nine museums, seventeen public squares, and twenty streets, which bore the name of Waterloo. How many more have been added since we can scarcely estimate.

We have already mentioned the toll-gate at Hyde Park Corner, and the old lodge adjoining it, which stood by the entrance into the Park. Appended to it was a small cottage, known to the public as the "Curds-and-Whey House." The lodge was joined on to Knightsbridge by a brick wall, which, as well as the old lodge and the "Curds-and-Whey House," was taken down about the year 1825, when a new lodge of stone was built, and the wall superseded by a light iron railing. About the same time, a small strip of ground was taken off the south-east corner of the Park, in order to form a garden for Apsley House; but the Duke of Wellington was not very popular at the time, and the encroachment on the public rights stirred up not a little bad feeling against him, an invidious parallel being drawn between his Grace and John, Duke of Marlborough, whose house was built on a site subtracted from St. James's Park.

"Hyde Park Corner is a worthy terminal mark to a great metropolis," observes Charles Knight. "To one who has been 'long in city pent,' the view from the Achilles along the elm row, towards the Serpentine, has a park-like appearance, that makes him feel out of town the moment he reaches it. To the traveller from the country, on the contrary, the view across the Green Park, towards West-minster Abbey, is truly courtly and metropolitan. The triumphal archways on either side corroborate the impression of stately polish; the magnificent scale of St. George's Hospital is worthy the capital of a great nation; . . . and Apsley House seems placed there in order that the 'hero of a hundred fights' may keep watch and ward on the outskirts of the central seat of power of the land whose troops he has so often led to victory."

In our view of this spot, on page 283, is shown the old toll-gate which formerly stood here. It had a milestone nestling under it, which gave it quite a rural appearance. It would have been amusing to have stood by the side of the old toll-gate, and to have seen the "quality," as people of rank and fashion were then styled, collecting just before the expected arrival of the great earthquake, which, it was prophesied vehemently, was coming to demolish the City and its suburbs. Charles Knight tells us, in his "London," that "for some three days before the date fixed, the crowds of carriages passing Hyde Park Corner westwards, with whole parties removing into the country, was something like a procession to Ranelagh or Vauxhall." This occurred in the month of April, 1750, and is thus recorded in a newspaper of that date:—

"Incredible numbers of people, being under strong apprehensions that London and Westminster would be visited by another and more fatal earthquake on this night, according to the predictions of a crazy life-guardsman, and because it would be just four weeks from the last shock—as that was from the first—left their houses, and walked in the parks and the fields, or lay in boats all night; many people of fashion in the neighbouring villages sat in their coaches till day-break; others went off to a greater distance, so that the roads were never more thronged, and lodgings were hardly to be procured even at Windsor; so far, and even to their wits' end, had their superstitious fears, or their guilty consciences, driven them."

This going off to Kensington, or Hounslow, or Windsor, to avoid the earthquake, reminds one of the old Duchess of Bolton, who, on Whiston's prophecy of the approaching destruction of the world, prudently resolved to be off to China, in order to escape so inconvenient an accident. Lady Hervey writes to her friend, Mr. Morris, with reference to this silly panic: "The Ides of March are come, and will, I am persuaded, be past in all safety before you receive this letter, in spite of prophets and prophecies. The newspapers are filled with accounts of a hundred little subaltern earthquakes which have been felt in many different places, but which I take to be only the ghosts of the more considerable one which haunt the timorous. . . . . Fear is an epidemic distemper; there is scarcely anything that is more contagious. I dare say at this minute nine parts in ten of the inhabitants of Westminster are shaking as much from this fear as they would from the earthquake if it was really to happen." That this curious instance of a "popular delusion" was not altogether a groundless panic, may be gathered from the following account,

read in the *London Magazine* for 1773 :—" Paris, May 14.—A report which had prevailed here that this city was to be destroyed by a comet in the night between the 12th and 13th of this month, so terrified many weak and credulous people, that whole families actually quitted Paris on that account, and are gone into foreign countries."

But it is time for us to resume our perambulation. Leaving Apsley House, we now travel north-

APSLEY HOUSE IN 1800. (*From Mr. Crace's Collection.*)

quoted from another publication, printed in the above year :—" On the 8th of March, at half-past five in the morning, the sky being very clear and serene, and the air very warm, the inhabitants of London, and to a great extent round the City, were alarmed by the shock of an earthquake, that came with great violence, especially about Grosvenor Square. This was preceded, about five o'clock, by a continual though a confused lightning, till within a minute or two of its being felt, when a noise was heard resembling the roaring of a great piece of ordnance, fired at a considerable distance, and then instantly the houses reeled, first sinking, as it were, to the south, and then to the north, and with a quick return into the centre."

A parallel to this " popular delusion " may be

wards, and following in the main the course of Park Lane, we shall, before long, find ourselves at Tyburn, which, for the present, must be the limit of our journeyings in the west of the metropolis, as we are bound to find our way back to the central regions of Bloomsbury, by a route embracing Oxford Street and the large district which lies to the north of it.

Park Lane, in the reign of Queen Anne, was a desolate bye-road, generally spoken of as "the lane leading from Piccadilly to Tyburn." The thorough-fare is, for the most part, open on its west side to Hyde Park, the other side being chiefly occupied by lofty and splendid mansions and terraces. Towards its southern extremity, the "lane" was formerly very narrow and inconveniently crowded;

but in 1871 it was widened by the Board of Works, by the removal of one of the mansions in Piccadilly, and the throwing open of Hamilton Place. Before the extension of London so far westward, when this was nothing more than a country lane, or bye-road, shaded here and there by trees, and winding its way along by the park palings, from the toll-gate at Hyde Park Corner to Tyburn, it must have presented a very rural appearance. So lately the property of a lady who died intestate, and whose wealth came into possession of the Government. It having been understood that she had often in her lifetime advocated the erection of a fountain here, this was thought the most desirable way to spend the money. The fountain stands on a very advantageous site, between the new and the old roads leading into Piccadilly, some twenty yards in advance of the point of bifurcation. The space

ENTRANCE TO GROSVENOR STREET FROM HYDE PARK, ABOUT 1780. (*See page* 370.)

as the beginning of the last century, the lane was almost, if not quite, destitute of habitation, for in it lived, moping away their existence in an unfinished house, commenced by their eccentric father, the sons of George Bushnell, who sculptured the statues which adorn Temple Bar. "This strange abode," says Mr. Walter Thornbury, in "Haunted London," "had neither staircase nor doors. . . . . Vertue, in a MS. dated 1728, describes a visit which he paid to the house, which was 'choked up with unfinished statues and pictures,' the sad relics of their father's wayward and eccentric genius."

At the point where Park Lane and Hamilton Place meet, there was erected, in 1875, at the cost of £5,000, an ornamental fountain by Thornycroft. The money expended on it was a part of is necessarily somewhat triangular, and the sculptor has adapted his design to the place by making it tri-frontal. The great feature in the work is, in accordance with this form of composition, a group of three heroic-size marble statues of the greatest of English poets—Shakespeare, Milton, and Chaucer ; and the summit of the monument, twenty-six feet from the ground, is a gilded bronze-winged figure of Fame, poised with one foot on a globe, blowing her trumpet, and bearing the wreath. Below the columnar pedestal on which these portrait statues stand, are three bronze figures of Muses, seated, and holding their attributes as Tragedy, Comedy, and History. These are so arranged that the Shakespeare is supported by the figures of Tragedy and Comedy, while the Milton stands between

Tragedy and History, and the Chaucer with Comedy and History on each side. The principal front is naturally given to the Shakespeare, facing across the Park, while Fame, lifting her trumpet high in the air, looks upward in the same direction. The statue of Milton faces the spectator coming down Park Lane; while Chaucer, his tablets and stile in hand, greets him with a pleasant half-humorous, half-reflective look, as he passes up the old narrow way from Piccadilly. Thus the sculptor has, with the happiest sense of the harmonies arising from mere position, availed himself of every coigne of vantage, and added interest and meaning to his work beyond its ostensible purpose of a fountain. The poet of all time faces the wide expanse of space, while Milton and Chaucer look over the western paths of busy practical life and work.

The first large mansion as we go up Park Lane is Holdernesse House, at the corner of Hertford Street. It is the residence of the Marquis of Londonderry, and stands on a site formerly occupied by the town mansion of the D'Arcys, Earls of Holdernesse, a title long since extinct. It is said that the father of the first Lord Londonderry travelled in the north of Ireland as a commission agent for a Scottish house of business, and that when his son rose to the surface in the political world, he was glad to petition the Earl of Galloway for leave to hook himself on to an obscure branch of the family tree of the Scottish house of Stewart.

The mansion—one of the most spacious and splendid in London—though little known to the world outside, was built, about the year 1850, from the designs of Messrs. S. and B. Wyatt, and commands a charmingly rural view over the expanse of Hyde Park. Here is a magnificent picture-gallery, containing, among other pictures, some full-length portraits of British and foreign monarchs of the present century by Sir Thomas Lawrence, as also a collection of articles of *virtu*—some of which were presented to the second Marquis of Londonderry by the Allied Sovereigns — vases, and tables of malachite. The sculpture-gallery contains several works by Canova and other great masters.

Great Stanhope Street, a broad thoroughfare, leading up, like an avenue, to the front of Chesterfield House, immortalises the family name of the old Earl of Chesterfield, its builder. Lord Palmerston lived, for many years prior to 1840, at No. 9. Next door, was living Mr. Alexander Raphael, the first Roman Catholic sheriff of London and Middlesex, whose money largely helped to ensure the return of O'Connell to Parliament as member for Carlow. No. 5 was, for many years, the residence of the Duke of Wellington's friend, Lord Fitzroy

Somerset, afterwards Lord Raglan; and from this house he started, in the spring of 1854, to take the command of our army in the Crimea, where he died in 1855. No. 15 was for some time the town residence of the gallant Field-Marshal, the first Viscount Hardinge, formerly Governor-General of India, and successor of the Duke of Wellington as Commander-in-Chief of the British Army. Facing the entrance to this street, and opening into the park, is Stanhope Gate.

Tilney Street, the next turning northward, connects Park Lane with South Audley Street. At his house in this street, in 1787, died, at an advanced age, Soame Jenyns, the well-known man of letters, essayist, poet, and convert from infidelity, and many years M.P. for Cambridge. His kindly and genial character made him very popular in society; but his various writings have come, for the most part, to be forgotten. It is said that no words of ill-nature or personality ever passed his lips, except his memorable epigram and epitaph—for it is both —on Dr. Johnson:—

> " Here lies Sam Johnson. Reader, have a care;
> Tread lightly, lest you wake a sleeping bear.
> Religious, moral, generous, and humane
> He was; but self-sufficient, proud, and vain;
> Fond of, and overbearing in, dispute ;
> A Christian and a scholar—but a brute !"

The house No. 6 in this street was the last town residence of Mrs. Fitzherbert, who was, no doubt, the lawful wife of George IV. She died in 1837, leaving her house to the Damer family. At No. 5, lived the Lord Yarmouth of the Regency, before his father's death raised him to the House of Peers as Marquis of Hertford.

Dean Street is the name by which a narrow and winding thoroughfare, leading behind Dorchester House into South Audley Street, is dignified. It is clearly only an enlargement of a rural bye-road, probably worn by the wheels of carts and wagons proceeding from the market-gardens of Pimlico to the market in the Brook Field, already mentioned. It consists of some half-a-dozen small houses, on one side only of the street, and has few reminiscences, social, literary, or political.

Dorchester House, the residence of Mr. R. S. Holford, the gardens of which face Park Lane on the one side, and Dean Street on the other, is one of the handsomest of the many modern mansions of London. It is in the ornate Italian style, and stands on the site of an older mansion of the same name, which was one of the residences of the late Marquis of Hertford, who died there in 1842. This nobleman, who, as Earl of Yarmouth, was a well-known figure under the Regency, married Mademoiselle

Fagniani, the daughter, according to some, of the Duke of Queensberry ("Old Q."), according to others, of George Selwyn, or George Selwyn's butler. Selwyn, it is recorded, left her a fortune of £30,000, two-thirds of which were to pass to Lord Carlisle's family if she should have no children. Lord Yarmouth was a *roué* and a profligate, but he had one redeeming quality, and that was wit. When Lord Granville resigned his post as ambassador at Paris, Lady Granville gave an evening party, jocosely adding that it was her "funeral." "I believe in a resurrection," said his lordship.

The present mansion was built in 1851-2, from the architectural designs of Mr. Lewis Vulliamy. It is faced with Portland stone, and in plan forms a parallelogram, about 105 feet wide by 135 feet in depth, very nearly the size of Bridgewater House. The grand staircase is of marble, and the interior generally is fitted up with great completeness. The arrangement of the west front, facing Park Lane, is original and effective, the mouldings and dressings generally having been carefully studied. The principal cornice displays a large amount of carving, and its size may be judged from the fact that the stones composing the chief projection of it are each upwards of eight feet square. There is a bold stone screen wall round the house, with a lodge at the south-west corner. "This mansion," says the *Builder*, "is a very good specimen of masonry, and is built for long endurance. The external walls are 3 feet 10 inches thick, with a cavity of about 5 inches, and the proportion of stone is great, and the bonders numerous; the stones are all dowelled together with slate dowells; and throughout, the greatest care appears to have been taken by the architect to ensure more than usually sound construction. If the New Zealander, who is to gaze on the deserted site of fallen London in some distant time to come, sees nothing else standing in this neighbourhood, he will certainly find the weather-tinted walls of Dorchester House erect and faithful, and will, perhaps, strive to discover the meaning of the monogram which appears on the shield beneath the balconies, 'R.S.H.,' that he may communicate his speculations to some 'Tasmanian Society of Antiquaries,' perhaps not more pugnacious, if less erudite, than our own."

Scattered through the principal apartments of Mr. Holford's mansion is a splendid collection of pictures, mostly by the ancient masters, many of them being of first-rate celebrity. The gallery contains, *inter alia*, fine specimens of Titian, Velasquez, Tintoretto, Vandyke, Murillo, Teniers, Wouvermans, and other artists. Among the pictures are two of the Caracci series, painted for the Giustiniani Palace, by Agostino and Ludovico Caracci. These famous pictures came to England in the Duke of Lucca's collection, and not being purchased for the National Gallery, after some negotiation with the trustees, they were subsequently exhibited in most of the cities of the United Kingdom, before they were separated to pass into the hands of private gentlemen. Then there are several of Rubens' exquisite sketches, among them the slight one for his "Entry of Henry IV.," in the Luxembourg collection, and the "Assumption of the Virgin," for the picture over the high altar in Antwerp Cathedral. Claude and the two Poussins are represented by brilliant landscapes. Altogether, the gallery ranks among the most important private collections in England. Mr. Holford has also a magnificent library, well stored with rare and curious books, among which are the *editio princeps* of Walton's "Compleat Angler," and Bunyan's "Pilgrim's Progress," and an extensive collection of English and foreign classics.

On the north side of Dorchester House is South Street, which runs into Hill Street, Berkeley Square. In this street stood the Roman Catholic chapel belonging to the Portuguese Embassy, and called after it the Portuguese Chapel. The building was removed about the year 1845, when it was superseded by the Jesuit Church in Farm Street, as already mentioned. In this street (at No. 39) lived Lord Melbourne, while occupying the post of Premier. In 1835, Mdlle. D'Este, daughter of the Duke of Sussex, lived at No. 36; and at No. 33, Lord Holland. In this street, also, lived Vice-Chancellor Sir John Leach.

Chapel Street is so called on account of its proximity to Grosvenor Chapel. In it, in 1841, lived General Sir Robert Thomas Wilson, who, having gained laurels in Egypt under Sir Ralph Abercromby, and subsequently in the Peninsula under Wellington, became involved in the unfortunate matter of Queen Caroline, and for his censure of the course pursued by the members of the Crown, was degraded and dismissed from the army; he was, however, subsequently reinstated, and attained the rank of general. He was for many years M.P. for Southwark; and for some time, just before his death in 1849, he held the post of Governor of Gibraltar.

Of Mount Street, which runs parallel with Chapel Street, across the middle of South Audley Street, we have spoken in a previous chapter.

A fine and spacious mansion, No. 21, between Mount and Upper Grosvenor Streets, was for many years the residence of the Marquis of Breadalbane,.

and afterwards of Lady Palmerston, who lived here in her widowhood.

In Upper Grosvenor Street lived William, Duke of Cumberland, more frequently known as "the butcher," on account of his wholesale massacre of the conquered Jacobites after the battle of Culloden, in 1746. Here he died, somewhat suddenly, at the end of October, 1765.

brother of George III., for whom it was originally built. It is separated from the street by a handsome open stone colonnade or screen, of classic pillars, connecting a double arching entrance, above which are pediments sculptured with the family arms, and panels with the four seasons above the foot entrances; the metal gates, and other portions of the screen, are enriched with foliage, fruit,

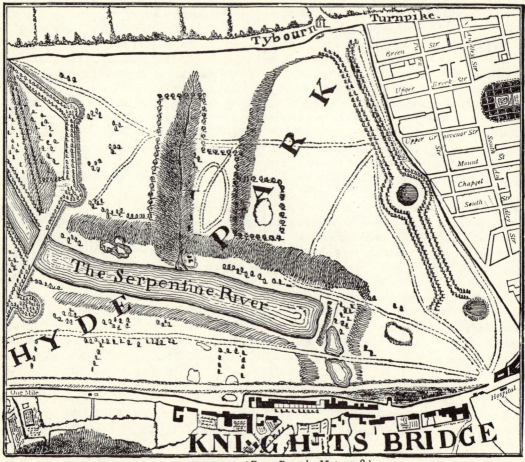

HYDE PARK. (*From Rocque's Map*, 1748.)

The corner house of Park Lane and Upper Grosvenor Street, formerly numbered 1, Grosvenor Gate, was the residence of Lord Beaconsfield, for more than thirty years, including the period of his first Premiership. It had belonged to Mr. Wyndham Lewis, for a short time his colleague in the representation of Maidstone, whose widow (afterwards Lady Beaconsfield) he married in 1839, soon after her first husband's death. He occupied it down to the year before his second Premiership.

On the south side of this street is Grosvenor House, the town residence of the Duke of Westminster. It was formerly called Gloucester House; and in it lived the Duke of Gloucester, younger

flowers, and armorial bearings. This screen was completed in 1842, from the designs of Mr. T. Cundy, who also erected, in 1826, after a beautiful example of the Corinthian order, the western wing of the mansion, containing the picture-gallery, one of the finest private galleries in Europe. Few sights are more attractive to strangers than galleries of paintings and statues; and although we are sadly deficient in public collections of such works of art, yet it may safely be asserted, that no country in Europe can boast of such magnificent private galleries as England, and no capital as London. Unlike Paris in this respect, most of the picture-galleries in London are the property of private individuals; but they are generally accessible by special application or a personal introduction.

The celebrated "Grosvenor Gallery" was commenced by Richard, first Earl Grosvenor, by the purchase of Mr. Agar's pictures, as a nucleus, for 30,000 guineas. The collection has since been considerably increased by various purchases. The gallery contains specimens of Claude, the Poussins, Raphael, Murillo, Snyders, Rembrandt, Rubens, Velasquez, Titian, Guido, Paul Veronese, Vandyke, Cuyp, Gainsborough, Reynolds, Hogarth, Vandervelde, and, indeed, of nearly all the great masters, ancient and modern. Hogarth's "Sigismonda," which is among them, as we know from one of the painter's private letters, was executed in 1764, the last year of his life, at the earnest request of Sir Richard Grosvenor.

In the words of Dr. Waagen, in his "Art and Artists in England," Grosvenor House gallery "makes a truly princely appearance, by its extent, the value of the pictures, and the manner in which they are hung. . . . . It is rich in the works of the great painters of the Dutch and Flemish schools of the seventeenth century, and in works of Rembrandt it is perhaps the first in England, after the private collection of royalty." Dr. Waagen also singles out for special commendation pictures by Paul Potter, Gerard Dow, Salvator Rosa, Claude Lorraine, Murillo, and Velasquez. The gallery is a magnificent and lofty apartment, lit only by a lantern from above; a faint and subdued light consequently reaches the lower part, to the great disadvantage of the pictures which are hung low. It contains five fine specimens of Rubens, including "The Wise Men's Offering," "Ixion," and "Sarah sending away Hagar;" the "Visitation of St. Elizabeth," and four others, by Rembrandt.

The following extract from Mr. H. C. Robinson's Diary, under date May 31, 1833, will give a good idea of the merits of this gallery :—"I accompanied ——— to the Marquis of Westminster's, to see his pictures. The pleasure of seeing them was rather enhanced than diminished by my better acquaintance with the great master-pieces in Italy. There are here some delightful specimens of Claude, which are equal to any on the Continent; there are also capital Rembrandts and Rubenses. It is true that there are but few of the great Italian masters, yet Guido's 'Fortune' (a duplicate) is one of the most beautiful pictures that I know. Westall was here with ——, and I could hear him giving the preference in colouring to Sir Joshua's 'Mrs. Siddons' over every picture in the room. The 'Blue Boy' of Gainsborough is a delicious painting."

It only remains to add that the duke very freely allows the gallery to be seen by the working classes; and that, with this end specially in view, has allowed access to it, under certain conditions, on Sundays, an example of liberality and consideration which might be followed in other quarters.

The Duke of Westminster is the head of the family of Grosvenor—a house which, although its connection with the English peerage is scarcely a century old, can lay claim to as noble a descent as any of our Norman houses. In fact, the Grosvenors have been of knightly dignity since the Conquest. Its head was the individual who, towards the close of the fourteenth century, carried on, for five long years, the memorable controversy of Scrope *versus* Grosvenor, before the High Court of Chivalry, the judges being the Lord High Constable, Thomas of Woodstock, Duke of Gloucester, youngest son of Edward III., and the Earl Marshal, Thomas de Mowbray, Earl of Nottingham. "Kings, warriors, mitred abbots, bishops, statesmen, and poets, appear on the scene. Four hundred witnesses, not one of lesser degree than 'a gentleman having knowledge of arms,' were called on to give evidence—among them John of Gaunt, Owen Glendower, Hotspur, and Geoffrey Chaucer. The question before the Court was such as may well raise a smile now-a-days, when everybody is, forsooth, a 'gentleman,' and when everybody who likes to pay the tax can assume what armorial bearings he pleases, without fear of punishment; it was simply the right to bear a particular plain coat of arms, heraldically described as '*Azure, a bend or*.' The plaintiff was Sir Richard de Scrope, of Bolton, the friend and comrade of the Black Prince; the defendant was Sir Robert Grosvenor, a Cheshire knight. We will not attempt to give an outline of the pleadings: suffice it to say, that the decision of the Court was in favour of Scrope, the same arms, '*within a plain bordure argent*,' being allowed to Grosvenor—the present arms of the family."

The Grosvenors were raised to a baronetcy in 1621, but did not attain the peerage till the early years of the reign of George III., when Sir Richard Grosvenor was created Baron Grosvenor of Eaton, in the County Palatine of Chester. His lordship was advanced to the dignities of Viscount Belgrave and Earl Grosvenor twenty years later. The second earl was raised to the Marquisate of Westminster at the coronation of William IV. The ducal title was conferred by Her Majesty in 1874. The title chosen by Earl Grosvenor for his marquisate is, at all events, appropriate; for it is from within the boundaries of the fair City of Westminster that the largest portion of the princely rent-roll of the family is derived. It is often said, and generally believed, that the Duke of Westminster's income exceeds that of any other nobleman of the age.

Continuing our walk up Park Lane, we pass, at No. 35, the residence of Sir Moses Montefiore, Bart., the venerable and indefatigable champion of the religious and social interests of the Jewish race in every part of the world.

administration, was somewhat of a *bon vivant*, as may be guessed from some of the anecdotes handed down about him. During the general depression in 1825–7, Lord Dudley remarked to a friend that his coal-mining income had fallen off during one year, £30,000; "but," he added, "I am a moderate man, and don't feel it. Lord Durham, they tell me, has not bread!"

On one occasion, when the *carte* of a forth-

THE FRONT OF GROSVENOR HOUSE. (*See page* 370.)

Dudley House, at the north-western corner of Upper Brook Street, is the residence of the Earl of Dudley, and is also noted for containing a gallery of pictures of the Flemish and Italian schools. The collection formed here by the late earl is described by Dr. Waagen in 1835 as a very mixed one. He enumerates a few by Bellini, Francia, Cuyp, Rysdale, &c., adding, "I looked in vain for the 'Three Graces,' by Raphael, which Passavant saw there." It is understood, however, that the present earl has added considerably to his gallery. There are also several fine specimens of sculpture, including a "Venus" by Canova.

Here lived the eccentric Earl of Dudley, who died in 1833. His lordship, who was Secretary of State for Foreign Affairs under Mr. Canning's

coming dinner at the "Clarendon" was discussed in his presence, his lordship observed: "My wants and wishes are moderate in such matters. I consider a good soup, a small turbot, a neck of venison with asparagus, and an apricot tart, is a dinner for an emperor—when he can't get a better."

Of his lordship's extraordinary absence of mind, and his unfortunate habit of "thinking aloud," many amusing anecdotes have been in circulation. It is told, as a fact, that when he was in the Foreign Office, he directed a letter, intended for the French, to the Russian Ambassador, shortly before the affair of Navarino; and, strange as it may appear, it obtained him the highest honour. Prince Lieven, who possibly never made any mistakes of the kind, set it down as the cleverest *ruse* ever attempted to be played off, and gave himself immense credit for not falling into the trap laid for him by the sinister ingenuity of the English Secretary. He returned the letter with a most polite note, in which he vowed, of course, that he had not read a line of it after he had ascertained that it was intended for Prince Polignac; but could not help telling Lord Dudley at an evening party, that he was "*trop fin*, but that diplomatists of his (Prince L.'s) standing were not so easily caught."

In 1826, No. 40 was occupied by the wealthy and eccentric Mr. Ball Hughes. In 1841, No. 27 was the residence of the celebrated engineer, Sir John Burgoyne; and at No. 49 lived Lord Ashley (since Earl of Shaftesbury). In this street, too, at one time, resided the Hon. Mrs. Damer, the sculptor. She was a daughter of General Conway, and the widow of Mr. John Damer, who, as we have seen,* whilst quite a young man, shot himself at a tavern in Covent Garden. She was a great friend

CAMELFORD HOUSE, 1820. (*See page 375.*)

With high birth, wealth, and everything in his favour, Lord Dudley ended in a ridiculous failure. He is tersely described by one of the ladies of the Court of George IV., as "a man who promised much, did little, and died mad." Madame de Staël, however, said of him, that "he was the only man of *sentiment* whom she had met in England."

Upper Brook Street, which connects Park Lane with the north-west corner of Grosvenor Square, has had at different times some distinguished residents; among others, William Gerard Hamilton, M.P., known as "single-speech Hamilton." In 1763, Lady Molesworth, her brother, and seven other persons, were accidentally burnt in their house in this street.

of Horace Walpole, who left her a life interest in Strawberry Hill.

Portugal Street, which runs north and south from Mount to Chapel Streets, parallel to Park Lane, still commemorates the name of the queen of Charles II. Our readers will not have forgotten that, at one time, this name was given to Piccadilly; and, in all probability, when thus quietly dropped out of use for the great thoroughfare, it was preserved in connection with this modest and retiring street by some lover of the Stuart line of kings. The street is narrow, and consists of little more than a dozen houses, all old-fashioned, and rather

* See Vol. III., p. 258.

gloomy; and there is little more to be said about it.

Park Street, which extends northwards from South Street to Oxford Street, crossing Mount Street, Upper Grosvenor, and Upper Brook Streets, has numbered among its residents at various times a few names which have become famous, such as Sir Humphry Davy, the greatest chemist of his age, who lived at No. 26; Mr. William Beckford, of Fonthill celebrity, who, in 1841, occupied No. 27; Mr. Serjeant Goulburn, who lived at No. 21; and Miss Lydia White, who, in 1827, died at her residence, No. 113. This lady, Mr. Peter Cunningham tells us, was "celebrated for her lively wit and for her blue-stocking parties, unrivalled, it is said, in the soft realm of *blue* May Fair"—except, it may be supposed, by Mrs. Montague. Sir Walter Scott writes, in his diary, under date of 13th May, 1826, that he "went to poor Lydia White's, and found her extended on a couch, frightfully swelled, unable to stir, roughed, jesting, and dying. She has a good heart and head, and is really a clever creature; but, unhappily, or rather, happily, she has set up the whole staff of her rest in keeping literary society about her. The world has not neglected her. She can always make up a circle, and generally has some people of real talent and distinction." At No. 56, now pulled down, lived, for many years, Baron Parke, both whilst a judge, and subsequently to his creation, in 1855, as a "peer for life," by the name, style, and title of Lord Wensleydale.

In Green Street, which runs eastward from Park Lane into North Audley Street, lived and died the Rev. Sydney Smith, the witty canon of St. Paul's. A native of Woodford, in Essex, he was born in the year 1771, and having entered the Church, became curate of Amesbury, in Wiltshire. "The squire of the parish," says Sydney Smith, "took a fancy to me, and requested me to go with his son to reside at the University of Weimar; before we got there, Germany became the seat of war; and, in stress of politics, we put into Edinburgh, where I remained five years." Here, in 1802, in conjunction with a few literary associates, he projected the *Edinburgh Review*. In the following year he removed to London, where he soon became "the delight and wonder of society." After holding various preferments, he was appointed, in 1831, one of the canons residentiary of St. Paul's. He published several pamphlets and sermons, and also his contributions to the *Edinburgh Review* in a collected form; but the work by which he is best remembered is "Peter Plymley's Letters," written to promote the cause of Catholic emancipation, and abounding in wit and irony. Sydney Smith died in February, 1845.

In this street lived Lord Cochrane, whose name became notorious in connection with a certain stock-jobbing fraud of a most extraordinary kind, which was played off in the metropolis, and of which we have already given the particulars,* but which may be briefly summarised here. It appears that between eleven and twelve in the forenoon of Monday, the 21st of February, 1814, a person, wearing a white cockade, passed rapidly by the Royal Exchange, in a post-chaise, drawn by four horses, and decorated with sprigs of laurel. Much about the same time a chaise similarly decorated, and a person of the same description within, was seen in the vicinity of Downing Street—not proceeding directly thither, but wandering about, apparently in want of a guide. Much excitement was caused by the appearance of these individuals, coupled with the rumours which had been spread abroad, to the effect that the mission of the man with the cockade was not to the British Government, but to the French princes here; and that he had certainly arrived at the residences of the Prince of Condé and the Duke of Bourbon. One of the actors engaged in this conspiracy, named De Berenger, was traced to the house of Lord Cochrane, in this street. After some lapse of time in consequence of investigations of the committee appointed by the Stock Exchange, these two persons, together with some four or five others, were brought to trial before Lord Ellenborough, "for conspiring to defraud that body, by circulating false news of Bonaparte's defeat, his being killed by the Cossacks, &c., to raise the funds to a higher price than they would otherwise have borne, to the injury of the public and to the benefit of the conspirators." All the persons indicted were found guilty; Lord Cochrane was sentenced to pay a fine of £1,000 to the king, to be set upon the pillory in front of the Royal Exchange, and to be imprisoned for twelve calendar months; one of the other prisoners received the same judgment, and the remainder were sentenced to a year's imprisonment in the Marshalsea. Lord Cochrane was one of the last persons sentenced to the pillory. This punishment he had not to bear, for Sir Francis Burdett vowed that, if necessary, he would stand by his side; and his presence was, in itself, protection from the mob.

Crossing Green Street, at right angles at its western end, is Norfolk Street. No. 22 in this street was once the residence of Lord Overstone, the eminent and wealthy banker, who here had a fine gallery of pictures. In this street lived the Duchess of Gordon. Though strictly pious in her

---

* See Vol. I., p 478.

later years, as a middle-aged matron she was a leader of fashion, and the admiration of West-end circles. If it be true that she was ambitious and vain, her ambition and vanity must have been gratified by seeing three daughters married to the Dukes of Bedford, Richmond, and Manchester, and a fourth to the Marquis Cornwallis.

In this street resided Lord William Russell, brother of the fifth and sixth Dukes of Bedford, who, on the 6th of May, 1840, was murdered in his bed by his valet, Courvoisier. From the confession which Courvoisier made, after finding his case was hopeless, it appears that, in the middle of the night, when the family had retired to rest, Lord William, feeling indisposed, dressed himself, and went down stairs, where he found the valet busy in packing up the valuables, apparently with intent to carry them away. He taxed him with his crime, and, telling him he should be discharged the next morning, returned to his bed. Courvoisier, in despair, after waiting some time, seized a carving-knife, went up to his master's room, and, finding him fast asleep, savagely cut his throat. The murderer was tried at the Old Bailey, and, being found guilty, was executed in the following July.

Passing once more into Park Lane, we have to direct our attention to two or three more houses before closing this chapter. The first of these, No. 16, was, in 1826, the residence of the late Lord Ellenborough, some time Governor-General of India; at No. 8 were living the Misses Berry, Horace Walpole's friends; and the large house at the northern end, next to Oxford Street, and backing on to Camelford House, was for many years the residence of the late Duke of Somerset, whose wife, one of the fair trio of Sheridan sisters, sat as the "Queen of Beauty" at the Eglinton Tournament. Camelford House, so called after Pitt, Lord Camelford, has nothing to command special attention, unless it be its mean and dingy appearance. The front of the house is towards Oxford Street, and the entrance at the side, whilst the court-yard at the back is open to Norfolk Street. The second Lord Camelford's body, after his death, in a duel fought near Holland House, was brought back hither, in 1804, and was taken hence to be deposited in St. Anne's Church, Soho, as we have already stated. The house then passed to his only sister, Lady Grenville, who lived here, with her husband, the Premier. She died, aged ninety, in 1863. At one time the house was let to Prince (afterwards King) Leopold and the Princess Charlotte. It has been for many years the residence of Sir Charles Mills, Bart., of Hillingdon Court, Middlesex.

Having now reached the northern extremity of Park Lane, we have on our left the Marble Arch; but of this, and also of Cumberland Gate and Tyburn, we shall speak in subsequent chapters.